AN INTRODUCTION TO WELSH POETRY

AN INTRODUCTION TO WELSH POETRY

From the Beginnings to the Sixteenth Century

by

GWYN WILLIAMS

PHILADELPHIA

DUFOUR EDITIONS / ALBERT SAIFER

1952

Printed in Great Britain

For Daisy,

llygad fy nydd

CONTENTS

★

APPENDIXES

ACKNOWLEDGEMENTS

★

I wish to acknowledge a debt of thanks to Professor Idris Foster, of the University of Oxford, and Professor Thomas Jones, of the University College of Wales, Aberystwyth, for many helpful indications and corrections ; and to the other Welsh scholars of this century, chiefly Sir Ifor Williams, whose lifetime of work on the old texts has widened our understanding of early Welsh poetry.

ABBREVIATIONS

★

BBC : *The Black Book of Carmarthen.*
BBCS : *Bulletin of the Board of Celtic Studies.*
BE : *Blodeuglwm o Englynion*, W. J. Gruffydd.
BM Add MS : British Museum Additional Manuscript.
BT : *The Book of Taliesin.*
C : Cardiff.
CA : *Canu Aneirin*, Sir Ifor Williams.
CD : *Cerdd Dafod*, Sir John Morris-Jones.
CIGE : *Cywyddau Iolo Goch ac Eraill*, H. Lewis, T. Roberts and Sir Ifor Williams.
CLl : *Cynfeirdd Lleyn*, Myrddin Fardd.
CLlH : *Canu Llywarch Hen*, Sir Ifor Williams.
CRhC : *Canu Rhydd Cynnar*, T. H. Parry-Williams.
DE : *Dafydd ap Edmwnd*, T. Roberts.
DGG : *Dafydd ap Gwilym a'i Gyfoeswyr*, T. Roberts and Sir Ifor Williams.
DN : *Dafydd Nanmor*, T. Roberts.
DWP : *The Development of Welsh Poetry*, Sir Idris Bell.
EWGP : *Early Welsh Gnomic Poetry*, Kenneth Jackson.
G : Gwyneddon.
H : Hendregadredd.
HLlG : *Hanes Llenyddiaeth Gymraeg*, T. Parry.
LEWP : *Lectures on Early Welsh Poetry*, Sir Ifor Williams.
Ll : Llanstephan.
LlC : *Llên Cymru*, T. Gwynn Jones.
M : Mostyn.
Pen : Peniarth.
RBH : *The Red Book of Hergest.*
THSC : Transactions of the Honourable Society of Cymmrodorion.
WLl : *Barddoniaeth William Llŷn*, J. C. Morrice.
YFN : *Y Flodeugerdd Newydd*, W. J. Gruffydd.
YGG : *Y Gelfyddyd Gwta*, T. Gwynn Jones.

Chapter I

THE POSITION OF THE POET IN WELSH SOCIETY

★

I have called this book an introduction to Welsh poetry because I think there must be a large number of intelligent users of the English language who know little or nothing about this subject, and a large number of Welsh people who are not able to read their own language. For them this book will therefore literally be an introduction. For scholars and students I can only attempt to express in another form what has already been argued, discovered and established, whilst sometimes permitting myself a modest heresy and sometimes drawing on not very widely known material for specimens in illustration.

There is a difference today between the attitude of the English and the Welsh towards poetry and the poet, and I think that this difference has been observable since the seventeenth century. In spite of the interest in poetry taken by young people during the last war, most Englishmen, if warned that a man is a poet, expect to find someone dreamy or fantastic, unpractical and useless. In Wales, on the other hand, to say that a man is a poet immediately induces an attitude of respect towards him, however ill-informed this attitude may be. This is perhaps because in England poets are rarely to be met with, whereas in Wales they announce themselves shamelessly in almost every village and county town. A village as little as Ffair Rhos in Cardiganshire today boasts of several poets and a man whose farming is criticised by the agricultural authorities replies in scathing verse which is repeated in bus and tavern. The ordinary Englishman is shy of poetry and unaware of the qualities that go to the making of a poet.

The poetry of a person who is conscious of such an attitude of unsympathy towards him on the part of the society in which he lives will inevitably be affected (though not necessarily for the worse), and this common attitude may be the reason why great English poetry has often not been recognised quickly and early enough in the poet's career for him to be given adequate honour and encouragement, whereas in Wales general appreciation has come more quickly and the poet has reaped honour if no great financial reward. It may also be the reason why much great English poetry is more personal and less social (since the poet is made to feel that he is apart from society) than Welsh poetry, which does not show the same swing from classical to romantic but in which the personal and social elements are more consistently and continuously blended.

It has seemed to me therefore that for anyone not living in a Welsh community or not familiar with Welsh social history some account of the relationship of the Welsh poet to those amongst whom he lives, a rapid survey of his function in that society, may help towards an understanding of the nature of the work produced and the phases of its development.

[i]

Just as it is impossible to indicate any one point at which Greek drama emerges from religious observance, so it is difficult for us, with the limited knowledge we have of the condition of Britain before the coming of the Romans, to distinguish between the functions of priest and poet in pre-Roman Britain. The inventions of Iolo Morganwg in the 18th century and, as a result, the dignified nonsense of the Gorsedd ceremony associated annually with the National Eisteddfod have helped to throw a mist of unreliable antiquarianism about the subject which scholarship has not the means completely to dispel.

It seems likely that the activities of bard and priest-prophet did occasionally overlap, but it is unlikely that we shall ever know to what extent. Some degree of overlapping is suggested by Julius Caesar when he speaks of the education given by the

Druids to the young Gauls and Britons who sat at their feet.[1] *Magnum ibi numerum versuum ediscere dicuntur. Itaque annos nonnulli vicenos in disciplina permanent.* (It is said that they learn there a great number of verses. And some remain in this discipline for twenty years.) Caesar had little first hand acquaintance with British Druidism, but since he is said to have been friendly with a Druid of the Aedui tribe in Gaul and since his information service was probably reliable, this statement can be taken as accurate. All we can assert, however, on the basis of this statement is that poetry was associated with religious and political education in Britain in the first century B.C. This is far from meaning that the druids and bards were the same persons, but that the technique of versification already developed by the poets was used as a pedagogical device.

To judge from the first clear reference we have to the Celtic poets, in the *Library of History* of Diodorus Siculus,[2] their task seems to have been much the same at the dawn of history as it continued to be officially in Wales up to the end of the thirteenth century and unofficially until the eighteenth century, that is to praise and to censure. This fascinating account of Britain and Gaul, written in the middle of the first century B.C. but partly based on the journey and report of Posidonius about the beginning of that century, though an important source of knowledge of the Celts and their way of life, is not entirely secure ground for generalisation on early British poetry. Diodorus distinguishes very clearly between Britain and Gaul, using the terms Brettania and Brettanikes for Britain and the Britons, and Galatia and Galatai for Gaul and the Gauls. The passage on the bards in the *Bibliotheke* comes in the section on Gaul, after the author has clearly finished with Britain. The applicability therefore of his remarks about the bards to Britain depends on the extent to which Britain had at that time been occupied by Celts of the same kind as those of Gaul. Not much notice has been paid to the fact that Posidonius

[1] *Gallic War*, vi, 14.
[2] *Bibliotheke*, v, 31–2.

reported that poets in Britain were called *bardoi*,[1] showing that the present Welsh word for poet, *bardd*, was already the name used one hundred years at least B.C.

The Celtic princes of that brilliant La Têne world which is reflected in the *Mabinogion* had their poets and musicians. Luerius, King of the Arverni, when he travelled in the second century B.C. went in a silver-mounted chariot and was accompanied by huntsmen, hounds and minstrels. If the poets did indeed censure as well as praise it is not unlikely that they influenced the policy of their masters and the temper of their fellow-countrymen. There is no doubt that the priests were important politically and the destruction of the Druids of Anglesey by Suetonius Paulinus was as necessary to the Romans as was the original decision of Julius Caesar to invade Britain because as the home of Druidism it continued to inspire Gallic resistance. After the christianising of Britain and during the long years of struggle against the English, the prophetic and exhortatory function of the druid was taken up by the poet, as is clearly shown in the considerable body of vaticinatory verse written from the eighth to the fourteenth century A.D. And as the Romans had gone to one of the main fountain heads of resistance in suppressing Druidism, so the English kings, Edward I and Henry IV, later made edicts against the poets, partly, at least, because of their influence in stiffening the Welsh national temper.

W. B. Yeats in his preface to Lady Gregory's *Cuchulain of Muirthemne* says, "The Irish poets had also, it may be, what seemed a supernatural sanction, for a chief poet had to understand not only innumerable kinds of poetry, but how to keep himself for nine days in a trance. They certainly believed in the historical reality of even their wildest imaginations." In that splendid, if decaying, civilisation which existed in Britain before the coming of the Romans the duties of poet and priest seem to be interwoven, but the degree to which this happened and the period when the overlapping took place (perhaps as at the present day only at moments of national danger) cannot be ascertained.

[1] Posidonius 23, *Fragmenta Historicum Graecorum*, vol. III, p. 259.

We are on surer ground, however, when we approach the more normal function of the ancient Welsh or British poet and his place in the society which clung to its integrity through the bloody centuries which followed the coming of the English to the island of Britain. Let us attempt then to consider by what kind of men Welsh poetry has been written, what their position in society has been, and how many of them have depended on the writing of poetry for a living.

The survey must of necessity begin before the term Welsh, bestowed by the English, can properly be used, and when even the term British may be misleading, for the early references we have to the Celts apply rather more to Gaul than to Britain and hardly at all to non-Celtic Britain, that is, the North and West. The chieftains of pre-Roman Britain had poets in their retinue but it is unlikely that their work, whether of praise or obloquy or of more trivial matters, was ever written down. Some of the poetry composed during the millennium after the landing of Julius Caesar certainly was recorded, but no poetry has so far been found in any manuscript dating earlier than the ninth century, though there is plenty of evidence of the existence of professional poets from the seventh century onwards.

The earliest known Welsh poetry (and here the term Welsh must be used for convenience sake) was composed in what we today call Scotland by Taliesin and Aneirin in the sixth century. Taliesin writes as a *penkerdd* or chief poet attached to a princely house, so that this early poetry seems to have been professionally written. He praises Urien, the king of Rheged (identified as the counties of Wigtown and Kirkcudbright today) and after Urien his son Owain, whose death in battle he laments. In the tradition of the house poet he praises their courage in battle and their generous hospitality at home.

Aneirin is not so easy to place socially. In some capacity he belonged to the household of Mynyddawg, who ruled in Edinburgh, but in his poem *Y Gododdin* there is less praise of the prince and more lamentation for the three hundred young men who made the spectacular but disastrous attack on the English of Deira at Cattraeth (Catterick). He knew them all, he had drunk and trained with them, and he speaks as a witness of their exploit. He may therefore have been one of them, a survivor endowed with the gift to record their bravery, and thus he may well foreshadow the warrior poets of the twelfth century.

The third great name in ancient Welsh poetry is that of Llywarch Hen. Llywarch was a prince of the North and a cousin of Urien, king of Rheged, but he ended his days in Powys and for the first time we have Welsh poetry associated with Wales, in the body of verse connected with his name. These poems lament the death of Llywarch's sons in battle and his own miserable old age, whilst others in the name of Heledd lament the killing of her brothers. Sir Ifor Williams has shown these poems to be an accretion of work by several hands between the seventh and the twelfth century about the stories of Llywarch and Heledd, verse sections of story cycles which may have been mostly in prose, but it is difficult to abandon entirely the possibility of a princely old poet and of a first poetess in the case of the indubitably old sections, for there is in these poems such intensity of personal feeling. A similar problem, though much nearer to us in time, arises out of the Sonnets of Shakespeare. In some sonnets the poet may be writing to order and speaking on behalf of another person. It is quite easy to believe this of Sonnets 1–17 for example, but what reader of any sensitivity would question the personal note in, to give just one example, Sonnet 30? This, I think, is a valid argument against the theory of bardic schools and multiple authorship in the case of *Y Gododdin* and at least some of the Llywarch and Heledd verse, the strong feeling one has that the poet is talking about his own loss.

The names of other poets of this period are remembered in later writing. Nennius, in his eighth century *Historia Britonum*, mentions Talhaearn, Neirin (obviously Aneirin), Taliesin, Bluchbard and Cian. Other names of poets who are said to have written in the seventh century are Myrddin, Morfran and Golyddan, and though their work has been lost there is no reason not to believe that they lived and wrote. Arofan is said to have been the poet of Selyf ap Cynan who fell in 615, and Afan Ferddig was the poet of Cadwallon ap Cadfan. The Domesday Book tells us that Gruffydd ap Llywelyn, king of Wales 1055–1063, had as his bard a poet called Berddig. Gildas, the first and one of the most severe critics of Welsh society, looking at Wales from his exile on the continent, had some centuries before this complained that the princes listened too much to the flattery of their poets.

A happy picture of conditions which quite understandably induced poets to extremes of praise is preserved for us in a poem called *Edmyg Dinbych* (Praise of Tenby) written about the year 900, in which we are told of the welcome given to poets by Bleiddud, Lord of Tenby, and in which we catch a glimpse of them being regaled with mead and wine in this safe castle overlooking the western sea.

In the Ireland too of the first millennium after Christ the poet was treated with a general respect and his position as a teacher regularised, but the Irish poet seems for the most part to have been either peripatetic or settled in a bardic school of a type which continued to function until suppressed by Elizabeth. In Wales there seems to have been more settlement of poets in the houses of the great and that is how we see them referred to in the statement of their privileges in the Laws of Hywel Dda.

[ii]

The fine code of law associated with the name of this tenth century king gives so complete a picture of the position of the poet in pre-Norman Welsh society that I propose to assemble here the references it makes to the different grades of poet. A warning must first of all be made. Though everything indicates conclusively enough that this code was formulated by Hywel Dda in the tenth century, the earliest version we have of it today is in a manuscript of the late twelfth century, so that the original code has probably suffered some Norman modification.[1] Hywel had visited Rome and frequently attended

[1] v. A. W. Wade-Evans, *Welsh Mediæval Law*, O. U. P., 1909.

sessions of the Wessex Witenagemot, and he codified existing Welsh practice into a body of law in emulation of Charlemagne, Alfred the Great and Rhodri the Great, his grandfather. It may be accepted that this code fixed and clarified what was already conventional to varying degrees in Wales before the tenth century, and that it regulated Welsh justice up to the end of the thirteenth century.

Three grades of poet are mentioned in the Laws of Hywel Dda, the *penkerdd* or chief poet, the *bardd teulu* or house poet, and the *cerddor* or minstrel-jongleur. Of these the minstrel seems to have been too lowly to have his rights defined by law and was therefore probably not a free man.

A poet became a penkerdd or chief poet when he won a chair, that is a seat in the immediate entourage of the king or prince. In hall he then sat next but one to the edling, or heir to the throne, the priest sitting between them. The chief poet sang first in hall. He received twenty-four pence from each virgin when she married. He had authority over the other poets and certain responsibilities when their daughters married. When the king asked for a song the chief poet sang two songs of God and one of princes. (This of course sounds like a modification by monkish scribes and, in fact, one manuscript (Cott. Cleo. X. 80) makes him sing three songs of Camlan, one of Arthur's battles.) The legal value of the chief poet's harp was one hundred and twenty pence, like that of the king, and of his tuning horn twenty pence.

The king's house poet was one of the twenty-four officers of the court and as such he had the right to woollen clothing from the king and linen clothing from the queen three times a year, at Christmas, Easter and Whitsun. He had the right of protection over a man until that man was conducted to the chief of the household. With the king's doctor he was given lodging in the house of the chief of the king's household, which was the biggest house next to that of the king. In the traditional passing on of the garments of lenten penance the poet received those of the steward and handed on his own to the doorkeeper. He got a steer from each spoil when he accompanied the household on a raid. On the day of battle it was his duty to sing *Unbeinyaeth Prydain* (The Sovereignty of Britain). When soliciting the king he sang one song, and two when soliciting a nobleman, but if he solicited a churl he should sing till he was tired!

The king gave him land and a horse, and in hall he sang second after the chief poet. When appointed he received a harp from the king and a gold ring from the queen. He was never to part with the harp. If the queen wished to hear a song in her apartment, the house poet should sing her three songs quietly, so as not to disturb the hall.

The conventional legal dues of the house poet are fixed, the insult fine, the murder fine, the land dues, and the three dues, *gobr*, *cowyll* and *agweddi*, connected with the marriage of his daughter. There were three arts which a churl was not permitted to teach his son, to be a scholar, a poet or a blacksmith. If the youth managed to practise one of these arts without detection he became a free man.

Kerddorion or minstrels are only mentioned together with almsmen as part of the retinue of the king.

Poets therefore ranked high in the civil service of the Welsh kings and once the poet had gained his rank as chief poet or house poet he was at least as secure as his master. And poetry was one of the three means, precarious though they may well have been, of rising into the class of freemen.

This code was law in Wales until 1285 and even after the last king of Wales held court it must have regulated the conduct of landowners towards their house poets, for the spirit of this law was followed for centuries after its sanctions no longer operated. A better way of putting it may be to say that the attitude towards poetry which informed this part of the law continued to be valid at least until the seventeenth century in some of the old houses of Wales. Noble houses continued to receive poets and some religious houses were equally hospitable. Cwrt y Brodyr in Carmarthen welcomed the visits of Tudur Aled in the fifteenth century. But from the end of the thirteenth century the poets had to depend on patronage and hospitality rather than on their legal rights. The effect of this upon their work will be discussed later in the book.

Great poetry was written by the house or court poets of the twelfth century and now for the first time we have not only the names of professional poets but some part at least of their work, and the splendid names of Gwalchmai ap Meilyr and Cynddelw Brydydd Mawr go with their equally splendid verse. Some of the poets must have become rich and it is a pleasant suggestion of Professor W. J. Gruffydd that place names like Llanfihangel Tre'r Beirdd, Tre Walchmai, Tre Feilir, and Gafel Prydydd y Moch (Saint Michael, the town of the poets, the town of Gwalchmai, the town of Meilir, the holding of the poet of the pigs) are evidence of their landowning.

There is evidence too that many, if not all, of these court poets of the twelfth and thirteenth centuries were nobly born and that they fought as well as wrote. According to the elegy written by Bleddyn Fardd, Dafydd Benfras died in battle at Llangadock in South Wales. They were not beyond falling out with their patrons and Professor Lloyd-Jones sees evidence of such a quarrel in one of Gwalchmai's odes to Owain Gwynedd and in the subsequent absence of an elegy by the poet to his former patron.[1] It is possible that the *Rhieingerddi* (poems in praise of girls) of Cynddelw and Prydydd y Moch are sincere love poems of courtship, something more than the *amour courteois* of the troubadour, in which case the court poets of this period were well enough born to propose marriage to a princess.

At a time when the professional poet was so little removed in social position from the prince it is not surprising that the princes themselves should occasionally practise the art of poetry. The twelfth century has given us great amateur writing in verse by two princes of North Wales, Hywel ap Owain Gwynedd and Owain Cyfeiliog, lord of Powys. These two men had obviously studied versification and the poetic vocabulary under master poets and they are steeped in the old traditions, Owain

[1] J. Lloyd-Jones, *The Court Poets of the Welsh Princes*. Proceedings of the British Academy, vol. XXXIV.

Cyfeiliog to the extent of borrowing freely from *Y Gododdin*, but their work is very different from that of the professional poets. The effect of this princely incursion into poetry must be left for later discussion.

Since we know that poetry had often been recorded and preserved in monasteries and that some religious houses patronised poets after the day of the poets' disestablishment, we would expect to find religious verse written by monks and priests. We know the name of one monkish poet, the Brother Madog, author of a charming poem on the birth of Christ, but most of the religious poetry written during the Middle Ages is the work of the regular poets who were apt to prepare for their end by a type of poem known as *Marwysgafn*, or poem of the death bed. To adumbrate a conclusion which will be argued later it may be said here that poets living officially under the law of Hywel Dda were conservative in their slow evolving of metrical technique, whereas those outside this controlled grading, princes, priests and the wandering poets of the centuries of disorder, wrote more freely and were the instruments of innovation, or, if you look at the matter from another point of view, of decadence.

[iii]

English law was not imposed upon Wales until 1536 so that, after the death in battle of Llywelyn ap Gruffydd, the last prince of all Wales, in 1282, no one system of law was generally applied throughout Wales for over two centuries, and the country fell into a state of confusion and disorder. It is not surprising that there are corresponding signs of confusion in the categories of poetry. The greatest poets are sometimes forced to a wandering way of life. The distinction between chief poet and house poet fades, though, as we shall see later, the bards at their irregular meetings try to keep up the old order, and the matter of poetry, notably in the work of Dafydd ap Gwilym, comes closer to that of the wandering poets of France.

The position of Dafydd himself, writing during the middle

part of the fourteenth century, is not easy to define. He was of noble birth and for most of his writing years he seems to have had Ifor Hael, a nobleman of South Wales, as his patron, but it is impossible to say exactly on what terms he lived at Ifor Hael's house. From the evidence of the poems we know that Dafydd ap Gwilym made love in almost every part of Wales, but we do not know the reason for his wanderings.

From now on we occasionally find women who master the rules of versification. Some religious verse as well as *cywyddau* and *englynion* of considerable indecency are ascribed in different manuscripts to a poetess called Gwerfyl Mechain, who, from the evidence of her own verse, kept an inn near a ferry. A bawdy exchange in verse is attributed to her and Dafydd ap Gwilym. Very different in tone is the work of three girls who call themselves three deer of Denbigh in some charming *englynion* addressed to their prospective lovers.[1]

The introduction of English law and the poets' loss of their ancient legal rights did not prevent some of the noble families of Wales from keeping house poets in the old manner well into the sixteenth and, in one case, into the eighteenth century. But most poets from now on depend on more than one patron and wander about the country from one house to another. There were other poets of the fourteenth and fifteenth centuries, Dafydd ap Edmwnd and Tudur Aled for example, who were of noble descent but who wandered about the country like the professional poets. Poets not actually resident depended on patrons for help in all sorts of ways and many poems were written to ask for help. The *cywydd* of asking or of thanks for the granted request became one of the most common kinds of poem and we find requests for a black bull, a red bull, a bow and arrows, a hawk, a pair of greyhounds, a pair of peacocks, a stallion, a sword and a swan. Even so the poets kept their ancient pride and there is not much humility in these poems of asking.

From the sixteenth century on there are records of the work of the *clerwyr*, the wandering poets of the lowest order, whose

[1] MS. Mostyn 131, p. 9.

verses had not previously been thought worth writing down. The Welsh *clerwyr* were the counterpart of the continental *cleri* or *clerici vagantes*, the goliardi, and a Welsh translation from Latin of the middle of the fourteenth century gives *joculatores* as *y glêr*.[1] We are given amusing accounts of the journeys they undertook, the varied reception they were given, a big stick in the hands of a surly housewife, wine and gold at Carmarthen, a churlish welcome by an English household in Ludlow. One of the most popular of these wandering rhymesters of the sixteenth century, Robin Clidro, was killed by a highwayman whilst on his rounds in South Wales.

With the classical tradition of poetry falling on evil days attempts were made to preserve the old order. We know that the bards met occasionally during the sixteenth century, sometimes by royal commission as at Caerwys in 1523 and 1568, to decide on matters concerning their craft, but how the order or guild of poets was regulated is not known, though it is recorded that grades of bardhood were granted to successful aspirants at marriage feasts.

[iv]

The sixteenth century gives us a new type of poet, the gentleman writer of occasional verse, new only because from this time onwards more manuscripts have been preserved for us and for the first time we have occasional and satirical verse of a kind which must have been written before but which was either not formally recorded or has been lost in the decay and destruction of manuscripts, for our view of early Welsh poetry is of necessity conditioned by the comparatively small body of work which has survived. The satirical function of the poet noted by Diodorus Siculus had been represented in the later Middle Ages in the work of Adda Fras, Rhys Fardd and others, in criticism of noblemen, in anti-English writing and in praise of outlaws, which involved contempt for the foreign law. In the fifteenth century Sion Cent wrote nobly against godlessness and

[1] *Dafydd ap Gwilym a'i Gyfoeswyr*, ed. I. Williams and T. Roberts, Bangor, 1914, p. lvi.

immorality in the lives of landowners, and Lewys Glyn Cothi was outlawed for taking sides as a poet in the Wars of the Roses.

The coming of Henry Tudor to the English throne and the subsequent union of England and Wales brought a flood of young Welshmen to the English court, and, in a century and atmosphere in which Henry VIII, the Earl of Surrey, Sir Thomas Wyatt and Sir Philip Sidney concerned themselves with poetry, these Welshmen were probably encouraged there to write in their own language as well as in English, in tune with the new Renaissance attitude towards the vernacular languages. The anonymous author of *Araith Ddichan ir Gwragedd* (a satire against women) has picked up the Skeltonian manner. Dic Huws (Richard Hughes, Equerry to Queen Elizabeth) writes Elizabethan lyrics in Welsh. Other gentlemen go to the Tudor court and fight its battles abroad but continue to write in as traditional a Welsh manner as those staunch conservatives at home in Wales who refuse to acknowledge the Renaissance. Captain Tomas Prys writes an elegy to his dead love in the conventional form but with a new simplicity and directness of language. Kynrig Hanmer from the wars in France sends a well-turned *englyn* of farewell to Tournai as he threatens to go back to look for his bright girl. There are *englynion* on the fall of Thomas Cromwell, in praise of Mary Tudor, and any number of poems to Queen Elizabeth. Lewys ap Edwart, a gentleman of the Queen's guard, suffers from an affliction contracted in a venereal encounter and is unable to keep an appointment to dine with some of his fellow-countrymen in London, so he sends them by letter nine *englynion* explaining his unhappy predicament in vigorous but as yet unprintable Welsh.

Many parsons were writing and in a variety of metres, for they too were clearly not bound by the reactionary control of the guild of bards, though some of the more scholarly ones, like Sir Davyd Johns, the seventeenth century vicar of Llanfair Dyffryn Clwyd, kept to the established *cywydd* form. Edmwnd Prys, graduate of Cambridge, translated the Psalms, and by 1595 William Middleton, a captain of the Queen's navy, had completed his translation of the Psalms of David, both books intended for vernacular worship in the new Church. Middleton also wrote an interesting elegy on the death of the Countess of Pembroke, whom he refers to in the language of the age as his lady mistress. Every type of educated man, towards the end of Elizabeth's reign, was tackling the task of widening the scope of Welsh poetry and of making it more generally comprehensible.

The ancient practice of writing poems of praise was falling into disrepute since the flattery involved was becoming more and more out of proportion with the facts, and we see an amusing parody of this kind of verse written by Sion Tudur, who died in 1602. By the seventeenth century the wandering poets were being forced by economic necessity to settle down to more regular occupations and verse is written by farmers, cattle-drovers and craftsmen, men who in an earlier age would have given all their time to rhyming and peddling their rhymes up and down the country. But they still occasionally write poems of praise or of asking to wealthy patrons. The more popular free style of the *penillion* was widely used for religious and moral purposes by Catholic, Anglican and Puritan worthies of the seventeenth century.

In the eighteenth century the urge to rhyme was still strong in the farmers, drovers and craftsmen of Wales and a considerable body of ballads results from this urge. The wandering *clerwr* had finally settled down to the land, the smithy and the cobbler's last, and every community had someone capable of a song about an unusual happening or a stanza for a tombstone. Some such rustic poets still studied the classical metres and not, in this century of antiquarianism, as a re-discovery of the past but in a direct and in some cases still traceable line of tutelage from the great practitioners of the fourteenth century. The bards would still meet in tavern eisteddfodau. But the work which literary historians pay most attention to in considering the eighteenth century is the product of parsons and scholars who brought to their traditional poetic lore an awareness of European movements and of other literatures. Such were the members of the Morris circle, Goronwy Owen and David Davies, Castell Hywel. The influence of contemporary English writing is observable in their work, though perhaps more on the subject matter than the manner. Later in the century London became the centre of Welsh antiquarianism, and the exchange of views between these writers was almost entirely through the medium of letters.

One other clerical poet of this century must be mentioned but this time one of a much more unscholarly type, William Williams, Pantycelyn, the hymn writer. He wrote in the free metres and, whether or not he is the greatest Welsh poet of modern times, he gave the Welsh people its most popular poetry. There is hardly a big rugby match today at which his words are not sung.

A man could no longer make a living or even materially supplement his income by writing verse, so that serious poetry became the province of people with some leisure and of some education, that is to say parsons and schoolmasters. As the livelier members of this class turned to Methodism, the end of the eighteenth century brought a resulting contempt and detestation for the more popular and more pagan kind of writing, for the ballad, the interlude and the traditional stanzas sung to the harp.

[v]

The type of man who writes Welsh poetry has not changed much since the eighteenth century, for most of the poetry of this present century has been written by Nonconformist ministers and university professors. Poets have, of course, arisen from other sections of society. The nineteenth century had its drink-loving architectural mason Talhaiarn, its correct station-master Ceiriog. In our century rural poets have continued to become masters of the classical metres. The tradition of the *clerwr* was alive within living memory in the Aeron valley in Cardiganshire and never-printed scraps of verse by the redoubtable Cerngoch and his circle are still quoted in those parts.

In the English-speaking South Wales town where I was bred tradesmen and master craftsmen and workmen studied the rules of versification and one of my early memories is of a coal merchant and my father composing *englynion* before the fire on a winter's evening. A young man I met recently at a railway station spoke no Welsh himself but, hearing me talk Welsh to my companion, offered to repeat a stanza he had learnt from his father and which I have never seen recorded. A barmaid at Tregaron capped my *englyn* with another and the county road surveyor had to read the copies I had made of fourteenth century *cywyddau* at the National Library. When I recited to a friend of mine, headmaster of a West Wales school, the epitaph of a seventeenth century bishop, he repeated it to a bank manager who the next morning passed it on to a solicitor and a shopkeeper, so that in a day or so it was being told in all its bright paganism all over the little town.

Interest in poetry and respect for it as a necessary and important part of the life of any complete community have therefore been fostered along two levels in Welsh-speaking Britain, the strict conventions of the chief poet and house poet passing on to the priest and the scholar, the freer tradition of the minstrel and the wandering singer persisting in the work of the village rhymester. But these two categories, in spite of mediæval law and more recent snobbery, have probably never been quite distinct, and they are happily not so today.

Chapter II

600—850

★

The earliest Welsh poetry which has come down to us, that of the end of the sixth century, is so old in comparison with poetry in other Western European languages that doubts have often been cast upon its antiquity. There have been reasons which justify such doubts. There is, first of all, the unfortunate fact that so much early poetry has completely disappeared, leaving the names of poets as though suspended in a vacuum which is preserved by tradition. The same is true of English literature, except that the very names of the poets have there disappeared with their work, for the Norman Conquest interfered much more with the continuous literary tradition in England than in Wales, where its effect was ultimately beneficial and not in the least retarding. Let me quote from Professor George Sampson's Introduction to his *Cambridge Book of Prose and Verse* (pp. xxi–ii). "If the reader will glance again at the contents of these manuscripts, and consider how many poems owe their existence to a freak of chance that has saved alive four old and perishable books from the wrecks of a thousand years, he should wonder, not that there is so little Old English literature, but that there is so much. What has vanished we cannot begin to conjecture . . . Of all the literature produced in the six hundred years between the coming of Hengist and the death of Harold no more has survived than a single generation could have written."

Another source of doubt is that we have no contemporary written versions of early poetry in English or in Welsh. At least four centuries separate the composition of *Beowulf* from its transcription in the form we have it today. The gap is even greater in other cases. The Indian epic *Mahabharata*, although probably composed by the year 200 B.C., does not exist in any manuscript older than the fifteenth century. It is not likely ever to be proved whether or not the *Chanson de Roland* was really sung by a minstrel as the Normans landed in England. In all these cases changes, additions and omissions may have been made by the many copyists, especially if they happen to have been poets. It has been the task of scholarship progressively during the last two hundred years, since the antiquarian movement of the eighteenth century first indicated the importance of these manuscripts, to detect the changes and to establish and to date the earliest form of the poems in question. Forgeries have been exposed, but in the study of early Welsh poetry the task of the scholar has been complicated, strangely enough, by the very continuity of the poetic tradition. For the poets of the twelfth and thirteenth centuries were themselves antiquarians and often made their work deliberately archaic. Less scholarly copyists of the thirteenth, fourteenth and fifteenth centuries would sometimes risk an ascription when they were not certain of the authorship so that we have poems over the name of Taliesin and Myrddin which were not written by them.

The study of language and of prosody has reached, however, such a point by today as to enable a good deal of dependable light to be thrown upon this puzzling field. In this chapter on early Welsh poetry I shall attempt to convey the findings of the best Welsh scholars of our day, findings which may well be definitive.

Aneirin

The work of Aneirin has come down to us in a manuscript of the thirteenth century called *Llyfr Aneirin*, the Book of Aneirin, now MS Cardiff I, and the main problem connected with it has been to establish the authentic antiquity of this poet's work, a task which has been performed by Sir Ifor Williams in his excellent edition.[1] He argues from the language and the form of the poetry, from annals and chronicles and

[1] *Canu Aneirin*, Welsh University Press, 1938.

persistent tradition, that the greater part of the work known as *Y Gododdin* dates from the end of the sixth century.

Aneirin wrote in Edinburgh. That Welsh poetry should have been written in Scotland is perhaps sufficiently startling to require some immediate explanation, for of the many languages that have been spoken in that country Welsh is not often remembered as a notable one. Under the Roman occupation a Brythonic language, which towards the end of that occupation was developing into the language we know today as Welsh, was spoken throughout Britain south of a line drawn roughly from the Clyde to the Forth. During the first centuries, therefore, of the Anglo-Saxon penetration of Britain, Welsh was the language of southern Scotland.

Aneirin was a poet at the court of Mynyddawg Mwynvawr, chieftain of the Gododdin tribe, whose capital was Edinburgh, known then as Eidin or Dineidin, and in the poem called *Y Gododdin* he recorded an attack made by a sort of commando force, trained by Mynyddawg, against the English of Deira and Bernicia. Let me briefly tell the story of this raid as it can be pieced together from the poem, for there is no narrative continuity in the poem itself. Mynyddawg gathered to his court at Eidin youthful representatives of Brythonic Britain. There they trained and drank mead and wine for a whole year until they were ready, three hundred resolute young men, to set out southwards, gold-torqued and brightly armed, on horseback. They attacked the English at Catterick and fought against heavy odds for a week, except for truces on Friday and Sunday to count the dead. Only one returned, the poet himself (another section of the poem gives the number of survivors as four), but they had killed many times their number of the enemy. This is not incredible if it is remembered that these English may not yet have learnt from the Britons the use of the horse and of body armour in warfare.

The poet takes the warriors one by one or in groups and concentrates on their valour, for this is poetry of the heroic age, but at the same time a variety of character emerges. Some are blusteringly bold, others shy and gentle. All are brave in battle.

One seems to have been bashful when he met a girl, but he fought and died as bravely as any.

Kayawc kynhorawc men ydelhei
diffun ymlaen bun med a dalhei.

Diademed and to the fore wherever he went,
breathless before a girl, he paid for his mead.

The poem begins in the middle of things with a lament for a youth whose name is not given except as the son of his father. We see him setting out on his swift horse, his tunic threaded with gold at the edge.

Gredyf gwr oed gwas
gwrhyt am dias
meirch mwth myngvras
a dan vordwyt megyrwas
ysgwyt ysgauyn lledan
ar bedrein mein vuan
kledyuawr glas glan
ethy eur aphan . . .
kynt y waet e lawr
nogyt y neithyawr
kynt y vwyt y vrein
noc y argyurein
ku kyveillt ewein
kwl y uot a dan vrein
marth ym pa vro
llad vn mab marro. [ll. 1-8 and 13-20]

The instinct of man with the age of youth
courage for fighting;
fast long-maned stallions
under thighs of a fine youth;
light broad shield
on the slim swift crupper;
clean blue swords,
garments bordered with gold . . .
Sooner his blood flows
than there's a wedding;
sooner he's crow's food
than there's a burying;

sweet friend to Owain,
shame that crows perch on him.
It's a horror to me,
the killing of Marro's one son.

We are given pictures of the youths at the court of Mynyddawg, drinking mead and wine from horns and cups of gold and silver. There is poetry and music to entertain them in the hall, and garments of purple and gold. At more than one point in the poem there is a suggestion that too much mead was drunk, but, as one less puritanical critic has remarked, even if they were drunk setting out they had a week to sober up. The bitterness with which the poet looks back upon the mead drunk is not due to any detrimental effect of the drinking on their performance in battle, but to his realisation that they paid for this mead with their lives, in returning service to Mynyddawg for his hospitality. This is how the whole company is described.

Gwyr a aeth gatraeth oed fraeth eu llu
glasved eu hancwyn a gwenwyn vu
trychant trwy beiryant en cattau
a gwedy elwch tawelwch vu
ket elwynt e lanneu e benydu
dadyl dieu agheu y eu treidu. [ll. 68–73]

The men who went to Catterick were a cheerful band,
fresh mead their sustenance, it became bitterness.
Three hundred in order embattled
and after feasting there came silence.
They went to churches to do penance
but death the ineluctable struck them down.

As the old Welsh proverb says, Mead is sweet but bitter when paid for.[1] Bitterer still is the memory of a man whose friends have made the payment of their lives.

Ket yvem ved gloyw wrth leu babir
ket vei da e vlas y gas bu hir. [ll. 138–9]

We drank bright mead by candle light;
though it tasted good, it's been long detested.

[1] *Chweg medd, chwerw pan daler.*

Sometimes a group of them is taken together as in the following section with its fine list of names which includes the first reference in literature to Peredur, the Perceval of later Arthurian romance.

Gwyr a gryssyassant buant gytneit
hoedyl vyrryon medwon uch med hidleit
gosgord vynydawc enwawc en reit
gwerth eu gwled o ved vu eu heneit
caradawc a madawc pyll ac yeuan
gwgawn a gwiawn gwynn a chynvan
peredur arueu dur gwawrdur ac aedan
achubyat enggawr ysgwydawr angkyman
a chet lledessynt wy lladassan
neb y eu tymhyr nyt atcorsan. [ll. 353-363]

The men who attacked had lived together,
in their brief lives were drunk on distilled mead,
Mynyddawg's army famous in battle.
Their lives paid for their feast of mead.
Caradawg and Madawg Pyll and Ieuan,
Gwgawn and Gwiawn, Gwynn and Cynvan,
Peredur of steel weapons, Gwawrdur and Aedan,
they had their shields broken in the battle;
and though they were being killed they killed.
Not one came back to his belongings.

One of them, at least, was about to be married, but his blood flowed before the time of his wedding. Many Englishwomen are widowed and mothers weep. There are passages as grim and brutal as the battle must have been, as in the following lines, where one of the rare similes of the poem occurs.

Yt ladei a llauyn vreith o eithin
val pan vel medel ar vreithin
e gwnaei varchlew waet lin. [ll. 309-311]

He killed with sharp blade spotted with blood,
as when harvesters reap in uncertain weather,
thus Marchlew made blood flow.

One of the heroes of the *Gododdin*, Tudfwlch by name, is celebrated in a separate poem called *Gwarchan Tudfwlch*, one of the most splendid things in the *Book of Aneirin*. Tudfwlch's eyes were like spears, "bright as a snake's from a snake's earth", he loved danger in his life, he was the wildness of the sea in the vanguard of men, he was a net for foes and for the love of girls.

Parts of the *Book of Aneirin*, are clearly later than Aneirin himself. We are told of his death in lines 647–8 and then how much his poetry is missed.

> Er pan aeth daear ar aneirin
> nu neut ysgaras nat a gododin. [ll. 654–5]
>
> Since earth has covered Aneirin
> now song has left the land of Gododdin.

Another later addition to the poem is the charming lullaby *Pais Dinogad*, with its quick movement and bright picture of early British domestic life, but so clearly incongruous is it here that I shall deal with it in a later chapter.

The *Gododdin* is a heroic poem made up of a series of lyrical fragments, thus seeming to conform with Stage One of Chadwick's classification of epic development,[1] but even though there is not the architectural form required of an epic there is in the poem a high degree of poetic craftsmanship in the writing of the disjointed sections. Even if the early date of the sixth century is accepted for most of the poem, this artistry does not surprise us when we remember that we have evidence that the poetic art had been practised in Britain for at least seven centuries before the *Gododdin* was written.

There is a considerable variety of metre, including rudimentary forms of several of the measures classified later, and the poem is rhymed throughout. In the section quoted above, beginning *Gwyr a gryssyassant*, may be observed end rhyme, internal rhyme, alliteration and assonance. Most of the sections of the poem consist of a series of lines with one rhyme, as far as

[1] H. M. Chadwick, *The Heroic Age*. The stages are briefly these: 1. Court-poems of the Heroic Age. 2. Epic and narrative poems based on these. 3. Popular poetry of the ballad kind. 4. Later treatment of heroic material.

we know the earliest poetic form in Welsh. It is interesting that the *Chanson de Roland* is written in this same form of one-rhyme sections.

The style of the poem is simple and direct, much use being made of arresting contrasts, as in the very first line of the poem, where the youth of the warriors is set alongside the maturity of their virtue and again in the tremendous line *a gwedy elwch tawelwch vu*—and after feasting there was silence. The language shows frequent signs of the romanisation of the British way of life, the chieftain is referred to as *dragon ducawt* and *rector*, and in hall he will sit on a *lleithic* (Latin, lectica), but as yet there is no trace at all of borrowing from English.

The civilisation depicted is that of the heroic ages of the Aryan world. The qualities admired in a man are courage, fidelity, the keeping of a promise and the payment of mead, which, as in the Anglo-Saxon *Finn* fragment, means faithful service to the chieftain whose mead you have drunk,[1] even though the payment required be the bitter one of death and the leaving behind of friendship and love, as Aneirin makes clear with terrible irony.

Taliesin

The main source for poems ascribed to the sixth century Taliesin is the thirteenth century manuscript, *Llyfr Taliesin*, the *Book of Taliesin*. Opinions of the authenticity of these poems have swung from too enthusiastic claims of unexceptional antiquity to an insistence that they are entirely mediæval. We now await Sir Ifor Williams' edition of the Taliesin poems, but enough of his research into the matter has been made public for us to be able to distribute this fascinating collection of poetry with some historical accuracy, for the work of this scholar has helped us to ascribe some poems to centuries which have until now appeared strangely barren of literary achievement.

Of the fifty eight poems in this manuscript seven are religious

[1] v. Professor Bruce Dickens. *Runic and Heroic Poems of the Old Teutonic Peoples.* Translation of the *Finn* fragment in *Cambridge Book of Prose and Verse.* To the Cycles of Romance, p. 22.

or biblical, probably of early mediæval authorship and inserted by monkish scribes as an act of penance for the pagan nature of much of the other poetry. Ten of the poems are of the prophetic sort and were probably all written after the year 900, and with one of these, *Armes Prydein*, I shall deal later on. There are some riddle poems, a list of proverbs, a poem in praise of Tenby which dates probably from the tenth century, and poems in praise of mead and beer.

Then, to come closer to Taliesin himself, there are two groups of poems more credibly associated with his name, one group of twelve historical poems which alone are likely to have been written by the sixth century poet and another group which Sir Ifor Williams claims to belong to a Taliesin saga and to a later period, most likely the ninth century.[1]

The twelve historical poems are set, like the *Gododdin* of Aneirin, in the North Britain of the late sixth century and are mostly in praise of Urien, king of Rheged, and of his son Owain. During the last quarter of that century Urien and Owain fought against Deodric, king of Bernicia, and against Hussa. Taliesin outlived both Urien and his son, but he immortalised them in song, and, with Arthur and Cynan and Cadwaladr, Urien and Owain grew into legendary figures during the Middle Ages.

Taliesin praises Urien in battle and at home. He calls him *angor gwlad*, the country's anchor or sustainer, and his sons *haelaf dyneddon*, most generous of men. We are told of his successful raids into enemy country, his burning of homesteads and carrying off of booty. This is poetry in the Aryan heroic manner and, as Professor W. J. Gruffydd has said,[2] there is none of the Roman influence to be observed here which he claims to detect in the Llywarch poetry.

The poems are short, the style bare, economical and striking. There are very few similes and metaphors, but when they occur they are powerful. This is how the English dead, lying on the battlefield, are described.

[1] *Lectures on Early Welsh Poetry*, pp. 50–5.

[2] *Barddoniaeth Cymru cyn Dafydd ap Gwilym*. Trans. H. S. C. 1937, pp. 262–3.

kyscit lloegyr llydan nifer
a leuer yn eu llygeit.
A rei ny ffoynt hayach
A oedynt hyach no reit.[1] [BT pp. 67–8]

The English sleep, a wide host,
with light in their eyes.
And those who fled not quicker
were braver than was needed.

The above lines are from a poem on the death of Owain, son of Urien Rheged. Urien himself is praised in a number of other poems for the characteristic heroic virtues of generosity to friends and ferocity towards enemies. Chadwick, in classifying heroic poetry, says, "To Stage I we may assign not only laudatory poems dealing with the victories and valour of living princes, but also such compositions as Gelimer's dirge and choric songs like the funeral chant over Attila."[2] Later, in dealing briefly with the poems to Owain and Urien which are attributed to Taliesin, he says, " . . . the poems themselves, even in the corrupt and often unintelligible form in which they are presented, plainly show all the marks of Stage I of our scheme. Their characteristics are those of court-poetry, but they never attain to true narrative. For analogies to the poems which deal with Urien we can hardly do better than turn to the court-poetry of the Viking Age."[3] Here is a specimen of how Urien Rheged is praised in the *Book of Taliesin.*

Uryen yr echwyd.haelaf dyn bedyd.
lliaws a rodyd.y dynyon eluyd.
mal y kynnullyd yt wesceryd.
llawen beird bedyd tra vo dyuuchyd.
ys mwy llewenyd gan clotuan clotryd.
ys mwy goginyant vot vryen ae plant.
Ac ef yn arbennic yn oruchel wledic.
yn dinas pellennic. ynkeimyat kynteic.
lloegrwys ae gwydant pan ymadrodant.
Agheu a gawssant a mynych godyant.
llosci eu trefret a dwyn eu tudet . . . [p. 57]

[1] I propose *hya* to make *hyach* as the most likely filling of the three-letter lacuna at the top of page 68 in the MS. J. G. E.'s effort is absurd.
[2] H. M. Chadwick, *The Heroic Age*, Camb. Univ. Press, 1926, p. 94.
[3] Chadwick, *op cit.*, p. 108.

Urien of Echwyd, most generous of Christians,
much do you grant to men in life;
as you gather so do you scatter;
the poets of Christendom[1] are happy whilst you live.
More happiness to the praiseworthy and famous,
more glory that Urien and his children live.
He the outstanding, the supreme chieftain,
refuge of the stranger, foremost in battle.
The English know this when they discuss matters,
death they have suffered and frequent pain,
their houses burnt, their garments taken.

For Britons at the end of the sixth century the Celtic parts of the island would constitute Christendom, since the English were still pagan at this time. One suspects that Christianity had not penetrated very deeply into the native way of life in Scotland and Wales (or, more correctly, North and West Britain), for Gildas says that the old Celtic idols were still standing in his day, and, if he is to be believed, the chieftains were a barbarous lot of scoundrels, but Christianity was one of the relics of the Roman civilisation which gave the Britons a feeling of superiority over the Teutonic invaders and thus qualified as an element in the flattery of a prince.

Stark boasting typical of the heroic age characterises a poem which is given the title of *Marwnat Uthyr Pendragon*, *On the death of Uthyr Pendragon*, Arthur's father according to later legend, in the *Book of Taliesin*.

Neu vi a torreis cant kaer.
neu vi aledeis cant maer.
Neu vi arodeis cant llen.
neu vi aledeis cant pen. [p. 71. ll. 16–18]

I have broken a hundred forts,
I have killed a hundred seneschals,
I have given a hundred garments,
I have cut off a hundred heads.[2]

[1] Literally *beird bedyd* means bards of baptism.
[2] cf. *lladd pen* meaning to cut off a head in *Branwen verch Llyr*, White Book (MS Peniarth 4), p. clxxxv.1.4.

The other group of poems which seem to form part of a Taliesin saga, the versified elements of unrecorded prose tales, is far more difficult to understand, has given rise to much more speculation than the earlier historical poems[1] and is therefore rather better known. In the form in which we have them they may have been written at any time from the eighth to the eleventh century, but they will be touched upon at this point, at the risk of suspicion of an attempt to anticipate the date of composition. Sir Ifor Williams, in his *Lectures on Early Welsh Poetry*, has drawn attention to a prose account of the life of Taliesin, a version of which Lady Charlotte Guest translated for her *Mabinogion*. This tale, recorded in a sixteenth century manuscript but probably of greater age, provides a framework for the strange knowledge which Taliesin claims in his verse and for his transformations from salmon to dog, then to stag and so on until he is a grain pecked up by a hen. This does not explain these mysterious utterances, for the tale seems to be a mediæval attempt to rationalise the poetry. To quote Matthew Arnold, "the writer is pillaging an antiquity of which he does not fully possess the secret," and these things are memories, such as Miss Jessie Weston discovered in the Perceval story, of ancient Celtic pre-Christian ritual which had lost its meaning when the tale came to be told but which retained its hold on the imagination, as indeed it still does.

The following transformations form part of a long poem called *Angar Kyvyndawt* or The Community of Hell.

Eil gweith ym rithat.
bum glas gleissat.
bum ki bum hyd.
bum iwrch ymynyd.
bum kyff bum raw.
bum buell yn llaw.
bum ebill yg gefel
blwydyn ahanher.
bum keilyawc brithwyn
ar ieir yn eidin.

[1] e.g. Robert Graves, *The White Goddess*.

Once more transformed,
I was a blue salmon,
I was dog, I was stag,
a roebuck in the mountains,
I was a stock and a spade,
I was a drill in a smithy
for a year and a half.
I was a speckled white cock,
desirous of hens.

Of his birth Taliesin speaks in an equally mysterious way.

Nyt o vam athat
pan ymdigonat.
Am creu am creat.
o naw rith llafanat.
o ffrwyth o ffrwytheu.
o ffrwyth duw dechrreu.
o vriallu a blodeu bre.
o vlawt gwyt a godeu.
o prid o pridret
pan ymdigonet.
o vlawt danat
o dwfyr ton nawvet. [p. 25]

Neither mother nor father
was my maker;
my source and my mould
were the senses, ninefold,
springing from fruits,
the fruit of God's roots,
primroses and hill bloom,
of tree and shrub blossom,
of earth and of clay,
on my birth day,
of nettle bloom
and the ninth wave's foam.

The ingredients remind one at once of the making of the beautiful and heartless Blodeuwedd in the *mabinogi* of *Math son of Mathonwy*, of the oak blossom, broom flowers and meadow-sweet out of which the enchanters Math and Gwydion made a wife for Llew Llaw Gyffes. The same magicians are in fact associated with the charming into life of Taliesin in the lines which continue this passage of the poem known as *Kat Godeu*.

Another famous poem is the riddle poem *Canu y Gwynt* or *Song of the Wind*, the occasion of which is said to have been an attempt to set free Taliesin's friends Elffin and Gwyddno from their imprisonment by Maelgwn Gwynedd in the castle of Deganwy. There is, however, nothing in the poem to justify this explanation, which springs from a later variant text translated by Lady Charlotte Guest in her *Mabinogion* and noted in the *Myvyrian Archaiology*. A need was no doubt felt for the rationalising of this poem, for it is the only riddle poem in Welsh. It is distinguished from the considerable body of late Latin, early Norse and English riddle poetry only by its much greater length.

Another poem which fits easily into a widespread type of primitive poetry, the catalogue poem, is the *Aduwyneu* or *Pleasant Things*, of Taliesin. The Chadwicks in their *Growth of Literature* relate this poem to early Greek and English catalogue poems and particularly to No. 13 of the Homeric Epigrams. The list of Taliesin's loved things offers a charming variety of objects. Pleasant to him are berries at harvest time, wheat on the stalk, flowers on an aromatic shrub, a long-maned horse, mead in the hall for the minstrel, the sun swift-rising in the sky, the moon shining on the world, fine Welsh and finally, a word cried out to the Trinity and a penance for sin.

In this tradition followed the fine poem in praise of Tenby, to be dealt with later, the *Gorhoffedd* poems of the twelfth century, particularly that of Hywel ap Owain Gwynedd and his shorter poems beginning with the words *I love* (*Karafy*). Prose lists of this kind were set as exercises in literary expression by masters to their apprentices in the craft of poetry during the Middle Ages and many of their products, the *Dewisbethau* and *Casbethau* (*Chosen and Detested Things*), were thought of sufficient interest to preserve in manuscript.[1]

[1] v. D. Gwenallt Jones, *Yr Areithiau Pros*. Welsh University Press, 1934.

Llywarch Hen

The third great name in early Welsh poetry seems, as the name of a poet, to have been struck a mortal blow by Sir Ifor Williams' edition of the poetry associated with the name of Llywarch Hen.[1] These poems record the tragic experiences and the prolonged grief of the old chieftain, Llywarch, and of the girl, Heledd, daughter of Cyndrwyn, a chieftain of Powys. As historical characters they may be placed towards the end of the sixth and the beginning of the seventh centuries respectively, but it would appear that the poems put in their mouths in the old manuscripts, chiefly the *Red Book of Hergest*, are of a later date and form part of story cycles which grew about their names during centuries in which Llywarch became the stock example of the old man who has outlived his glory. Sir Ifor Williams shows how these were probably prose tales with verse interpolations for greetings and epitaphs and for the conveying of emotion, and he finds remains of similar story cycles in the *Black Book of Carmarthen*. There are traces of this mingling of verse with prose in the *Mabinogion*, and in the manuscripts of the sixteenth and seventeenth centuries an *englyn* or sequence of *englynion* is sometimes introduced by the story which gives it background and *raison d'être*.[2] According to this theory the stories, or *cyfarwyddyd*, of Llywarch Hen and Heledd have been lost, perhaps never having been written down, and the verses only remain, having been recorded by some lover and collector of poetry.

Sir Ifor Williams considers the verse form, the primitive three-line *englyn* in this case; the language, as far as is possible when the alterations and modernisations of mediæval copyists have been taken into account; finally the stages in the struggle between the Welsh and the Saxons, and proposes some time about the year 850 for the composition of these poems. He omits much gnomic verse which is ascribed to Llywarch Hen in old manuscripts, limiting his selection to those poems or brief

[1] *Canu Llywarch Hen*. Welsh University Press, 1935.

[2] The use of occasional verse in prose tales is to be found in early Irish literature too, e.g. *The Adventures of Suibhne Geilt*. See also early French Arthurian romances.

fragments which refer to the families of Llywarch and Cyndrwyn.

Of the historicity of Llywarch the man there is little doubt, even if he never wrote a line of verse. He began his life in North Britain and some of the *englynion* lament the death of Urien Rheged, prince of what is today South-West Scotland and the patron of Taliesin, the Urien who, like Arthur, became a legend in the Middle Ages. The speaker in the poem carries the head of Urien from the battlefield.

Ry thyrvis vym breich, ry gardes vy eis.
  Vyg callon neur dorres.
 Penn a borthaf am porthes. [CLlH. p. 14]

My arm shakes, my breast trembles,
  my heart breaks.
 I carry a head by which I was fed.

Llywarch ended his life in Powys, North Wales, and there he saw his twenty-four sons killed one after another in the relentless war against Mercia. So he outlived his children and became the famous Old Man of mediæval Welsh literature. He laments especially the death of Gwên and Pyll, two favourite sons, and then bewails his own destiny in a bitter and famous poem of old age.

This is how Llywarch's *Lament* begins:—

Kynn bum kein vaglawc bum kyffes eiryawc
keinmygir uy eres
gwyr Argoet eiryoet am porthes.

Kynn bum kein vaglawc bum hy
am kynwyssit yg kyuyrdy
Powys paradwys Gymry.

Kynn bum kein vaglawc bum eiryan
oed kynwaew vym par oed kynwan
wyf keuyngrwm wyf trwm wyf truan.

Baglan brenn neut kynhayaf
rud redyn melyn kalaf
neur digereis a garaf.

Baglan brenn neut gayaf hynn
Yt wyd llauar gwyr ar llynn
neut diannerch vy erchwyn.

Baglan brenn neut gwannwyn
rud cogeu goleu e gwyn
wyf digarat gan uorwyn . . . [CLlH. pp. 8–9]

Before my back was bent I was a ready speaker,
my fame was great;
the men of Argoed always gave me to eat.

Before my back was bent I was bold,
welcome in beer houses
of the paradise of the Welsh, Powys.

Before my back was bent I was brilliant,
my spear was first, I was spearhead.
I'm round-backed, heavy and wretched.

Wooden crook, it is autumn;
ferns are red, grass is yellow;
him I refused is now my fellow.

Wooden crook, it is winter;
drinking men are talkative;
my bedside is not festive.

Wooden crook, it is spring,
cooks are red, there's feasting light.
I am no more the girls' delight.

He continues thus to address his stick, his only companion now, thinking back to the fighting, the stallions and the girls he once took delight in and hating himself for the plight in which he finds himself. The four things he hates most now attack him, coughing, old age, disease and longing. The poem ends thus.

Nym kar rianed nym kenniret neb
ny allaf darymret
wi a agheu nam dygret.

Nym dygret na hun na hoen
Gwedy lleas Llawr a Gwen
wyf annwar abar wyf hen.

Truan a dynghet a dynghet y Lywarch
yr y nos y ganet
hir gnif heb escor lludet.

The girls don't love me, no one frequents me;
this is captivity.
O, death, why don't you set me free?

No sleep nor mirth comes to me now
that Llawr and Gwên are killed.
I'm rotting carrion now, I'm old.

A wretched fate was doomed for Llywarch
on his birth night,
a long labour of grief that never grew light.

Another sequence of stanzas is put into the mouth of someone who lies sick, perhaps of leprosy, at Abercuawg. This man, whose name is not given, for he is referred to only as the Sick Man of Abercuawg, has time in the imprisonment of his sickness to look at nature and to feel very sorry for himself.

Gordyar adar gwlyb neint
llewychyt lloer oer deweint
crei vym bryt rac gofit heint. [CLlH. p. 24]

The birds are loud, the brooks are full,
the moon shines, the night is cold,
my mood is sad with the sadness of sickness.

The sick man is prevented from going to battle, yet, even though death in battle was the expected and honoured end, he thinks with greatest regret of the happy things of peace.

Alaf yn eil meil am ved
nyt eidun detwyd dyhed
amaerwy adnabot amyned. [p. 25]

Cattle in the shed, a cup for mead;
the happy do not ask for fighting.
Patience is the fringe of knowing.

The other important group in this body of poetry belongs to the girl Heledd. She too, like old Llywarch, is a desolate wanderer, her home destroyed, her brothers all dead. The hall of her favourite brother Cynddylan at Pengwern, in present-day Shropshire, has been burnt by the English and her brother killed. In the first stanza attributed to her she calls thus to her attendants:—

Sefwch allan vorynnyon a syllwch
    Gyndylan werydre
  Llys Bengwern neut tande
  gwae ieueinc a eidun brotre. [CLlH. p. 33]

Stand out, girls, and gaze
    towards Cynddylan's land;
  the hall of Pengwern burns,
and for her coverlet a sad girl yearns.

Her finest, most agonised poem is on this hall of Cynddylan and each stanza of the sixteen begins with the words *Stavell Gyndylan.*

Stauell Gyndylan ys tywyll heno
    heb dan heb wely
  wylaf wers tawaf wedy. [p. 35]

Cynddylan's hall is dark tonight;
    no fire, no bed.
  I'll weep awhile and then be still.

She remembers the feasting, the songs, the wisdom and the security, but now her brothers are dead and she is left to lament. This is no wild keening but a controlled agony of a kind which is rare in literature.

More frightening is Heledd's poem on the Eagle of Pengwern which is eager for flesh she has loved and which will tonight feast on Cynddylan.

Eryr Penngwern penngarn llwyt heno
  aruchel y euan
 eidic am gic Kynndylan. [p. 38]

Eagle of Pengwern, grey-beaked, tonight
  its call is high,
 eager for Cynddylan's flesh.

Five stanzas turn upon this terrible thought.

And this is how she speaks of the White Town, probably Whittington near Oswestry, where they lived together in the days of their happiness.

Y dref wenn yn y thymyr
y hefras y glas vyuyr
y gwaet a dan draet y gwyr . . .

Y dref wenn rwng Trenn a Throdwyd
oed gnodach ysgwyt tonn yn dyuot o gat
nogyt ych y echwyd.

Y dref wenn rwng Trenn a Thraual
oed gnodach y guaet ar wyneb gwellt
noc eredic brynar. [pp. 39–40]

White town of this countryside,
green mounds are now your honour
and blood men trample under . . .

White town between Trenn and Trodwyd,
more torn shields came from battle
than homing cattle.

White town between Trenn and Trafal,
there was more blood on your field's face
than ploughshare's trace.

So great seems to me the personal anguish in some of the utterances given to Llywarch Hen and to Heledd that it is difficult even in the face of confident scholarship to abandon entirely the sixth century Llywarch and the early seventh century Heledd as the original composers of at least the kernel of the poetry in the story cycles which clearly grew up about their names in the centuries that followed their unhappy lives.

In style the Llywarch and Heledd poems show many of the qualities we have already observed in the *Gododdin*, the striking, briefly stated contrast, the concise expression of grief, the economy of words which was made easier by the grammar of Welsh in that day. There are repetitions, with and without variation, which suggest lamentation, but which also, when they occur at the beginning of stanzas in a sequence, were aids to the reciter's memory. There is abundant assonance and alliteration, though not yet systematised, and internal and end rhyme. The stanzas are either in the form of variants of the primitive three-line *englyn* or stanzas of three lines united by a rhyme, most lines carrying three stresses. The *englynion* are similar to those of the Cambridge *Juvencus* manuscript, the date of which is about 850.

Myrddin

Of the work of Talhaearn, Cian, Dygynnelw, Morfran, Arofan and Afan Ferddig, poetic bearers of splendid names, of whose existence in the sixth and seventh centuries we have some evidence, nothing certain remains. Poems are sometimes ascribed to them in the manuscripts, but this is thought today to have been merely the fathering of work upon ancient names either by copyists and recorders uncertain of the authorship of what they were handing on, or by reciters who wished to enhance the value of their repertoire.

In the case of Myrddin, the tradition is much stronger and more consistent, and the ascription of poems more frequent. Myrddin, the Merlin of Arthurian legend, was probably a warrior bard of North Britain who lived towards the end of the sixth century. The legend which grew about his name says that he went mad in battle and retired to a wood in Scotland called Coed Celydon (the name is remembered in *Caledonia*), where he lived alone and wrote prophetic verse. For this reason he was known later as Myrddin Wyllt (or Myrddin the wild) and

Merlinus Silvanus or Silvestris. There are resemblances in the story of Myrddin to those of the Irish Suibhne Geilt and the Scottish Lailoken, so that the basic story may well have had a common Celtic source much older than the historical Myrddin of the sixth century, with whom it later became associated. Miss Enid Griffiths[1] points out the similarity of the name Lailoken to the Welsh word *llallogan*, which meant twin or brother or lord, and the fact that in an early poem in the *Red Book of Hergest*, *Cyfoesi Myrddin a Gwenddydd*, Gwenddydd addresses her brother, Myrddin, as *llallogan*, whatever the word means. More recent work by Mr. A. O. H. Jarman and Mr. James Carney has confirmed the basic identity of Myrddin, Lailoken and Suibhne Geilt. The later story of Tristram too has elements in common with these three.

The core of one of the four ancient books of Wales, the *Black Book of Carmarthen*, was the work traditionally ascribed to Myrddin, whose name occurs in the Welsh form, Caerfyrddin. This is mostly prophetic verse and is thought today to refer almost exclusively to events of the eleventh and twelfth centuries, and therefore to have been written as bogus prophecies in those centuries to encourage resistance against the English and the Normans. Myrddin, in spite of all this, is not so easily disposed of as a figure of legend only and a convenient name for giving authority to political utterances. It seems more and more likely that the twelfth century *Vita Merlini* was based on older Welsh material, and Giraldus Cambrensis testifies in the same century to an oral tradition connected with Myrddin in North Wales. Then there is a reference to Myrddin in *Armes Prydain*, a prophetic poem occurring in the *Book of Taliesin*, which poem Sir Ifor Williams now dates about the year 930.

It would seem therefore that legendary accretion and the inaccurate fathering of work has occurred in large measure to an historical Myrddin who was probably a poet. Any prophetic verse he himself may have written has been altered to fit later events, altered perhaps time after time, so that it is doubtful whether the original core of poetry may at this late age be laid

[1] *Early Vaticination in Welsh*, p. 75.

bare of the additions and changes of copyists and adapters. The problem has not yet been thoroughly tackled, but the strength of the tradition associated with his name suggests that, the Druids having disappeared with the christianising of Britain under the Romans, Myrddin, like Taliesin but not Aneirin, was one of the poets who united the functions of druid and bard.

Not all the poems given to Myrddin are prophetic. The following poem, which I cannot pretend to understand fully, must refer to some person and incident of early Christian times in our island.

Du dyuarch du dycapan
du dy pen du duhunan
iadu ae ti yscolan.

Mi iscolan yscolheic
yscawin y puill iscodic
guae ny baut a gaut guledic.

O losci ecluis a llat buch iscol
allyvir rod y voti
vy penhid ystrum kynhi.

Creaudir y creadureu
porthideu muyhaw kyrraw de imi vy geu
ath vradaste am tuyllas ynneu.

Bluytin llaun im rydoded
ym bangor ar paul cored
edrich de poen imy gan more pryued.

Bei yscuypun ar un
more amluc guint y vlaen bric guit fallum
arav vneuthume bith nys gunaun. [BBC. p. xii]

Black your stallion, black your cap,
black your head, black yourself,
black skull, is it you Ysgolan?

I am Ysgolan the learned one;
the frightened man is light in judgement;
a pity that churlish deed was done.

For burning a church and killing school cattle
and the drowning of a gift book
my penance is heavy upon me.

Creator of all creatures,
our greatest help, forgive my wrong;
he who betrayed you cheated me.

I was given a full year
at Bangor on the stake of a weir;
see the pain the sea worms gave me.

If I had known what now I see,
obvious as wind in the top twigs of a tree,
I should never have done what was done by me.

Sir Ifor Williams takes these stanzas to have formed part of yet another *cyfarwyddyd* or prose tale with occasional verses and points out the element of dialogue in them.[1] History records no Ysgolan Ysgolhaig, but in a late sixteenth century poem in praise of the Welsh translation of the Bible the following lines occur:—

pob kelvyddyd a dysc ffraeth, ddoedd gwir wybodaeth ganto
nes y Scolan gythrel gay ddinistro llyfray'r kymro.

Every art and fluent learning, he had every knowledge,
till the false devil Scolan destroyed the Welshman's books.

Another version of this poem states that this Scolan had been sent by the Pope and that, encouraged by his success, the proud Augustine used the English to destroy the great schools of Wales. The incident of the drowning of the books is similar to the Irish Suibhne Geilt's flinging of a psalter into a lake in his persecution of Christianity, and both stories belong to the early days of that religion in Celtic Britain.

The prophetic poems of the *Black Book of Carmarthen*, though they may well retain a core or framework of Myrddin's writing,

[1] *Canu Llywarch Hen*, p. xli. Gwenogfryn Evans (ed. BBC p. xviii) believes this poem to be a dialogue between the poet Taliesin and his father confessor, Yscolan, but I see little sense in this interpretation.

are so heavily overlaid with later political material that they must be left for later consideration.

The Juvencus Englynion

The oldest Welsh poetry we have in manuscript, though not necessarily, of course, the oldest in composition, occurs in twelve three-line stanzas (*englynion*) written in the margin of the Juvencus metrical version of the Psalms, now in the Cambridge University Library. These are now believed to be in the script and orthography of the first half of the ninth century.

Nine stanzas in praise of the Trinity, though not yet fully explained, form a complete religious poem, the earliest in this kind. The other three stanzas, occurring in another part of the manuscript, are taken by Sir Ifor Williams to be yet another fragment of an old story. The orthography, surely due to the scribe being more used to writing Latin than Welsh, makes the poem seem stranger and more remote than it need be, but even when modernised much in it is beyond ordinary comprehension. Here is the poem in the original spelling.

niguorcosam nemheunawr henoid
mitelu nit gurmaur
mi amfranc dam ancalaur.

nicanā niguardam nicusam henoid
cet iben med nouel
mi amfranc dam anpatel.

namercit mi nep leguenid henoid
isdiscirr micoueidid
dou nam riceus unguetid.

This is how I attempt to translate these stanzas which, at first sight, might seem to be a transliteration into the Latin alphabet of almost any language under the sun.

I shall not argue even for an hour tonight,
my retinue is not over great;
I and my Frank, about our kettle.

I shall not sing or laugh or kiss tonight
    though we have drunk flowing mead;
  I and my Frank, about our bowl.

Let no one ask me for mirth tonight,
    poor is my retinue.
  Two lords may boast together, one but speaks.[1]

So might old Llywarch have complained after a defeat, in the days before old age overtook him, and so did Suibhne Geilt lament. The Frank was a mercenary soldier (the word *frank* was used in Welsh a long time before the Norman Conquest!) and he was no equal companion for the unlucky but proud chieftain. Mead brings no jollity, therefore, tonight. They sit there, master and mercenary, sharing the food and the drink as they have shared the rigours of battle, but there can be no conversation, for that is something that takes place between equals. The benighted chieftain can only speak to his companion, not talk with him.

The lost story would have told us of the battle, perhaps of a return to a homestead, and we would know who this proud, gloomy man was. We can now only guess at all this and be thankful to the Latin scribe who thought enough of his native literature to record a favourite scrap.

This brief picture of the temporary gloom of a warrior and the more poignant visions of misfortune we get in the poetry of Llywarch Hen and Heledd appeal perhaps more to present-day taste than the greater starkness and brilliance of Taliesin and Aneirin, but, as Sir Idris Bell very well points out in his *Development of Welsh Poetry*, there is nothing here of the so-called Celtic twilight. Grief, regret and longing are expressed with the same jewelled clearness as courage and slaughter.

[1] They have been analysed by Sir Ifor Williams in the Bulletin of the Board of Celtic Studies, vol. vi, and the problems arising out of them discussed in his LEWP pp. 28–31. His brilliant interpretation explains this last line.

I have ventured to depart from Sir Ifor Williams' interpretation at a few points, but my understanding of the poem, especially of the last line, I owe chiefly to him

A similar economy, though by nature of the subject less stark and concrete and pagan, is to be observed in the nine religious *englynion* found in the same manuscript, of which the following is the last. I give it in its *Juvencus* form and then modernised according to Sir Ifor Williams' interpretation, before translating it.

un hamed hapuil haper
uuc nem isnem intcouer
nit guorgnim molim map meir.

Un a fedd a phwyll a phair
uwch nef, is nef, yn gywair;
nid gorwaith moli mab Mair.

One who has wisdom and authority
over and under heaven in harmony;
the praise of Mary's Son is no redundancy.

Chapter III

850—1100

★

These centuries were once considered a period nearly empty of recorded Welsh literature and it seemed almost hopeless with certainty to date within them any poetry which has come down to us. It has been accepted by some historians as a dark and unproductive age, whilst others have made the depredations of Norse robbers and burners, together with the internal disorders and feuds of Wales itself, the reason for this barrenness. In Wales, however, as in England, manuscripts have disappeared with the passing of the centuries. Only one copy of *Beowulf* survived the Middle Ages and that very nearly went in the fire of 1731, before it had been transcribed. Not a line of this poem occurs in any other manuscript, so that the only early English epic poem might have slipped from our grasp, as other things in fact did, as recently as the eighteenth century.

Llanbadarn, to make one guess, must have been rich in manuscripts before the ninth century, but everything that was not made of stone at Llanbadarn has gone, the gold and silver carried off, the manuscripts burnt, leaving only the tracery of the stone crosses where there must have been much fine writing. There is evidence in the *De Excidio Brittanniae* of Gildas that something must have been written down and some writers already famous by the last quarter of the sixth century, but whether they wrote in Welsh or in Latin he does not say. His intention is to make public certain evils he has observed in the Britain of his day. He will do it "not so much with the aid of native writings or records of writers, since they, if they ever existed, having been destroyed by enemy fire or carried away in the ships which took my countrymen to exile, are no available, but will follow the account of foreign writers."[1] The exile to which he refers was probably the move, in the face of Anglo-Saxon penetration, from South Britain to North Western France, and the foundation of Brittany and the Breton culture. Gildas, a peevish cleric writing from a continental monastery, could see no good in the sinful Britain of the sixth century, and is therefore sceptical about the existence of books in the island, but he would hardly have mentioned books and writers if there was not some evidence of their having existed.

When there was greater security under the princes of the twelfth and thirteenth centuries, new monasteries were established and there was much recording of poetry, so that it would seem on first consideration that a great renaissance took place in the world of writing about the beginning of the twelfth century. If the political and social history of Wales be taken into account, however, there should be little difficulty in accepting a continuous and developing tradition of writing through these dark years from the sixth to the twelfth century. Only this can explain the great technical advance to be observed in twelfth century poetry and the establishment of *cynghanedd*, a complex and increasingly strict system of alliteration, as the main element of prosody. Nor is the concern of the tenth century Laws of Hywel Dda with the rights of different grades of poets intelligible unless poetry was being written on at least three different levels.

During this period much of the poetry in the so-called Four Ancient Books of Wales must have been composed, then added to the earlier poetry in re-copying, so that when we have the work of six centuries jumbled together, as in the *Black Book of Carmarthen*, its extraction is no easy task. To perhaps the ninth century belongs, in its present form, one of the most charming

[1]Gildas, *De Excidio Brittanniae*, ed. Hugh Williams. Cymmrodorion Record Series 1899.
. . . non tam ex scriptis patriae, scriptorunque monumentis, quippe quae, vel si quae fuerint, aut ignibus hostium exusta aut civium exilii classe longius deportata, non compareant . . . Part I, section 4, p. 19.

things in Welsh, the song known by its first words—*Pais Dinogad*, Dinogad's petticoat. This lullaby occurs incongruously in the *Book of Aneirin*, amongst the *Gododdin* poems, but it has obviously no connection with the epic material. Sir Ifor Williams explains its presence by suggesting that it was written, like the Juvencus *englynion*, into the margin or some empty corner of an old manuscript and incorporated into the *Gododdin* by a later copyist, to whose uncritical slavishness we are now indebted for this gem.

Dinogad is a little boy who wears a petticoat or tunic of marten skins. His mother, probably, sings to him of his father's exploits as a hunter and a vivid picture is given of a happy, peaceful scene. Much poetry of this kind must have been composed in the heroic ages but not thought worthy of permanent record and some of our nursery rhymes are the broken memories of such lyrics. This little poem belongs originally to a time when Welsh was spoken in what is today England, for the fish in it are caught in the Derwent river, though which one, even possibly the Darent (they all derive from *derwen*—the Welsh for *oak*), it is now impossible to tell. Here is the poem.

Peis dinogat e vreith vreith
o grwyn balaot ban wreith
chwit chwit chwidogeith
gochanwn gochenyn wythgeith
pan elei dy dat ty e helya
llath ar y ysgwyd llory eny law
ef gelwi gwn gogyhwc
giff gaff dhaly dhaly dhwg dhwg
ef lledi bysc yng corwc
mal ban llad llew llywywc
pan elei dy dat ty e vynyd
dydygei ef penn ywrch penn gwythwch pen hyd
penn grugyar vreith o venyd
penn pysc o rayadyr derwennyd
or sawl yt gyrhaedei dy dat ty ae gicwein
o wythwch a llewyn a llwyuein
nyt anghei oll ny uei oradein. [CA. ll. 1101-1117]

Dinogad's speckled petticoat
is made of skins of speckled stoat;
whip whip whipalong,
eight times we'll sing the song.
When your father hunted the land,
spear on shoulder, club in hand,
thus his speedy dogs he'd teach,
Giff, Gaff, catch her, catch her, fetch, fetch!
In his coracle he'd slay
fish as a lion does its prey.
When your father went to the moor,
he'd bring back heads of stag, fawn, boar,
the speckled grouse's head from the mountain,
fishes' heads from the falls of Oak Fountain.
Whatever your father struck with his spear,
wild pig, wild cat, fox from his lair,
unless it had wings it would never get clear.

This is the earliest record we have in verse of hunting for sport and for the larder in western Europe, and the game and the methods had not altered very much in the fifteen thousand years or so which separate it from the cave paintings in south-western France. The most primitive weapons are here, the spear and the club, and the earliest form of little boat, the coracle, which is now perhaps in its last generation in West Wales. The child's clothing is made of skin, but the trained dogs bring it nearer to historical times. Even so, it should be remembered that Britain was famous as an exporter of trained hunting dogs before the Romans ever saw our shores.

Early Welsh poetry abounds in descriptions of nature, but it seems to me wrong to assemble truncated passages and to call that nature poetry, for that involves the monstrous surgery practised by Victorian criticism in its search for this sort of thing. There is little description of nature for nature's sake in old Welsh poetry. Landscape, birds and the weather are used for different purposes, sometimes to establish a mood, at other times to suggest contrasts, or to provide padding of a pretty kind, or lines which by their rhyme or initial letter aid the reciter's memory and so carry along the main theme of the poem. Here are two stanzas from the *Black Book*.

Kintevin keinhaw amsser
Dyar adar glas callet
Ereidir in rich ich iguet
Guirt mor brithottor tiret.

Ban ganhont cogeu ar blaen guit guiw
handid muy vy llauuridet
Tost muc amluc anhunet
kan ethint uy kereint in attwet. [p. xvii]

Month of May, the finest time,
birds are loud, growth is green,
ploughs are in the furrow, the ox in the yoke,
the sea is green, the lands many-coloured.

When cuckoos sing high in fine trees
the greater is my grief;
smoke hurts me, I clearly lack sleep
for the bitter going of my kinsmen.

Commenting on this poem in a very interesting passage of his *Lectures on Early Welsh Poetry* (page 13), Sir Ifor Williams points out that whereas in some literatures the cuckoo's note is associated with the gaiety of spring as the rebirth of nature (he does not mention the more ominous and equally widespread warning of cuckoldry—o word of fear!), in old Welsh poetry its cry induces melancholy and the memory of all that has passed with this and other winters. This he brilliantly derives from the old Welsh *cw* (pronounced like the English *coo*) which meant *where*, and which is cognate with the Latin *quo*, the Persian *ku* and the French *où*. The cuckoo comes asking, "Where, where?" *Où sont les neiges d'antan?* The sensitive listener is plunged into grief for the loss of friends and for the gay days that are gone, and spring, in spite of the incongruous brightness of nature, becomes a time of lamentation.

Statements about nature are sometimes mingled with truths of human behaviour in a kind of gnomic medley. Here are some stanzas of this kind from the famous *Eiry Mynydd* sequence in the *Red Book of Hergest*.

Eiry mynyd hyd ardes,
hwyeit yn llynn gwynn aches,
hwyr hen hawd y ordiwes . . .

Eiry mynyd brith bronn kreic,
krin kalaf alaf dicleic,
gwae wr agaffo drycwreic . . .

Eiry mynyd pysc ynryt,
kyrchyt carw culgrwm cwm clyt,
hiraeth am varw ny weryt.

Snow on the mountain, the stag in rut,
ducks on the lake, the water's white;
the old are slow and easy to catch.

Snow on the mountain, the rock breast's speckled,
reeds wither, cattle fear water;
woe to the man who gets a bad wife.

Snow on the mountain, fish in the ford,
the thin bowed stag seeks the snug valley;
longing for a dead one brings no joy.[1]

In the *Red Book* there are other similar three-line sequences called, after the repeated first word of their stanzas, *Bidieu* and *Gnodieu*, which are catalogue poems where the poet seeks to pin down the nature of a thing in an adjective or a statement. Similar too are the *Autumn* stanzas (*Kalan gaeaf*), the *Gorwynnion* (*the Brightly White Ones*) and the *Glaw Allan* (*Rain Outside*) stanzas, for in all of them moods or observations of nature are linked with human wisdom of the proverbial kind. Here are the *Glaw Allan* stanzas from the *Red Book*.

Glaw allan gwlychyt redyn
gwynn gro mor goror ewynn,
tec agannwyll pwyll y dyn.

Glaw allan y gan glydwr
melyn eithin crin euwr,
duw reen py bereist lyvwr.

[1] Professor Kenneth Jackson allots these stanzas to the early twelfth century in their present form, but this does not preclude a much earlier date for original composition with some twelfth century scribal redaction. v. *Early Welsh Gnomic Poems*, Welsh University Press, p. 7.

Glaw allan gwlychyt vyggwallt.
cwynuanus gwan diffwys allt,
gwelwgan gweilgi heli hallt.

Glaw allan gwlychyt eigyawn.
gochwiban gwynt ywch blaen cawn:
gwedw pob camp heb y dawn. [RBH. p. 1032]

Rain outside, it wets the ferns,
white the sea gravel, the edge of foam;
fair is the candle of prudence for man.

Rain outside, warmth within,
gorse is yellow, corn cockle withers;
Lord God! Why did you make the coward?

Rain outside, it wets my hair,
the weak man moans, the hill is steep,
pale white the sea, salt the brine.

Rain outside, it wets the sea,
the wind whistles loud over the reed grass;
all achievement is widowed without talent.

In the *Black Book of Carmarthen* there are stanzas of nature description which Sir Ifor Williams, in a very interesting analysis, has shown to be introductory material and sympathetic padding for a debate between warriors who are preparing to set out on a raid.[1] The poem, similar in style to the gnomic poems of the *Red Book*, begins with a fine description of a wintry landscape.

Lym awel llum brin.
anhaut caffael clid.
llicrid rid reuhid llin.
ryseiw gur ar un conin.

Ton trathon toid tu tir.
goruchel guaetev rac bron banev bre
breit allan orseuir.

[1] LEWP, pp. 15–16.

Sharp the wind, bare the hill,
it is hard to find shelter,
the ford is foul, the lake freezes,
a man may stand on a single stalk.

Wave after wave rushes towards land,
there are loud shouts against the hill's breast,
one can hardly stand outside.

The atmosphere of winter is insisted on for several more stanzas and then elements of conversation and story slip into the poem.

Ottid eiry tohid istrad.
diuryssint vy keduir y cad.
mi nidaw. anaw nimgad.

Snow is falling, the way is covered,
my warriors hurry on to battle,
I will not go, my wound won't let me.

More stanzas of this sort follow until at last we come to the raid itself and the talk is more openly and consistently of war. The unwilling and wounded leader has been induced to go on the disastrous expedition and now they ride out.

Y bore gan las y dit
ban kirchuid mug maur treuit.
nyd oet uagaud meirch mechit.

In the morning at break of day,
when we set out for Mug the great smiter,
Mechydd's horses were not petted.

The poem ends with a stanza of praise for this Mechydd, who was one of the sons of Llywarch Hen and who was killed on this raid by Mug's spearmen.

Mechit mab llywarch. dihawarch unben.
glvystec llen lliw alarch.
kyntaw affruin cluymus march. [BBC. xlv–xlvii]

Mechydd son of Llywarch, undaunted leader,
fair in his mantle of the swan's colour,
was the first to make fast his horse's bit.

A more sophisticated way of recording proverbial wisdom in verse was to make the proverb the last line of a three-line stanza and to attribute its authorship to a certain speaker. That these attributions, usually made to early British saints, need not be taken too seriously becomes clear when we meet a bird and a fish speaking. The saints were proper persons to utter such wisdom, but when their names failed to provide suitable rhymes, the thrush and the fish were pressed into service. The saints are therefore to be held no more responsible for these utterances than are those towns for the astonishing events for which, for rhyme's sake, they are made the locale in the English limerick. These stanzas, known as *Englynion y Clyweit, the Stanzas of Hearing*, were written down in the *Red Book of Talgarth* about the year 1400, and since the only purpose of each stanza is to carry a proverb, we have here the purest kind of gnomic verse, whereas the proverbial material in the *Red Book of Hergest* and the *Black Book* is very often, like the nature description, a filling out or conventional device for padding a verse form which has as its main purpose a dialogue or a story. Because of this comparative simplicity of intention the *Stanzas of Hearing* are much easier to understand. They are lively and sometimes very amusing. Here are four of them.

A glyweist di a gant y vronvreith
pan dramwych dros diffeith
na vit dy elyn dy gedymeith

A glyweist di a gant teilaw
gwr a vu yn penytyaw
a duw nyt da ymdaraw.

A glyweist di a gant ryderch
trydyd hael serchawc serch
gnawt rygas gwedy ryserch.

A glyweist a gant y pysc
wrth ymdraffill ymplith gwrysc
trech vyd anian noc adysc. [RBT. p. 161][1]

[1] v. I. W. and T. P-W. BBCS vol. III, p. 4 ff.

Did you hear what the thrush sang?
When you travel through wild country
don't let your enemy be your companion.

Did you hear what Teilo sang,
the man who was a penitent?
It is not good to strike against God.

Did you hear what Rhydderch sang,
the third generous lover of love?
Too much love makes too much hate.

Did you hear what the fish sang
as he floundered among the stalks?
Nature is stronger than education.

So, because the poet could find no holy man or hero whose name rhymes with *addysg* (education), the unfortunate fish has to lie on the bank of a stream gasping out this piece of wisdom. But even here there is a certain appropriateness, for the dying fish may well be thinking that if he had stuck to the usual flies instead of enquiring into new experience he would still have water, not air, in his mouth. Nature, perhaps, should be stronger than education.

The Stanzas of the Graves

In the *Black Book of Carmarthen* (pages xxxii–xxxiv) there is a remarkable series of seventy-three stanzas in the primitive *englyn* form which record the burial place of heroes. The recognisable names are of sixth century warriors, but many of the names given were probably detached from any known history when the stanzas were put into the form in which we have them today. They must belong to the earlier unrecorded centuries of the Roman occupation. Most of the graves seem to be in the open country, without reference to any kind of consecrated ground, like those I pass during the summer in walking over the ridge from my house to Llyn Eiddwen.

E betev ae gulich y glav.
gvir ny ortywnassint vy dignaw.
kerwid a chivrid a chav.

The graves that the rain wets
of men who stood no insult,
Cerwyd and Cywryd and Caw.

The most famous, of course, is the stanza that refers to Arthur, perhaps the earliest reference in literature to this hero.

Bet y march. bet y guythyr.
bet y gugaun cletyfrut.
Anoeth bid bet y arthur.

A grave for Mark, a grave for Gwythur,
a grave for Gwgawn Redsword.
The grave of Arthur will not be known.

Gwydi gurum a choch a chein.
A goruytaur maur minrein.
in llan helet bet owein.

After purple and red and fine clothes,
after great stiff-maned stallions,
in Heledd's ground is Owain's grave.

Gwydi gweli a gwaedlan.
a gviscav seirch a meirch cann.
Neud ew hun bet kintilan.

After the wound and the battlefield,
and the dressing of armour and white stallions,
this is the grave of Cynddylan.

Bet elchwith ys gulich glav.
maes meuetawc y danav.
Dyliei kynon yno y kiniav.

Rain wets Elchwith's grave,
the field of Mevetawg under it.
It was Cynon's duty to lament[1] him there.

[1] *kiniaw* of course means *to dine*, and the *Red Book of Hergest* version gives *cwynaw*, *to lament*. Though RBH is a century later than BBC, it seems obvious that the sources are different, that the BBC scribe here made an error in copying, and that RBH is the better reading.

In conformity with this theory of the origin of the Llywarch Hen poetry, Sir Ifor Williams believes this whole series to be not one long poem but a collection of final stanzas from tales of the life and death of famous warriors, the prose tales which they once punctuated now being lost to us. But if this is true, and support for it comes from the inclusion of a version of the Elchwith epitaph in the Llywarch Hen sequence in the *Red Book* (page 1048), then a considerable effort has been made by the collector of the stanzas to dramatise the series and to give it some artistic unity as a poem. Many of the stanzas begin with the question *Whose is the grave?* Such a stanza would seem less appropriate to a tale than to a list of graves with the question introduced occasionally to relieve monotony, just as Prospero keeps Miranda awake during his long recital of their past. At one point the compiler or poet, whichever he may be, steps forward to speak directly to his hearers.

Piev y bet hun.
Bet hun a hun. gowin ymi. mi ae gun.

Whose is this grave?
It's so and so's grave. Ask me. I know.

The scene springs to the mind's eye, the poet standing at the high table in hall, pausing in the recitation of his poem and, like a good entertainer, asking his audience for requests. Names are roared out, most of them unknown to us today, he picks out suitable ones and goes on with his list. The stanzas end abruptly at the foot of a page and, turning over, we meet a religious poem. Either the copyist abandoned the poem at this point or there is an order in this list of the graves of heroes which has not yet been detected. The last hero mentioned, buried in a great field, sounds more like a mythological than a historical person. He is Beli, son of Benlli the giant, and having gone as far back as that, the poet might well have thought his poem complete.

Certain things stand out significantly when one considers these impressive fragments. The heroes for whose historicity there is some evidence, such as the North Britons Owain ap Urien and Rhydderch Hael, all date from the sixth or early seventh centuries. It is possible, therefore, that the original compilation of the stanzas was made during the seventh century, though the form in which we have them will have suffered a succession of modernisations. Interesting too is the mystery connected with the burial of Arthur, which permitted the later evolution of the myth of his return, or the more convincing association of the myth of the returning or reborn hero with his name. But in these stanzas there is not the least hint of vaticination, bogus or otherwise, no stirring up of a nation to resistance and revenge, no use of any one of the heroes, even though Arthur and Cynon and Owain be among them, as leaders who will return from the grave to drive out the English.

Another very strong piece of negative evidence in favour of the great antiquity of these *Stanzas of the Graves* is the absence of any attempt to associate the heroes with any well-known ecclesiastical institution. Bédier has shown in *Les Légendes Epiques* that much of the mediæval heroic poetry of France was composed expressly to glorify and advertise religious houses on the pilgrim route to Compostella. If these *Stanzas of the Graves* were not already well known, or if they were of twelfth century composition, it is hard to believe that scribes of St. John's Priory at Carmarthen could have resisted the temptation to transplant at least one notable grave to within their precincts. There is no sign of this, and more signs of pagan than of Christian burial in most cases. In my translations above I deliberately rendered *llan helet* as Heledd's ground, not St. Heledd's Church as might be expected, for there is no known Saint Heledd and the word *llan* is used for many enclosures besides that of a church.

All this can only mean that these poems are in essence, if not in their present form, amongst the oldest things in Welsh literature. They stand out, grim, rain-washed and sad, like the menhirs of Pembrokeshire, a land where the atmosphere of the *Mabinogion* still seems to linger.

To the ninth century probably belongs a unique poem in praise of Tenby. All that remains of the title of this poem in the margin of the *Book of Taliesin* is *mic dinbych*, and Sir Ifor Williams proposes *Etmic Dinbych, Praise of Tenby* as the very acceptable title.[1] This is the happiest picture we have of the culture and security of a Welsh fortress in the dark ages which we know so little of. The poet celebrates the chieftains of the house of Erbin who have given him and his fellow poets such hospitality behind the battlements which overlook the Atlantic. Each stanza is an *awdl*, that is a sequence of lines with one rhyme (compare the *Chanson de Roland*), and each *awdl* begins with the words *Adwyn gaer yssyd*—There is a fine fortress. Here are the first three stanzas of this bright triumphant poem, excluding the introductory invocation to God.

Aduwyn gaer yssyd ar glawr gweilgi
bit lawen ygkalan eiryan yri.
Ac amser pan wna mor mawr wrhydri
ys gnawt gorun beird uch med lestri.
Dyhybyd gwanec ar vrys dybrys idi
Adawhwynt ywerlas oglas ffichti.
Ac am bwyf o deus dros vygwedi
pan gattwyf amot kymot athi.

Aduvyn gaer yssyd ar llydan llyn.
Dinas diachor mor oe chylchyn.
gogyfarch ty prydein kwd gygein hyn.
Blaen llyn ap erbin boet teu voyn.
Bu goscor a bu kerd yn eil mehyn.
Ac eryr uch wybyr a llwybyr granwyn.
Rac ud felyc nac escar gychwyn.
Clot wascar a gwanar yd ymdullyn.

Aduvyn gaer yssyd ar ton nawvet.
aduvyn eu gwerin yn ymwaret.
ny wnant eu dwynuyt trwy veuylhaet.
nyt ef eu defawt bot yn galet.
Ny llafaraf eu ar vyn trwydet.
noc eillon deu traeth gwell kaeth dyfet.
kyweithyd o ryd wled waretret.
kynnwys rwg pop deu goreu kiwet. [BT. pp. 42–3]

[1] The margin of the manuscript has obviously been cut at the expense of two or three letters. For arguments and discussion see Ifor Williams, *Trans H.S.C., 1940*.

There is a fine fortress above the sea,
gay at the kalends this bright promontory;
and whilst the sea performs its bravery
the bards are above over their cups of mead;
the wave rushes towards it in all haste;
they leave the Atlantic to the Pictish tribes.
I beseech God in my prayer
that I may keep my covenant with you.

There is a fine fortress over the wide water,
a bright homestead with the sea about it.
Ask Britain who is master here;
chief of Erbin's line, may it be yours.
There was gathering and song in a wattled place,
an eagle above the sky and a path for the pale-faced
before the wise lord, spur of the enemy,
of widespread fame, and a ready arraying.

There is a fine fortress above the ninth wave,
its men are splendid in a rescue;
they make no luxury out of shame,
nor is it their way to be hard-hearted.
I will tell no lie upon my visit—
better Dyfed's captivity than service in Deudraeth.
Its retinue, when the humble are feasted,
assures between each two guests the best concord.

We have much more detail in this poem than the *Gododdin* gave us of the kind of entertainment which Mynyddawg Mwynvawr must have provided for the three hundred who attacked at Catterick. There is more dwelling, perhaps the result of a period of comparative peace and security, on the delights of the days of peace, less concentration on the brutality of war and the bitterness of losing friends. This is much more social than heroic poetry, but there is yet a clarity in its hard brightness which is not easy to come by in later work, and the following two lines from the last stanza have the grim economy of Aneirin and Taliesin.

Dyf ieu bu gwartheu a amugant.
Ac yd oed vriger coch ac och ar dant.

Thursday there was dishonour which they refused,
there was blood on hair and a sigh on the harp.

Religious poetry

The Christian religion is but spasmodically reflected in early Welsh poetry. If Gildas, writing towards the end of the sixth century, was something more than a bad-tempered exile, then the princes of Britain after the departure of the Romans and during the years of early Saxon expansion were an ungodly and sinful set. Votiporix, whose tombstone with its Latin inscription now stands in the delightful Carmarthen Museum, can hardly have been the person to encourage his poets to sing of God, and although the young men of the *Gododdin* are said to have gone to church to confess before setting out on their expedition, there is much more of pagan preparation in the Aryan heroic way than of Christian mood about their year at the court of Mynyddawg Mwynvawr. Later, of course, when English paganism had cut off Wales from the other Celtic parts of the island, religion became involved in patriotism, which induced the reluctance of the Welsh to partake in the conversion of the English. Even centuries later, Giraldus, who can advise his Norman masters on methods of subduing the Welsh princes, still fights to his death for the independence of the Welsh church from Canterbury.

If considered from the point of view of religion, the *Book of Taliesin* presents a curious contrast. Whereas in the twelve early poems set in North Britain there are only six Christian references, the poems of what Sir Ifor Williams has called the Taliesin saga are full of terms belonging to every aspect of the Christian faith, even though the mythological content of these poems is clearly pre-Christian. Sir Ifor says, "The author or editor is conscious, uncomfortably conscious, of the clash between his theology and these mythological fancies. So he blends with them as much of the Christian faith and practice as he can." In this way monkish scribes overlaid the glorious paganism of the *Mabinogion* with incongruous Christianity and changed the Laws of Hywel Dda to make the bard sing of God instead of praising heroes. But let no one blame them. They preserved something at least for us, their modifications were modest enough in comparison with what has been done since their time, and the earlier material continues to shine through.

Some purely religious poems occur in the *Book of Taliesin* and in the *Black Book of Carmarthen*. There is one on the favourite mediæval subject of the Day of Judgement, attributed to Taliesin but more likely to have been written some centuries after his death. Here are some lines from *Yrymes Detbrawt, A Prophecy of Doomsday*.

pan discynho pater
y dadyl ae nifer.
Achyrn gopetror
ac enynnu mor
llwyth byt lloscetawr
hyny uwynt marwawr
lloscawt ynial ran
rac y vawr varan. [BT. p. 10 ll. 17–21]

When the Father descends
to judgement with his host,
horns at the four corners[1]
and a kindling of the sea,
the earth's people burning,
they will be embers;
the wilderness will burn
before the great doom.

An interesting object lesson in the degree to which a poem can be changed in successive modernisations is afforded by a comparison of this poem from *The Book of Taliesin* with a version of the same poem in the late sixteenth century Gwyneddon 3 manuscript. Although some phrases and the intention and atmosphere of the poem remain in the later version, the changes are considerable and the poem, as a result, is much more comprehensible, which was no doubt the purpose of the sixteenth century scribe. In spite of this, however, the attribution in MS Gwyneddon 3 is still to Taliesin.

The Prophecy of Doomsday, in company with many other poems of similar nature, is clearly in line with the view of the Day of

[1] cf. Donne, At the round earth's imagined corners blow
Your trumpets, angels . . .

Judgement common to Western Europe during the Middle Ages, and which was founded on the Apocalypse, the Sibylline Oracles and the warnings widely attributed to Saint Jerome. In the tradition of Welsh poetry they indicate to what degree the poet had taken over the monitory function of the Druid, the responsibility for moral and religious instruction, just as in the poetry of political prophecy he had taken over the duties of the Vates.[1] This poem, too, vividly foreshadows Sion Cent's insistence on the worthlessness of this world and his terrible pictures of death.

A famous poem is the following hymn of praise to God by an anonymous writer, from the *Black Book of Carmarthen*.

Gogonedauc argluit hanpich guell
Athuendicco de egluis a chagell
A kagell ac egluis
A vastad a diffuis
A Teir finhaun yssit
Due uch guint ac un uch eluit
A yrisgaud ar dit
A Siric a perwit
Athuendiguiste awraham pen fit
A vuchet tragiuit
A adar a guenen
A attpaur a dien
Athuendiguste aron a moesen
A vascul a femen
A Seithnieu a ser
A awir ac ether
A llevreu a llyther
A piscaud in hyderuer
A kywid a gueithred
A tyuvod a thydued
A y saul da digoned
Athuendigaf de argluit gogoned.
Gogonedauc argluit hanpych guell. [BBC. xviii]

[1] Strabo gives the three classes, Bard, Druid and Vates, but mediæval Welsh poets refer to the Druids as the prophets. v. *Book of Taliesin*, p. 18, ll. 3–4 and p. 76, ll. 7–10. See also *Llawysgrif Hendregadredd*, Welsh University Press, pp. 132 and 279.

Glorious Lord, all hail to you!
May the church and the chancel bless you;
may you be blessed by chancel and church.
May the plains and the hills bless you;
may you be blessed by the three wells,
two above the wind and one above the earth;
may the shadow and the day bless you;
may silk and fragrant shrubs bless you;
as Abraham, head of the faith, blessed you.
May the eternal life bless you.
May you be blessed by the birds and the bees;
may aftermath and growth bless you.
as you were blessed by Aaron and Moses.
May you be blessed by male and female;
may the seven days and the stars bless you;
may the air and the ether bless you;
may books and all inscription bless you;
may you be blessed by fish in water;
may you be blessed by thought and deed;
may you be blessed by sand and soil;
may he who has done good bless you;
and I will bless you, Lord of Glory.
Glorious Lord, all hail to you!

Prophetic verse.

In the *Book of Taliesin* and the *Black Book of Carmarthen* there is a great deal of vaticinatory verse ascribed to Taliesin and Myrddin, but which cannot have been written in their entirety by these two poets. The oldest of these is probably a poem of two hundred lines called *Armes Prydain* or *Arymes Prydein Vawr*, the Prognostication of Great Britain, which occurs in the *Book of Taliesin*. This violently anti-English poem is not so much a prophecy as a call to arms and an expression of hatred. There will be an agreement between the non-Saxon peoples of the British Isles.

achymot kymry agwyr dulyn
Gwydyl iwerdon mon aphrydyn
cornyw achludwys eu kynnwys genhyn.

An agreement of the Welsh with the men of Dublin,[1]
the Irish of Ireland, the men of Anglesey, the Picts,
the men of Cornwall and of the Clyde will join with them.

[1] This is a reference to the Danish settlement of Dublin. Hence the distinction between them and the Irish proper.

We are told of the trick by which the English got Thanet and how unhappy for the Britons was their increase in numbers. There will be a great battle and some will escape. Amongst these, possibly because they will not be in the van, will be a few of the hated stewards of Cirencester, at whose hands the Britons have suffered grievous inflictions.

dyhed yeu gwraged adywedant
eu cryssau yn llawn creu a orolchant.

They will tell their woes to their wives
who will wash the shirts that are full of blood.

Cadwaladr and Cynan will lead the army and there will be blood on the foreign faces.

achreu rud ar rud allmyn.
and red blood on foreign cheeks. [BT. p. 15]

The English have taxed them and trampled on their saints, but now men under the banner of St. David will drive the enemy into the sea at Sandwich (Aber Santwig). Cynan and Cadwaladr will rule from the Isle of Man to Brittany, from South Wales to Thanet, from the Roman Wall to the Atlantic. This is how the two heroes are described.

Deu unben degyn dwys eu kussyl
deu orsegyn saesson opleit dofyd
deu hael deu gedawl gwlat warthegyd
deu diarchar barawt unffawd unffyd
deu erchwynawc prydein mirein luyd
deu arth nys gwna gwarth kyfarth beunyd. [BT. p. 17]

Two terrible chieftains, weighty of judgement,
two will conquer the Saxons in the cause of God,
two bounteous ones, generous with the plunderer's land,
two ready, fearless ones, of one fortune, one faith,
two protectors of lovely, holy Britain,
two bears it were no shame to bait every day.

The lack of reference to the Normans, the references to the Danes, and a number of other details lead Sir Ifor

Williams to date this poem very convincingly about the year 930. It is a fine, spirited piece of work, the best of the poems of prophecy and one of the first expressions of Welsh, as distinct from British, nationalism, coming as it does from a Wales which has now been cut off from Cornwall and North Britain, but which has not abandoned the dream of an all-Celtic island.

Other prophetic poems in the *Book of Taliesin* are much more obscure than this. There are many references to heroes who will come over the sea to the rescue of the Britons. Cadwallawn will come from Ireland assembling armies and will avenge earlier defeats. This Cadwallawn was killed by Oswald in 635 and was the father of Cadwaladr, who appears much more frequently as the avenging hero.

Pan dyfu gatwallawn dros eigyawn iwerdon
yd atrefnwys nefwy yn ardnefon
keinyadon moch clywyf eu gofalon.
Marchawc lu mor taer am gaer llion
A dial idwal as aranwynyon
A gware pelre aphen saesson.
Ys trabludyo y gath vreith ae hagyfieithon
o ryt ar taradyr ym porth wygyr ymon. [BT. p. 73]

When Cadwallawn comes over the Irish sea,
he who planned a paradise in Ardnefon,
he will soon hear the distress of the chieftains;
the mounted host will press on to Chester
to take revenge for Idwal and Garanwynion,[1]
and they will play ball with English heads.
The speckled cat and her foreigners[2] will be fought
from Taradyr ford to Porth Mygr in Anglesey.

Besides this brindled cat there are other mysterious animals whose significance has been forgotten, a dog, a stallion, an ox, a sow and

pymhet llwdyn gwyn awnaeth iessu. [BT. p. 29]
the fifth white wether that Jesus made.

[1] The Battle of Garanwynion is mentioned in BT, p. 57, l. 1 and p. 14, l. 23. v. *Cymmrodor 28*, for J.M.J.'s attempt to situate it.
[2] *Anghyfiaith* means *speaking another language*.

In many of the poems I have referred to there is no reference to the Normans or to any event later than the tenth century. In others the Normans are mentioned, as in the *Kein Gyfedwch* poem where they occur with the Picts as enemies, whilst in yet another poem a strangely dressed Asiatic people will invade Britain (BT. page 78, lines 20–24).

In the *Red Book of Hergest* and the *Black Book of Carmarthen* there are more prophetic poems where not only is the coming of the saviour heroes, Arthur, Owain, Cynon and Cadwaladr, predicted, but a grim picture of the state of Britain is given. There will be planting without harvesting in an unpeaceful age; manners and morals will decay, for men will cease to blush, girls will go naked and women will be shameless and lustful. Families will fall out, again a safe enough prophecy in feud-torn Wales. Priests will get rich and poets poor.

> Gwacllaw bard hard effeiryat. [RBH. p. 385]
> Empty-handed the poet, splendid the priest.

Minstrels will go unrewarded from the door.

> Kertorion allan heb ran teithi
> Kyn safont iny drus tlus nys deupi. [BBC. p. xxxi]
>
> Minstrels outside without their rightful share;
> though they stand at the door the gift does not come.

Foreign fashions will enter the country and the women will wear four-cornered horns or towers on their heads (BBC. p. xxviii). Thus is the decay of morality associated with the progressive loss of control over the island of Britain and with the coming of foreign ways.

Three groups of prophetic poems, known usually as the *Bedwenni*, the *Afallenneu* and the *Hoianneu*, are attributed to Myrddin in the *Black Book of Carmarthen*. These titles mean respectively the *Birch Trees*, the *Apple Trees* and the *Greetings*, and they are so called because each stanza begins with an apostrophe to the birch or the apple tree, or with greetings to a little pig (*parchellan*).

The prophetic part of these poems, whether bogus prophecy, that is, written for political purposes after the event, or genuine but necessarily vague prognostication, has been shown to belong to the eleventh and twelfth centuries[1], but the stanzas often begin with Myrddin speaking about himself. These latter lines may therefore have originally been utterances of the historical Myrddin of the sixth century, with later vaticination interpolated and brought up to date time after time, the original matter and the legendary accretion being left to provide authority for the prophecies.

In the *Birch Tree* poems there are no elements of the Myrddin legend except that the poet in the first line of each stanza addresses trees in different parts of Wales, and Myrddin, of course, became Merlin Sylvestris, the madman of the woods. That these trees are all in Wales, whereas Myrddin went mad in Scotland, suggests a date when Welsh was no longer spoken anywhere except in West Britain. The Irish Suibhne Geilt, who has already been compared to Myrddin, also addressed the birch tree and called it blessed, just as Myrddin does.

Gwin y bid hi y vedwen in diffrin guy. [BBC. xxiv]
Blessed is the birch tree in the Wye valley.

In the *Apple Tree* and *Little Pig* poems, on the other hand, there is a good deal of information about Myrddin's unlucky life, as, for instance, in the following stanza.

Awallen peren atif in llanerch
y hangert ae hargel rac riev ryderch
amsathir inybon. maon ynychilch.
Oet aelav vt vt dulloet diheueirch.
Nu nym cari guendit Ac nimeneirch.
Oef kas gan gwassauc guaessaf Rydirch.
Ryrewineis y mab ae merch.
Aghev a duc paup. pa rac nam kyueirch.
A guydi guendolev nep riev impeirch.
Nym gogaun guarvy. nym goffvy gorterch.
Ac igueith arywderit oet eur wy gorthorch.
Kin buyf aelav hetiv gan eiliv eleirch. [BBC. xxv]

[1] E.M.G., *op. cit.*, Chapter III. An example is the hopelessness of ever getting rid of the Normans and their invasion of Ireland. BBC. XXVIIb.

Apple tree that grows in a clearing,
her nature protects her from Rhydderch's men.
There's been trampling round her trunk, men about her;
she was the treasure of a lord, lord of patterns of courage.
Gwenddydd loves me not, nor will speak to me;
Gwasawg, whose patron is Rhydderch, hates me,
since I killed her son and daughter.
Death takes everyone; why won't it call me?
After Gwenddoleu no lord respects me.
No play delights me, no wench will visit me.
In the battle of Arfderydd my torque was of gold
but today I'm not the swan-white girl's treasure.

Gwenddydd was Myrddin's sister (Ganieda in the *Vita Merlini*) and the battle of Arfderydd was fought by Rhydderch in 573, somewhere in North Britain. In the *Vita*, Gwenddydd is married to Rhydderch, but this relationship is not mentioned in any of the poems, where she is only vaguely associated with Rhydderch. Gwenddoleu, king of the Scots and Myrddin's patron, is dead, killed in this very battle of Arfderydd, according to a line in the *Red Book of Hergest*.

Other poems of this kind have much more prophecy in them, more hatred and more delight in the bloody details of battle.

Afallen peren per y chageu . . .
Ami disgoganave rac perchen machrev.
In diffrin machavuy merchyrdit creu
goruolet y loegyr gorgoch lawnev.
Oian aparchellan dy dau dywiev
gorvolet y gimry goruawr gadev.
In amuin kyminaud clefytaud clev.
Aer o saesson ar onn verev.
A guarwyaur pelre ac ev pennev.
Ami dysgogana fe gwir heb gev.
Dyrchafaud maban inadvan y dehev. [BBC.xxiv]

Apple tree of sweet branches . . .
I will foretell for the owner of Machreu
in the valley of Machavuy a Wednesday of blood,
a triumph for England and red blades.
Then, little pig, the dawn of Thursday,

triumph for the Welsh in great fights,
in defence of Cyminawd a quick sword blow,
a slaughter of the English on Beref stream,
and the playing of ball with their heads.
And I foresee truly, without deceit,
the raising of a youth in a corner of the South.

And here is a *Little Pig* poem which offers a fairly equal blend of legendary Myrddin material and of prophecy.

Oian aparchellan llimy vinet
Kyuuely anwinud panelhute y oruet
Bychan a wir ryderch hael heno y ar y wlet
aportheise neithuir o anhunet
Eiri hid impen clun gan cun callet
Pibonvy imblev blin wy rysset.
Ry dibit div maurth dit guithlonet
Kywrug glyu powis achlas guinet.
Achivod hirell oe hir orwet
y amvin ae elin terwin guinet. [BBC. xxviiib]

Greetings, little pig with the sharp toe nails,
indelicate in your lying down.
Little knows Rhydderch Hael at tonight's feast
what wakefulness I suffered last night;
snow up to my knees, amongst wild dogs of the woods,
icicles on my beard, my way weary.
Tuesday will come, a day of fury
between the lord of Powys and the land of Gwynedd.
And Hiriell will rise from his long lying
to defend Gwynedd's borders against her foe.

Hiriell was one of the many traditional heroes of North Wales called to come to his people's aid like the heroes of the other parts of Britain, Urien, Owain, Cadwaladr and Arthur; and to prophesy fighting between Gwynedd and Powys was, unhappily, a safe enough bet in the twelfth century, just as there were places where it was safe enough to predict a battle, border towns, fords and heads of estuaries. Though most of this vaticination is grim and violent, some poems strike a happier note such as that in the last *Apple Tree* poem which ends thus:—

Kaffaud paub y teithi. llauen vi bri brython.
Kenhittor kirrn eluch. kathil hetuch a hinon. [BBC. xxvib]

Everyone shall have his due, happy will be the Briton's fame;
there will be raising of towers[1] of rejoicing, and songs of
peace and of fair weather.

That, therefore, is the mixture we find in this prophetic verse, a mixture repeated in the *Cyfoesi Merddin* of the *Red Book of Hergest* and in many other poems, a foundation perhaps of the original complaints of Myrddin from his sixth century woodland retreat which has become a palimpsest for safely vague prophecy and for partisan historical writing after the event at any time from the sixth to the early thirteenth century.

The reader by this time may well be puzzled by the paucity of Arthurian material in the poems which have been discussed and by the more frequent expectation of the return of such heroes as Cynan and Cadwaladr than of Arthur himself. But few though the references to Arthur be, they are of great importance, for, to quote Professor George Sampson in the *Cambridge Book of Prose and Verse* (page 206), "To find any mention of him earlier than the twelfth century we must turn to Wales, where, in a few obscure poems, a difficult prose story, and two dry Latin chronicles, we find the first written references, meagre and casual, but indicating traces of ancient tradition." A treatment of the origins of the Arthurian cycle of legend will be found in an appendix at the end of this book.

[1] Perhaps *horns* of rejoicing, or even *chimneys*.

Chapter IV

1100—1300

★

More exactly, this period begins with a revolt against the Normans in 1094 and ends with the death of Llywelyn, last prince of Wales, in 1282. It was a period of great national self-consciousness and, for the most part, of independence. The power of the princes of North Wales gave stability and therewith encouragement to the arts. Monasteries were founded and flourished, and within their walls the poetry and history of the age and of previous ages were recorded and copied. At Strata Florida in Cardiganshire, founded in the twelfth century and endowed by the Lord Rhys, prince of Dyfed, there are slabs of slate incised with fourteenth century poetry, indicating a familiarity with contemporary literature suitable to the burial place of Dafydd ap Gwilym.

It was a period, too, when there were close contacts between Wales and Ireland, with a resulting interchange of influences which has not yet been fully worked out, though Professor W. J. Gruffydd has expressed the view that the example of Irish writing is responsible for the more lyrical note in the work of the princely poets of the twelfth century. Under their powerful masters the professional poets became powerful too, and their grip is strong on the form, matter and conventions of poetry. Most of the poetry which has survived from this period is therefore in the heroic tradition of Aneirin and Taliesin. Old metrical forms are used and the diction is archaic. The *englyn* form, certainly as old as the ninth century and probably much older, is only beginning to be thought suitable for work by chief poets, but alliteration is rapidly developing towards the perfected *cynghanedd* of the fourteenth century. Never in the history of

Welsh literature has poetry been so difficult for contemporaries to understand as it was during the twelfth and thirteenth centuries, for the protected poets delighted in the mysteries of their craft and echoes of the past satisfied their princes, since nothing seems to please monarchs more than to be associated with past glory. Training in the art of poetry was arduous and its products esoteric, for poetry was intended to make only a vague impact on the uninitiated mind.

The first of the great poets of this period is Meilyr, who in 1137 sang an elegy to Gruffydd ap Cynan, the leader chiefly responsible for the national revival and to whom tradition attributes the bringing from Ireland of poets and an Irish influence on Welsh writing. In an elegy of 172 lines, made up of three *awdlau*, or sections in one rhyme, he sings of the glory that has gone.

> Kyn myned mab Kynan ydan dywawd
> keffid yny gyntet uet a bragawd
> o olo Gruffut yn rut uedrawd
> kwynym dragon dwfyn dygyn diwyrnawd. [H. p. 2]

> Before Kynan's son went below the gravel
> there was mead and spiced ale to be had in his hall.
> For the burying of Gruffydd in the red grave
> we lament the lord of our world, grievous day.

His triumphant return from Ireland is pictured in the following lines, whilst the tragedy of his death is not forgotten.

> Gwedy tonneu gwyrt gorewynawc
> dyforthynt y seirch meirch rygygawc
> anu neud gweryd yn warweidyawc
> gwae a ymdiried wrth uyd bradawc. [H. p. 3]

> After the green waves topped with foam
> the ambling stallions carry the armour
> kicking up clods in their submission.
> Woe to him who trusts the treacherous world.

The elegy to Gruffydd ap Cynan ends on a religious note and it is for his pious *Marw Ysgafyn*, or death-bed poem, that Meilyr is most remembered. This is how the poem ends, with a prayer for burial in the holy island of Bardsey, still called Enlli by the Welsh.

Brenhin holl riet am gwyr nam gomet
am y drugraret om drygioni
keueis y liaws awr eur a phali
gan ureuawl rieu yr eu hoffi
ac wedy dawn awen amgen ynni
Amdlawd uyn tauawd ar vyn tewi
mi veilyr brydyt beryerin y bedyr
porthawr a gymedr gymhes deithi
pryd y bo kyfnod yn kyuodi
y ssawl y ssy met ar maa ui
As bwyf yn adef yn arhos y llef
y lloc a achef aches wrthi
ac yssi ditrif didreul ebri
ac am y mynwent mynwes heli
ynys veir uirein ynys glan y glein
gwrthrych dadwyrein ys kein yndi
Krist croes darogan am gwyr am gwarchan
rac uffern affan wahan westi
kreawdyr am crewys am kynnwys J
ym plith plwyf gwirin gwerin enlli. [H. p. 8]

The King of all lords knows me, won't deny me
his mercy for my wickedness.
I was often given gold and silk
by generous lords for praising them,
but after the lively gift of poetry
my wretched tongue is struck with silence.
May I, the poet Meilyr, pilgrim to Peter,
gatekeeper who judges the sum of virtue,
when the time comes for us to arise
who are in the grave, have thy support.
May I be at home awaiting the call
in a fold with the moving sea near it,
a hermitage of perpetual honour
with a bosom of brine about its graves.
Island of fair Mary, pure island of the pure,
image of resurrection, how lovely to be there!
Christ of the foretold cross knows me and will keep me
from the pain of hell, that remote guest-house.
The Creator who created me will take me in
to the good parish of Enlli's people.

The degree to which the technique of versification had progressed by the beginning of the twelfth century may be estimated from the two lines commencing *Krist croes darogan*, with their subtle blend of internal rhyme, multiple alliteration and assonance. Consider the line:—

rac uffern affan wahan westi.

Uffern is linked to *affan* by two consonants, *affan* to *wahan* by the repeated vowel and the rhyme, *wahan* to *westi* by the consonant *w*. The effect, and nothing could be more suitable to the quietly ecstatic prayer with which the poem ends, is one of incantation.

Gwalchmai, son of Meilyr, was chief poet to the great Owain Gwynedd. Professor Lloyd-Jones sees a sign of a possible quarrel between the poet and his patron in the absence of an elegy by Gwalchmai on the death of Owain Gwynedd[1]. Had Gwalchmai written such an elegy it would most probably have come down to us, for such poems were more carefully preserved than any other kind, and those princes who did not die in battle would retire confidently to a monastery which they had founded or succoured, in the knowledge that the library would be enriched after their death by fine poems in their honour. A quarrel between the poet and his patron may well have arisen from the two poems which Gwalchmai wrote to Madog ap Maredydd, Owain's rival, one a song of praise and the other an elegy on his death. This, however, is how Gwalchmai begins one of his many poems to Owain Gwynedd.

Ardwyreaf hael o hil Eneas
ardwyreaf glew llew lluch efras
ardwyreaf dechaf o deyrnet prydein
a theyrnaf kein ywein eur was. [H. p. 14]

I praise the generous one of the stock of Aeneas;
I praise the bold lion, the flash of honour;
I praise the most splendid of Britain's princes,
and the fine kingdom of golden Owain.

[1] The Court Poets of the Welsh Princes, Proceedings of the British Academy, vol. XXIV, pp. 17–18.

Gwalchmai's most remarkable poem is his *Gorhoffedd*, a title which means a great delight in which there is an unconcealed element of boastfulness. Love, war and nature are the things in which the poet delights, and the boastfulness, for which we have no cause to doubt there was justification, appears clearly enough in the following lines.

Gwalchmei ym gelwir gelyn y saesson
ar les gwledic mon gweint ym plymnwyd. [H. p. 17]

Gwalchmai am I called, enemy to the English;
at the call of Anglesey's lord I took part in battle.

As in so many old Welsh poems, a mood is established by a description of the season of the year. The *Gorhoffedd* begins thus:—

Moch dwyreawc huan haf dyfestin
maws llafar adar mygyr hear hin
mi ytwyf eur ddetyf diofyn yn rin
mi ytwyf llew rac llu lluch vyg gortin
Gorwylyeis nos yn achadw fin
Gorlas gwellt didrif dwfyr neud yessin
gordyar eaws awdyl gynneuin
Gwylein yn gware ar wely lliant
lleithyryon eu pluawr pleidyeu etrin
Pellynnic vyg khof yg kynteuin
yn ethrip caru kaerwys vebin
pell o uon uein ydwyti dwythwal werin
essmwyth yssyt ynn asserw gyfrin
yt endeweis eneu ynechlyssur gwir
ar lleueryt gwar gwery y lein
ac ar lles ywein hael hual dilin
dychysgogan lloegyr rac uy llain. [H. p. 17-18]

Quick rising the sun, summer hurries on,
splendid the song of birds, fine smooth weather,
I am of golden growth, fearless in battle,
I am a lion, my attack a flash against a host.
I watched through a night to keep a border;
murmuring ford waters in heavy weather,
the open grassland green, the water clear,
loud the nightingale's familiar song.

Gulls play on the bed of the sea,
their feathers glistening, their ranks turbulent.
My memory goes back to early summer
because of my young love from Caerwys.
You are far from the lively folk of little Anglesey,
secure in its bright secrecy.
I listened to lips on a true occasion,
to the gentle words of the virgin of the swords
and to the need of Owain, my fine fetter.
The English retreat before my sword.

The three themes of love, war and nature in summer continue to interweave without very much development or story, just as Celtic art entwines its themes into a pattern which has hardly any beginning or end and which avoids any central point of interest such as is required to make a composition based on the artistic traditions of the Mediterranean[1]. The poem ends thus:—

Ac amdawd o vun nenwawl defnyt
A dyfnwys a mi meith gerennyt
Ac ymdaerawd y dreul o dra newyt
Ac amrant hirwrwm a grut hirwlyt
Ac yn llys afneued ym eitunir
hynoeth oeth dybytaf a dybwyf ryt
Ac os duw o nef neu ym kynnyt
keinuod gan lywe ymy lawr ym hunyt. [H. pp. 21–2]

Having gone from a girl, stuff of heaven's light,
who contracted with me a long friendship
and was angry with new excess for this waste,
with her long brown lashes and long soft cheek;
in the bountiful hall I'll be desired,
tonight I'll be easy if I'm given freedom,
and if God in his heaven is on my side
being with my bright girl will be my lulling.

Other poems by Gwalchmai are an obscure set of verses perhaps to his wife Efa, an ode to God, and a dream poem which is full of piety. Once more it is extremely difficult to establish a

[1] cf. Collingwood and Myers, *Roman Britain*, p. 187, for general remarks on the difference between Mediterranean and Nordic (including Celtic) art.

connected development in reading his poems. This is the abstract art of the Celtic tradition in which images and thoughts are set like gems in a returning pattern, so that lovely, disconnected phrases remain suspended in the memory—*llywy lliw eiry ar goed* (a girl of the colour of snow on trees), *gwely a thy a thes aelwyd* (a bed and a house and the warmth of a hearth) and the horror of—

> a Menei heb drei o drallanw gwaedryar
> a lliw gwyar gwyr yn heli[1]. [H. p. 14]
>
> and Menai without ebb for the great flood of bleeding
> and the colour of men's blood in the brine.

Cynddelw, who flourished in the second half of the twelfth century, is in the manuscripts and by tradition given the title *Prydydd Mawr*, Great Poet, and he may well be the greatest of the poets of this period. He was either more prolific than the others or more of his work has been preserved, perhaps because of his accepted greatness or because of the unusual number of princes whom he praised in song. He wrote in praise of the greatest leaders of his day, Owain Gwynedd, the Lord Rhys, Hywel ap Owain Gwynedd, whom we shall soon meet as a poet, Madog ap Maredydd and Llywelyn the Great. Like Gwalchmai, Cynddelw was also a warrior and speaks familiarly and proudly of fighting.

As a chief poet, Cynddelw took very seriously his duty in the handing on of the poetic traditions, and he was obviously a stickler for the discipline of the poet's craft. Speaking of himself as a poet in his elegy to Cadwallawn ap Madog, he says:—

> As gwtant yn dysc yn disgyblon. [H. p. 131]
> And our disciples know our teaching.

Again he claims:—

> Ry dysgas disgywen veirtyon. [H. p. 105]
> I have taught splendid poets.

[1] This couplet occurs in a poem to Owain Gwynedd, of which Thomas Gray made a spirited mistranslation.

Time and again he speaks proudly of his own ability, of his position as chief poet, and of his rank as master teacher of the craft of verse, and it is thus that he crushes his rival Seissyll Bryffwrch in the disputation between them for the post of chief poet to Madog ap Maredydd. He is continuously aware of tradition and compares himself to the earlier Arofan and Afan Ferddig, poets with whose work he seems to be familiar, though the whole of it has been lost to us.

As the poets of Britain had been doing for at least thirteen centuries before him, Cynddelw praised his patrons for the lavishness of their provision in hall and for their success in battle. This, according to him, is the effect of Owain Cyfeiliog's onrush upon his enemies:—

taryf rac twryf glasuor a thewdor
a thoryf a theruysc diachor
a thrylew a thrylwyn urondor
a thrychyon a thrychan elor. [H. p. 137]

a scattering before the sea's roar and power
a throng and a fearful turmoil
a proofed and ready breastplate
and wounds and three hundred biers.

He must have been welcome in many of the great houses of Wales and the record provided by his work shows to what degree the spirit of Hywel Dda's laws was still mighty. In a series of *englynion* on the death of Rhirid Flaidd, he says,

Kelennic ruteur am rotei Ririd
nym rotes a uei lei
nyd aruanwl uut uytei
nyd ar uanarch yn parchei. [H. p. 179]

Rhirid would give me a gift of red gold,
nothing less would he give me;
he would not be too careful with bounty;
for no small cause did he respect me.

In spite of Cynddelw's respect for and dependence on tradition, and even though he was the greatest craftsman in the classical metres of his age, yet some of the new elements that were entering into Welsh poetry are prominent in his work, for like Gwalchmai, he broke away from the epic severity of conventional poetry to write in praise of a woman. He is also responsible for some metrical inovations, such as the writing of an elegy in the *englyn* form, but this, Professor Lloyd-Jones suggests, was made possible for him by his functioning in two capacities, as chief poet (*pencerdd*) and as house poet (*bardd teulu*), so that in his lesser professional status he was able to depart from the strict *awdl* form which was alone considered suitable for momentous occasions.

The poetry of Cynddelw is full of blood and of corpses on which the crows feed, but in his song of love to Eva, daughter of Madog ap Maredydd, there is little mention of war and less boasting of the poet's prowess in battle. The poet sends a proud, lusty stallion to bear his message of love to the girl, who is thus described:—

Kymraec laesdec o lys dyfrynt
kyfleuer gwawr dyt pan dwyre hynt
kyfliw eiry gorwynn gorwyt Epynt.

Fair supple Welsh girl of the hall in the valley,
like the light of dawn when day's course begins,
colour of whitest snow on Gorwydd Eppynt.

The poet boasts that young girls have fallen in love with him, but he returns again and again to this one girl's praise.

Gwery vanon vanwl gwar uetwl ueith
gorne gwawr vore ar uor diffeith.

Virginal exquisite queen, of long gentle thinking,
the colour of breaking day on a deserted sea.

Towards the end of this same poem to Eva he announces himself thus:—

Bart llywelyn hael hud ym gelwir
geleurut gelyn y bop enwir
enwawc ym keinyoes ym keinmygyr
anwar uy llachar o nym llochir. [H. p. 125]

I am called the poet of generous Llywelyn,
red, leech-like enemy of all lying,
I am famous, treasured and respected,
fierce my flashing anger unless I'm made much of.

It is important to remember that in spite of his being a professional poet and a famous teacher of the craft, Cynddelw was of noble birth and a warrior of repute. He could petition proudly for the love of his prince's daughter.

We come now to the work of two poets who were themselves princes and notable warriors, Hywel, son of Owain Gwynedd and Owain Cyfeiliog, prince of Powys.

Hywel ap Owain Gwynedd, writing in the second half of the twelfth century, is a poet who foreshadows Dafydd ap Gwilym and Huw Morus in his handling of love and nature. Here is a poem to one of the many girls whose love he enjoyed, full of delicate play upon the idea of choosing, brilliantly coloured and yet simple and conversational in its tone.

Uyn dewisy riein uirein ueindec
hirwenn yny llen lliw ehoec.
am dewis synhwyr fynhyaw ar wreicyeit
ban dyweid o ureit weteit wouec
am dewis gydrann gyhydrec a bun
a bod yn gyurin am rin am rec
Dewis yw gennyfy hartliw gwanec
y doeth yth gyuoeth dy goeth gymraec
Dewis gennyfy di beth yw gennytty ui
beth a dewi di dec y gostec
Dewisseisy vun ual nad atrec gennyf
yawn yw dewissaw dewistyn tec. [H. p. 319]

My choice, a slim, fair, bright girl,
tall, lovely in her heather-coloured gown;
my choice knowledge, to look at womanliness
which quietly utters a seemly thought.

My choice is to share with and be with a girl,
privately, with secrets and with gifts.
My choice is you, colour of the foam,
your wealth your wisdom, and your fine Welsh.
You are my choice: how do I stand with you?
What, are you silent, my pretty silence?
I've chosen a girl of whom I'll not repent;
it's right to choose a lovely girl of choice.

But it is when Hywel mingles his love of girls with his love for the mountains and shores of his home in North Wales that he writes most memorably. This he does beautifully in his *Gorhoffedd*, which has much more gaiety and delight and less of boasting and of battle in it than Gwalchmai's poem of the same title. This is how the poem begins and ends, with four lines taken from near the middle.

Tonn wenn orewyn a orwlych bet
gwytua ruuawn bebyr ben teyrnet
caraf trachas lloegyr lleudir goglet hediw
ac yn amgant y lliw lliaws callet
Caraf am rotes rybuched met
myn y dyhaet myr meith gywrysset
Caraf y theilu ae thew anhet yndi
ac wrth uot y ri rwyfaw dyhet
Caraf y morua ae mynytet
ae chaer ger y choed ae chein diret
a dolyt y dwfyr ae dyfrynnet
ae gwylein gwynnyon ae gwymp wraget
Caraf y milwyr ae meirch hywet
ae choed ae chedyrn ae chyuannet
Caraf y meyssyt ae man ueillyon arnaw
myn yd gauas faw fyryf oruolet
Caraf y brooet breint hywret
ae difeith mawrueith ae marannet . . .
Caraf y morua y meiryonnyt
men y bu ureich wenn yn obennyt
Caraf yr eaws arwyryaws wyt
yg kymer deu dyfyr dyffrynt iolyt . . .

Moch gwelwyf am nwyf yn etein y wrthaw
ac ym llaw uy llain
lleucu glaer uy chwaer yn chwerthin
ac ni chwart y gwr hi rac gortin

Gortin mawr am dawr am daerhawd
a hiraeth a sywaeth y ssy nawd
am nest dec debic afallulawd
am berw eur beruet uymhechawd
am enerys wyry ny warawd ym hoen
ny orpo hi diweirdawd
am hunyt ddefnyt hyd dytbrawd
am hawis uy newis deuawd

Keueisy vun duun diwyrnawd
keueisy dwy handid mwy eu molawd
keueisy deir a phedeir a phawd
keueis bump o rei gwymp eu gwyngnawd
keueis chwech heb odech pechawd
Gwenglaer uch gwengaer yt ym daerhawd
keueisy sseith ac ef gweith gordygnawd
keueisy wyth yn hal pwyth peth or wawd yr geint
ys da deint rac tauawd. [H. pp. 315–18]

The foaming white wave washes over a grave,
the tomb of Rhuawn Pebyr, regal chieftain.
I love today what the English hate, the land of the North,
and the varied growth that borders the river Lliw.
I love those who gave me my fill of mead
where the seas reach in long contention.
I love its household and its strong buildings,
and at its lord's wish to go to war.
I love its coast and its mountains,
its castle near the woods and its fine lands,
its water meadows and its valleys,
its white gulls and its lovely women.
I love its soldiers, its trained stallions,
its woods, its brave men and its homes.
I love its fields under the little clover
where I found a place of triumphant joy.
I love its regions to which valour entitles,
its wide waste lands and its wealth . . .
I love the coastland of Meirionnydd
where a white arm was my pillow.
I love the nightingale in the wild privet
where two waters meet in the valley of worship . . .

Early I see my vigour wing to the stirrup
    and my sword to my hand;
  bright Lleucu, my sister, laughing;
  her husband won't laugh before my onrush.

Great violence has involved me in payment,
    and longing, alas, is natural,
  for pretty Nest, like apple blossom,
  for the golden pear tree, heart of my sin.

For the virgin Generys there's no end to my pain;
    she clings to her chastity;
  for Hynud there's matter till Doomsday
  and for Hawis, my chosen ritual.

I had a girl of the same mind one day;
I had two, their praise be the greater;
I had three and four and fortune;
I had five, splendid in their white flesh;
I had six without concealing sin;
Gwenglaer, daughter of the White Tower, brought strife;
I had seven and a grievous time of it;
I had eight, paying part of the praise I sang.
  Teeth are good to keep the tongue quiet.

In these poems we glimpse a happy man living a full life in the vivid world of twelfth century North Wales, hunting and fighting in its woods and mountains and along its bird-bright shores, finding, more often than not, a white-skinned girl in every stout castle overlooking sea and moorland, and yet finding time to study the art of poetry and to write these joyous lyrics. The sharpness and clarity of the North Wales landscape has never been so well caught in words, nor have tenderness and humour been better mingled in the expression of love.

Owain Cyfeiliog, our second princely poet, ruled in Powys from 1149 to 1195 and died in 1197 at the Cistercian monastery of Ystrad Marchell, which he himself had founded. Little remains of his writing but what is left is remarkable and splendid, and it is impossible not to believe that he wrote much more, for he shows such mastery of the poetic craft and his work is steeped more than that of any other mediæval poet in the manner of Taliesin and Aneirin, whose heroic poetry echoes continuously through Owain's work. His poem, *Hirlas Owain*, is named after the Hirlas horn, the long blue mead horn, which, by its circling of the hall, gives the poem its plan.

Owain Cyfeiliog is feasting his retinue after a night expedition, the purpose of which seems to have been the freeing of a prisoner. He calls upon the mead-bearer to carry the horn around the hall and to pour out plentifully, and as the horn goes from man to man he praises them for their exploits. Then the horn comes to an empty place. Moreiddig has been killed in the fight and his loss is deeply felt.

What brings the poem so completely to life is this dramatic, periodical calling upon the mead-bearer, so that the taper-lit hall with its drinking company is recreated in our mind's eye. Befitting its importance in the poem, the horn itself is given ample description. It has a cover of thick silver. It is a horn of a hundred honours. Let us break in upon its circling of the hall.

Dywallaw di y corn argynvelyn
anrydetus vetw o vet gorewyn
ac or mynni hoedyl hyd yn blwytyn
na didawl i barch can nid perthyn
a dytwe i Rufut waywrutelyn
gwin a gwydyr goleu yn i gylchyn
dragon Arwystli arwystyl tervyn
dragon Owein hael a hil Kynvyn
dragon iw dechreu ac niw dychryn cat
cyvlavan argrat cymyw erlyn
ketwyr yt aethant er clod obryn
kyvoedon arvawc arvau Edwyn
talassant i met mal gwyr Belyn gynt
teg i hydrevynt tra vo undyn.[1]

Pour out the horn for Cynfelyn,
honourably drunk with foaming mead,
and if you wish to live another year,
don't stint his praise, that wouldn't be proper.

[1] Texts in *Llyfr Coch Hergest* and the *Myvyrian Archaiology*.

And give to Gruffydd of the ruddy spear
wine in a clear-walled glass,
the leader from Arwystli, pledge of the border,
leader of bountiful Owain of Kynvyn's breed,
a leader who starts and who fears no battle,
slaughter in moving, affliction in pursuing;
warriors who went over there for glory,
of the same age, in Edwyn's armour.
They paid for their mead like Belyn's men of old.
May their autumn be fair as long as they live.

What story there is in this poem must be gathered piecemeal, as in the *Gododdin*, but it is wrong to judge this poem as a narrative. It was composed in the first instance for men who knew the story since they had taken part in the fight. It is a poetic commentary on a shared experience by the bard of the company, who is in this case the prince himself. It is difficult to allot this poem to any one of Chadwick's stages of epic development, for though its style is a twelfth century revival of a sixth century epic manner, yet the poem was written after an expedition by the man who, quite probably, led that expedition, and therefore qualifies to belong to a primary stage in epic writing. Owain Cyfeiliog's men pay for their mead with fearless service and sometimes with their lives in the same way and in the same terms as did the young men of the *Gododdin* and Hnaef's warriors in the *Finn* fragment. There is no anachronism here, but a prolongation of the heroic age.

This echoing of earlier epic material by a mediæval poet imposes upon us a consideration of the relevance of the revolutionary studies of Joseph Bédier[1] to early Welsh poetry. Bédier has shown that the *Chansons de Geste* were written as a kind of touristic propaganda for religious houses in the South of France. The clerics employed poets to versify legends which glorified heroes who were canonised after their death and whose shrines and relics they housed. In this way pilgrims along the Via Tolosana, on their way to Compostella, were induced to turn aside and to make visits which brought profit and

[1] *Les Légendes Epiques* and other works.

renown to lesser shrines. Bédier has proved, and in a way which is as fascinating as any detective story, that the *Chansons de Geste* were composed during the eleventh and twelfth centuries, so that all belief in earlier authorship must be abandoned.

Bédier claims that for a legend to persist it must be tied to a locality and, in fact, to a religious house, for the monasteries were the only repositories of history and legend in the Middle Ages. This, however, does not apply to Wales. The early Taliesin poems carry no reference to specific saints or shrines, and the *Gododdin*, apart from vague reference to certain practices, is hardly Christian at all. These poems cannot have been preserved from antiquity or forged in an antique manner to the greater glory of any shrine or monastery. In Wales, as we have seen, the bardic order was responsible for the handing down of poetry and the poetic skill, and the bards themselves, without clerical encouragement or help, were sufficiently capable of preserving or of forging poetry.

Were the findings of M. B´dier true of early Welsh poetic legend we should expect to find direct pointers to such places as Strata Florida, Cymmer, Margam, Aberconwy and Cwm Hir in the Llywarch Hen and Heledd verse, but they are not there. And what an opportunity was provided by the *Stanzas of the Graves* for the accumulation of heroes and saints in one burial place. But most of the heroes are buried in the open country and can hardly have been the objects of pilgrimage. In particular, what an opportunity was lost with the greatest of them, Arthur. It seems therefore impossible to question the antiquity of the *Gododdin* and some of the Taliesin poetry by comparison with the *Chansons de Geste* and by applying M. Bédier's method. Religious modification of earlier material undoubtedly took place, and it is easy to believe that from the beginning of the twelfth century the monks would above all preserve poems in praise of a prince whose burial within their precincts was to their glory. We may, for instance, be indebted to the monks of Ystrad Marchell for the perpetuating of the work of their patron Owain Cyfeiliog, but the *Gododdin* and *Beowulf* take us beyond this kind of indebtedness.

Another consideration which must arise from the study of the verse of Hywel ap Owain Gwynedd and Owain Cyfeiliog is the influence they exerted on the subsequent course of Welsh poetry. It is clear that they were both thoroughly grounded by their bardic teachers in the craft and traditions of poetry but since they could hardly have been classed as either house or chief poets, and since their rank gave them greater freedom, they were able to venture beyond the limits of ordinary poetic practice, and, in so doing, to widen the scope of poetry for those who followed them. It would be wrong, however, to exaggerate their originality in employing a wide range of personal experience as subject matter. Nothing could be more intensely personal than some of the Llywarch Hen and Heledd poems, or the complaint of the chieftain in the Juvencus manuscript, whilst in their own century Gwalchmai had pointed out the way of extension to his princely successors in his *Gorhoffedd* and his *Ode to Eva*. Poetry had before the twelfth century touched on many aspects of life, witness the lullaby interpolated into the *Book of Aneirin*, but verse which did not deal with war or the greatness of some prince was not then thought worthy of permanent record, so that some of the more lyrical utterances have been saved for us only by some lucky chance. The tenth century Laws of Hywel Dda speak of poems suitable to be sung by the house poet to the queen or to the lady of the house in her private apartment, but all these songs have been lost. When this kind of verse was produced by a great prince, the monks of a monastery which he had founded or succoured might well think it worth while to record it, even though to the order of bards it might savour of triviality.

The by now conventional subject matter, a poem to God, many to patrons, one to a girl, is once more to be found in the work of Llywarch ap Llewelyn, whose approximate dates are 1173–1220, and who is usually known by his bardic name of Prydydd y Moch, the Poet of the Pigs. In spite of this curious title, Prydydd y Moch was, if we are to accept the evidence of his poetry, a warrior as well as a professional poet, and, if the place name Gafel Prydydd y Moch has any meaning, a land-owner.

An interesting record of a quarrel between poet and patron is embodied in his two poems known as *Bwgwth Davyt*, the *Threatening of David*, and *Kyvarch Gwell Davyt*, the *Greeting of David*, both addressed to Dafydd ap Owain. *The Threatening of David* begins with four lines of nature description and it may be, and has been, argued whether the poet's intention is merely to begin elegantly in the old convention of using nature as padding, to create an atmosphere suitable to the subject matter of controversy, or to indicate the time at which the dispute took place.

Kalan hyturef tymp dyt yn edwi
calaf gan lloer uann llwrw uenegi
kyntwryf yn ebyr llyr yn llenwi
kyngyd gaeafawr hwyluawr heli
keluytodeu reen rannwyd a mi
megys na rannwyd am ryeni
kychwetyl am dothyw am dwythualch ri
kywychyawn am dawn om dielwi
A gwrt uyt adwyn a gwedi uyg kert
agarw y angert engyr a hi. [H. p. 262]

October kalends, season of withering day;
stalks in the moonlight tell where the path is,
in river mouths the turmoil of rising tide,
winter's hour prevails, the sea's mood is majestic.
Lordly accomplishments were given to me
such as were not given to my forefathers.
News has come to me that a lively lord,
splendid in his favours, has reviled me.
And instead of what should be, after my songs,
his violence is rough and terrible.

The poet then asserts his superiority to those others who quaver hoarsely in Dafydd's praise and asks for a return to favour, for no other lord will inspire him.

The next poem, the *Greeting*, ends with a grateful piece of flattery, for the poet has been restored to his position, in the form of an *englyn*[1].

[1] It should be noted that the modern *englyn* form has by now been established, replacing the primitive three-line *englyn* used in the Llywarch Hen and Juvencus poetry.

Ar gedyrn eur gedawl. Dauyd
o deuawd angertawl
Rwym kynnygyn kynnogyn ditawl
rwyf prydein prydyt ath uawl. [H. p. 265]

For the brave, bountiful gold. David,
out of incomparable custom
offerer of a bond to an exiled debtor,
Lord of Britain, a poet praises you.

Again, singing as house poet to Llywelyn ap Iorwerth, and therefore able to use the less official four-line stanza, Prydydd y Moch says:—

Eryr teyrnet yr yueisy uet
ar het ar dyhet ar deheu ri
yr yueisy win oe ualch vuelin
ae wisgoet eurin ar uynogi.[1] [H. p. 278]

Royal eagle, I have drunk mead
in peace and war at my lord's right hand;
I have drunk wine from his proud horn,
in the bright garments of his bounty.

In the list that follows of Llywelyn's victories, the place names are handled in a manner typical of the poets of this period, the name being sometimes broken into two by the insertion of a descriptive adjective. The effect in Welsh is curiously pleasant, whereas any attempt to do this in English would surely be doomed to ridicule, for it is hardly possible to contemplate such phrases as Birming cloudy ham or Canter gentle bury. Prydydd y Moch, however, delights us with *Caer vawr vyrtin*, *Aber tyner teivi*, and *Aber hydyruer hotni*, by which device Carmarthen, Cardigan and Brecon become euphoniously great, gentle and watered. The reason for the greater acceptability of this trick in Welsh may be the comparative

[1] This form may also be considered a kind of *rhupunt hir*. See the Appendix on Versification.

homogeneity of the constituent parts of the place names, and, as a result, the more general and immediate awareness of the etymology of such names, so that their breaking up is more natural and comprehensible.

Prydydd y Moch is one of the most violent and bloody of these writers of a period which took pleasure in the contemplation of the crow-picked corpses of its enemies through the medium of verse, and his description of the killing of the English at Swansea, in the poem to Rhys Gryc, sounds like the clang of armour.

His poem to Gwenlliant, daughter of Hywel, has in it the elements we observed in the *Gorhoffedd* of Gwalchmai, a love which burns in his breast and takes away his colour but which, I suspect, may here be a literary passion of the troubadour kind, a detailed awareness of the season of the year, and unusually arrogant boasting of his deeds against the English. To this is added a device which was later to become conventional in poems addressed to girls, the sending of some bird or beast as a messenger of love. In this poem, as in Cynddelw's poem to Eva, the messenger is a stallion, and just as a bird may in fact carry a message, a horse can carry a rider, so that the meaning here may go beyond the convention by promising or threatening a visit.

Yet another aspect of this poet's work is his criticism of man in society, for Prydydd y Moch was an acute observer of men and liked to talk about them, distinguishing and classifying with mediæval complacency. In his *Ode* to Rhodri ap Owain, he says,

Rannws duw deus donyon—anghymwys
agkymhes y veibyon
Rann y bawb y bobyl yadon
rei yn drud ereill yn doethyon
Rei tra llwfyr tra llafar eu son
Ac ereill taerlew termudyon
Rei digart yn hart yn haelon
mwy no rwy o rei kybytyon. [H. p. 265]

The Lord God shared out gifts—unsuitably,
  excessively to men,
a share for every one with a head on him,
some reckless, others wise,
some cowardly and too talkative,
others courageous and quite dumb,
some without blemish, fair and generous,
whilst many more are miserly.

When Llywelyn ap Iorwerth, known as the Great, died in 1240, Dafydd Benfras was amongst those who lamented his passing. Another elegy followed when news came of the unlucky death of Llywelyn's much loved son, Gruffydd, in attempting to escape from the Tower of London on Saint David's Day, 1244. A third elegy followed the death of Dafydd, Llywelyn's other son, in 1246, and then, when in 1248 Henry III gave permission for Gruffydd's remains to be transferred from London for burial in the Abbey of Aberconwy, which his father had founded, Dafydd Benfras wrote a fourth elegy on all three princes together.

In three stanzas on death, Dafydd Benfras struck a note which still echoes through Welsh poetry. The form of the poem, too, is significant, for it may be observed here, as in the work of Prydydd y Moch, that the *englyn* has reached a point beyond which there has been no development, in spite of seven centuries of continuous subsequent use. Here is one stanza of this fine poem.

Pob dyn oer dyddyn neut eiddaw agheu
  aghyueillwr iddaw
y veddu daear arnaw
y ved or diwed y daw. [H. p. 192]

To every man belongs death, cold tenement,
  death the unfriendly;
to own earth above him,
to the grave at last he comes.

Readers unfamiliar with the modern *englyn* form may in the Welsh of the above poem observe most of its characteristic features: the thirty syllables in all (ten, six, seven and seven), the four end rhymes, the linking word, beyond the rhyme at the end of the first line, which is echoed in the first word of the second line, the internal rhymes and the alliteration. The last line has two echoes subtly entwined, *ved* and *-wed* (*fedd* and *-wedd* in modern Welsh), and *diw-* and *daw*. These are all common features of the *englyn*, but not so common, and possibly accidental, is the half rhyme which runs down the middle of the lines, *oer*, *-wr*, *-ar*, *or*. One may, without over-stretching analysis, bring to light still more subtleties in this little poem, until, in spite of the simplicity of its statement, for the Welsh, apart from the archaic *neut*, is the ordinary Welsh of today, the poem is seen as a little piece of perfection, a minute triumph in an exacting craft.

The period with which we have been dealing may be said to end with the unlucky death in 1282 of Llywelyn ap Gruffydd, the last independent ruler of Wales, and the beastly execution of his brother David by Edward I in 1283. That the magnitude of this disaster was realised in its own day can be seen in the magnificent ode written to the last Llywelyn by Gruffydd ab yr Ynad Coch. This is a more passionate and more personal lament than any of the many odes composed on the death of earlier leaders, for, though it begins conventionally enough with the poet's own grief and with praise of the dead prince's generosity, it moves through the not unusual general grief, the wounds, the blood, the cries of widows and orphans, the burnt homes and ravaged lands, to a tremendous climax in which the poet's whole world comes to an end, and in which, as in the tragedies of Shakespeare, nature and the order of the universe seem to be imperilled by the disaster. Here is the passage.

Oeruelawc callon dan vronn o vraw
rewyd val crinwyd yssyn crinaw
Pony welwch chwi hynt y gwynt ar glaw
pony welwch chwi r deri yn ymdaraw
pony welwch chwi r mor yn merwinaw yr tir
pony welwch chwi r gwir yn ymgyweiriaw
Pony welwch chwi r heul yn hwylaw r awyr
pony welwch chwi r syr wedyr syrthyaw

Pany chredwch chwi y duw dynyadon ynvyt
pany welwch chwir byt wedyr bydyaw
Och hyt attat ti duw na daw mor tros dir
pabeth yngedir y ohiryaw
nyt oes le y kyrcher rac carchar braw
nyt oes le y trigyer och ortrigyaw
nyt oes nachyngor na chlo nac egor unfford
y escor brwyn gyngor braw. [RBH. pp. 1417–18]

The heart is cold under a breast of fear;
lust shrivels like dry branches.
See you not the way of the wind and the rain?
See you not the oaks beat together?
See you not the sea stinging the land?
See you not truth equipping?
See you not the sun driving the sky?
See you not the stars have fallen?
Do you not believe God, demented men?
See you not the end of existence?
A sigh to you, God, that the sea might come over the land!
Why are we left to linger?
There is no resort from the prison of fear.
There is nowhere to dwell, alas for the dwelling!
There is no counsel, no lock, no opening,
no way of escaping from terror's sad counsel.

To those who like to classify poets, who are embarrassed by this poem's departure from the usual conventions of the court poetry of the twelfth and thirteenth centuries, and who set it apart as a wild personal cry, it may be said that the occasion of the poem was the unluckiest day in the history of the Welsh, that in technique the poem is brilliant, that in its entirety it is one of the most splendid utterances in Western European literature.

Bleddyn Fardd, too, laments the death of Llywelyn the Last and his brothers in a more conventional ode. The time is, suitably, winter and the poem begins:—

Neud amser gaeaf gwelwaf gweilgi
gweilgig moradar hwylvar heli
neud oerllen aryen eryri weithyon
neud uchel gwenndonn gwyndir enlli. [H. p. 67]

> It is winter time with the sea at its palest,
> the sea birds' perch in an angry mood,
> Snowdon is now a cold veil of hoarfrost,
> the white wave high on the holy land of Enlli.

The poet is sad for the loss of the three chieftains whom he praises and names in turn with their victories, comparing them to Arthur. He ends with a prayer to God, to the powerful Saints David and Cybi, and finally to Mary and the prophets, that they may be granted "in the good eternal parish a guest house of mercy."

So, with this final repayment for mead and for fine garments, this blending of season and emotion, this pious prayer to the Celtic saints, this characteristic uniting of the tasks of the official poet, we may leave a period of great writing in the noble houses of a still unconquered Wales. The poets from now on will find it harder to make a secure and honourable living, and to resist inroads upon the technique of their craft.

Chapter V

THE FOURTEENTH CENTURY

★

The effect of the loss of Welsh independence is not immediately to be observed in poetry, which must be considered in the light of this political change for three centuries from 1282 for the process of disintegration in Welsh culture to become clear. The noble houses continued to sustain poets but the dignity of a chief poet's position was greatly diminished under English government, for the poet was no longer a secure paid official, high in the counsel of a prince. Poets, whether their patrons were great or small, came more and more to consider themselves as of the same class, the struggle and the rivalry being to win a wealthier patron and a more comfortable life. With this came an inevitable decline in the authority of the chief poet and bardic teacher, opening the way for innovation.

It is dangerous, however, to overestimate political and social changes as causes of change in poetry. Poetic practice rarely remains constant under any circumstances and new experiments come with new writers, for the poet though he must be a craftsman, is more than a craftsman. Even during the twelfth century and in the work of such conservative practitioners as Cynddelw we observe changes in the matter and manner of poetry.

But the way of life in Wales was changing, and Professor W. J. Gruffudd has admirably indicated[1] how the change must needs be reflected in the art of the age we are now to consider.

From about the year 1300 on there was to be less internecine and less national warfare for the Welsh (though Welshmen

[1] *Barddoniaeth Cymru cyn Dafydd ap Gwilym.*

were to play a prominent role in English armies), the blacksmith-armourer was to dwindle from his eminence in the community, iron work was to be less grim and more decorative, there was to be greater comfort in the great houses. Women were to see more of their menfolk and become more than a brief solace for the resting warrior or breeders of young partisans in the paternal feuds. This, as much as the influence of the troubadour singing of the Continent, brought women and love into greater prominence in poetry. How much is due, with all this, to the personality of such men as Madog Benfras, Dafydd ap Gwilym and Sypyn Cyfeiliog it is impossible now to say, but our debt to them must surely be great, for it is hard to believe that, whatever kind of society and age they lived in, they would not have delighted in the beauty of girls and the freshness of woods in early summer.

A notable development in the form of poetry is the final acceptance of the *englyn* as suitable for the highest purposes, which were, to the strict bardic mind, the praise of the great and the lamenting of the death of patrons. The *englyn* had previously been employed in tale telling, in the popular gnomic verse and in the praise of lesser persons. It had been the metre of the house poet rather than the chief poet, but now, in the work of Gruffudd ap Maredudd and Gruffudd ap Dafydd, the *englyn* achieves the highest rank in the metrical hierarchy[1], a position which it has kept until today.

So great is the volume of poetry produced from about 1340 to the present day, or perhaps it would be more exact to say so much has been recorded and preserved in contrast to the loss and destruction of much earlier work, that from now to the end of this book I can do no more than select outstanding or characteristic poets.

The language of the fourteenth century poets, particularly the innovators, is much closer to modern Welsh than anything we have so far considered, and the *cywyddau* are sufficiently

[1] The measures permitted to the official poet were in the fourteenth century classified as twenty-four. An account of these will be found in the Appendix on Versification.

comprehensible to a present-day Welshman who has no specialised training in the language. The language of the more traditional poets and of the older poetic forms, however, bristles with archaisms and there are anachronistic references to the world of Aneirin and Taliesin.

Gruffudd ap Adda was a friend of Dafydd ap Gwilym and, although little of his work remains to us, there is enough to establish him as a brilliant poet. He died in 1344 of a deep wound in the head received in a sword fight with a friend at Dolgellau. The skull, with a deep dent in it, was still to be seen early in the sixteenth century and was used to drink out of as a cure for coughing[1]. He was something of a musician, too, and the air known after his name, and to which he refers in an *englyn*, was preserved and printed in the *Myvyrian Archaiology.*[2]

Gruffudd ap Adda wrote a charming poem to a birch tree which was cut down to make a maypole for the town of Llanidloes. The poem is full of contempt for town dwellers and their petty commerce, and of love for the green woods and the hills. It is written in the new *cywydd* form and the seven-syllable couplet with its unaccented rhyme, the chief feature of this form, gave opportunity for the polishing of little gems of verbal music. The poem is full of craftsmanship such as we see in the following couplet:—

Ni chel y drem uchel draidd
y briallu ebrillaidd. [DGG. p. 118]

Nor will your features, reaching high,
hide April's primroses.

He ends by asking the tree where it would like best to be, in the confidence that the birch would agree with him in his feelings about town and country.

Ai cyrchu'r ffrith gadr adref,
ai crinaw draw yn y dref.

[1] MS. Gwyneddon 3, 153a.
[2] DGG., p. 120.

To seek your lovely woodland home
or shrivel down there in the town.

Another poem by Gruffudd ap Adda is full of gaiety, and of the happiness of confident love. It is called *Lleidr Serch*, *Thief of Love*, for as the poet lies in wait for a girl and thinks of what he is about to do, his mind turns upon the other illicit pleasures of raiding. This is how the poem ends.

Lleidr wyf, mae clwyf i'm clymu,
lleidr merch deg, nid lleidr march du;
nid lleidr myharen heno,
lleidr meinwen drwy ddien dro;
nid lleidr buarth gwartheg,
lleidr hon, wedd ton, dan wydd teg;
lleidr eres hudoles hy,
lleidr poendaith, nid lleidr pandy;
lleidr dirwyn morwyn nid mau,
lleidr purserch, nid lleidr pyrsau;
nid wyf leidr un llwdn carnawl,
arnaf ni bu hwyaf hawl:
lledrad gariad a'm gorwyf,
lleidryn, boen efyn, bun wyf. [DGG. p. 119–20]

I am a thief, a wound binds me,
thief of a fair girl, not a black stallion;
for tonight no thief of a ram,
thief of a maiden this happy time;
no thief of the cattle enclosure,
thief of her, wave-coloured, in the fair wood;
thief of a wonderful bold enchantress,
thief of a penance, not of a fulling mill;
thief to entwine a girl who's not mine,
thief of pure love, no thief of purses;
no thief of a hoofed heifer,
yet never was law so heavy upon me;
love's theft now overcomes me,
o daring pain, I am the thief of a girl.

Madog Benfras, another contemporary and friend of Dafydd ap Gwilym, though famous in his day as a master of the poetic craft, has left only a small body of work, once more in the new *cywydd* form. Little is known of his life, but one piece of tradition makes up for all other deficiencies, for it is said that he married Dafydd ap Gwilym to Morfudd in the woods according to bardic ritual. Equally with Dafydd, therefore, his religion must have been that of the woods and their inhabitants and, like Dafydd, he produced finely wrought poems in praise of girls. Of an unnamed girl he said:—

Pan ddel merched y gwledydd,
o rai teg i'r un oed dydd,
y bydd tebyg ei hoew loewbryd,
bun ymysg merched y byd,
fyth i'r lamp grair ddisgleirlan
ymysg y canwyllau man. [DGG. p. 125]

When the girls of all countries come,
the fair ones to one meeting,
her lovely lucent face,
maid amongst the girls of the world,
will be like a bright shrine lamp
amongst the little tapers.

Madog Benfras wrote an ode on the death of Dafydd ap Gwilym in which he calls him *eos Dyfed*—the nightingale of Demetia, *hebog Deheubarth*—the hawk of South Wales[1], and *pennaeth gwawd*—the chieftain of poetry. Dafydd wrote him an elegy in return, for it must be remembered that poets, in friendly or derisive manner, sometimes wrote laments for each other's death whilst they still lived.

I have thus briefly dealt with Gruffudd ap Adda and Madog Benfras before Dafydd ap Gwilym in order to make the latter's appearance about the middle of the fourteenth century[2] less isolated and exceptional than has often been suggested by historians of literature. Dafydd was perhaps not the first, and was certainly not the only one, to seek the consolation of the woods from the new order imposed by the English upon Wales.

[1] Iolo Goch calls Dafydd *hebog merched Deheubarth*—hawk of the girls of the South.
[2] Dafydd's dates are roughly 1325–1380. v. DGG., pp. xi–xxv.

In the new towns which clustered about Edward I's formidable castles, the privileges of commerce were not for some time accorded to the Welsh, and even when Welshmen came to enter fully into the guild organisation of these towns it was to be expected that the old aristocracy, together with the old order of bards, and Dafydd ap Gwilym was both a classically trained bard and an aristocrat, should regard the whole of the new urban way of life with contempt. The Celtic way of life, ever since the Romans first offered the temptations of towns, has always been anti-urban and remains so today, as is demonstrated by the peripatetic habits of the National Eisteddfod and the lack of centralisation in Welsh cultural organisation.

Dafydd ap Gwilym's life was one of continuous escape from the new political and economic tendencies of his age. He makes no explicit protest against government from Westminster or any prophecies, in the old manner, of the expulsion of the English, but neither does he, like Iolo Goch, accept and praise the English king. His attitude towards the English is one of contempt. He wants to have as little to do with them as possible and, with his country's way of life crumbling about him, he delights in the beauty and sublimity of nature, the loveliness of girls and the wit and poetic skill of his friends. To accuse him on these grounds of triviality, for this has been done, to compare him as a serious person unfavourably with Iolo Goch, seems to me a great error, for surely the kissing of a girl is no less dignified than the cutting off of a man's head, the song of a nightingale no less important than the terms of a statute, a storm no less terrible than a chieftain at the head of his men. Owain Cyfeiliog lived a life which justified his emulation of the *Gododdin* manner, but with the passing of the age of iron went the heroic standards, and for a poet of the fourteenth century to write of nothing but blood and ravaging would be an anachronistic absurdity.

There is no doubt that Dafydd ap Gwilym was acquainted, directly or indirectly, with the troubadour development in European writing, most probably through the poetry of the French trouveres. Dafydd may have made the pilgrimage to

Compostella, passing through *chanson de geste* and troubadour country, but even if he did not, Wales offered sufficient opportunities for contact with a style of writing which was well over a century old when he was born. As a young man Dafydd lived for some years with an uncle in South Wales who had become a government official, and the beginning of the fourteenth century saw the appearance of a crop of English love lyrics, which seem to have been written in South West England, not far, in fact, from Maesaleg, the home of Dafydd's chief patron, Ifor Hael.

The aubade and the serenade appear in Dafydd ap Gwilym's work, together with nearly all the characteristic elements of troubadour and goliardic writing[1], and Sir Ifor Williams argues very convincingly in *Dafydd ap Gwilym a'i Gyfoeswyr* that the poet may well have been one of the *clerici vagantes*. He frequently refers to himself as a member of *y gler*, the Welsh term (derived from *clericus*) used for these wandering scholars and poets. Continental goliardic poetry is full of love of the open air, and the connection between the church, the *clerici vagantes* and the *goliardi* may explain the frequency of ritual terminology in Dafydd's work, and his readiness to use religious ceremony for purposes of imagery and parody. It should always be remembered, however, that many of the outstanding elements of Dafydd's poetry are to be found in twelfth and thirteenth century Welsh writing. Poets had previously written in praise of girls and the landscape of North Wales had become much more than a background to human activity in the work of Hywel ap Owain Gwynedd. Had the work of the second grade of poets been handed down to us more completely, we should probably be able to trace the forerunning of Dafydd in the field of humour and parody, just as prototypes must have existed for the grosser humour of Madog Dwygraig.

From these not entirely profitable considerations of the source of Dafydd ap Gwilym's inspiration, whether his personality, his conscious working on elements already existing in

[1] See Chotzen, *Recherches sur la Poésie de D. ap. G.*, 1927.

Welsh poetry, the condition of Wales in his day or the achievements of the new way of writing in France, Germany and South West England, let us turn to the poetry itself.

Dafydd ap Gwilym, although most often thought of as an innovator, was fully trained in the intricacies of the bardic craft and, in the art of *dyfaliad*, or kenning, is closely linked to the earlier mediæval masters. Even towards the end of his life, when writing an elegy on the death of Angharad Hael, wife[1] of his patron Ieuan Llwyd of Llyn Aeron, Dafydd reverted to the *awdl* metres employed by his more conventional contemporaries and predecessors. Here are excerpts from the poem illustrating the two metres used and his command of each. The first quotation is in the *englyn* form, the second in the measure known as the *toddaid*.

Llawer bron am hon ym-Mhennardd a hyllt
ail Essyllt wiw lwyshardd,
llefain yw berf oferfardd,
llwyr wae ni chwarae, ni chwardd.

Ni chwardd gwirfardd cu wir-fad cwyn uthr
can eithyw Yngharad,
neu thyrr fy mron eithr fy mrad,
nod llif garw neud-llef girad. [G. p. 83a]

Many a breast for her in Penardd will split,
second Yseult, seemly, holy and fair;
to weep is the vain poet's verb,
full grief plays not nor laughs.

Nor laughs the true poet, fond goodness laments
for Angharad's going,
or my heart would break with my treachery
in bitter flood and cries of longing.

The poem, which consists of nine *englynion* followed by thirty-eight lines in the *toddaid* measure with one main rhyme, ends thus:—

[1] She is given as daughter to Ieuan Llwyd in MS. Gwyneddon 3, p. 82, b.

Gweddig argywedd ddeigr gawad a'm gwlych,
gwyrdd fyngrudd a chrych, fawr-nych farw-nad,
gwenwyn i'm ei chwyn, nychiad i'm hystlys,
gwanas gywir-lys gŵn yscarlad.

Gwaith drwg i'r olwg hir-wylad ynghaeth,
gwaith cyfing hiraeth cof Angharad. [G. p. 84a]

A fitting pain, a shower of tears wets me,
my cheek is sallow and withered by languishing grief;
a poison to me her lament, it consumes my side—
the clasp of a courtly scarlet gown.

Sad work for the sight, the long enforced weeping;
woeful work of longing, the memory of Angharad.

The *englynion* quoted above are full of the devices peculiar to the form, which may be picked out by the eye even in ignorance of Welsh. Of particular interest and not required by the rules of metrics in a sequence of *englynion* but adopted by the writer to tighten the form or to increase the difficulties of composition, is the repetition at the beginning of an *englyn* of the last word or words of the previous one, a device known in Welsh as *cyrch-gymeriad* (link-taking), which was at least a century old when Dafydd used it and which was used with great effect later by Dafydd Nanmor. Thus *ni chwardd* at the end of one *englyn* is echoed at the beginning of the following one, whose last word, *girad*, is in turn echoed by *Rhy irad* at the beginning of the subsequent *englyn*. One rhyme is used throughout the *toddaid* lines, but every other line is taken two or three syllables beyond the main rhyme, creating a new rhyme with the middle of the following line. This secondary rhyme varies with each couplet. Thus the main rhyme in this case is *-ad*, but *gwlych* rhymes with *chrych*, *hystlys* with *-lys*, and so on, so that the rhyme scheme weaves in and out like the tracery on a stone cross.

Another trick, known in Welsh as *cymeriad*, is the repetition of the first letter of one line at the beginning of successive lines. So, as though to make the thing more difficult still, and this is not infrequent in mediæval Welsh poetry, each of the *toddaid* lines quoted begins with *gw-*. The consummation of the artistry occurs in the last line, where every syllable is linked in some way to another. Let us analyse it. *Gwaith* repeats *gwaith* of the previous line; the first five consonants of *cyfing hiraeth* (c, f, ng, h, r) are repeated in that order in *cof Angharad* of the second half of the line; the *-aeth* of *hiraeth* rhymes with *ynghaeth* of the previous line, and the *-ad* of Angharad rhymes with *-wylad.* Nothing could possibly be more complex and deliberate than this, and yet, and here is the inexplicable and untranslatable miracle, the line runs off the tongue as easily and fluently as a customary greeting.

So much for Dafydd's skill in the traditional verse forms of the official poet, but the form in which he made himself the greatest poet in Welsh is the *cywydd*[1], which he certainly established, much as Dryden did the heroic couplet, as the main poetic form for succeeding generations, even if he did not invent or perfect it. The origin of the *cywydd* form is mysterious although probably only made so by our ignorance, once again, of the work of the lower poetic orders before the fourteenth century. Dafydd ap Gwilym must have taken advantage of the new freedom, or licence, to raise this form to the level of the *awdl* measures and the *englyn*. The *cywydd*, in the work of Dafydd ap Gwilym, his contemporaries and his successors up to the present day, is a poem of usually not less than thirty and not more than a hundred lines in length. The lines are usually of seven syllables and rhyme in couplets, one of the rhyming syllables being accented, the other unaccented, as though, in English, sulking rhymed with king. The main feature of the *cywydd* development is the elaboration and regularisation of the device known as *cynghanedd*,[2] which consists of controlled

[1] Pronounced like the English words—cow with.

[2] In English spelling this would be written cunghanneth, the th as in breathe. v. Appendix on Versification.

variations of multiple alliteration, with occasional internal rhyme. The *toddaid* line analysed in the previous paragraph affords a good example of a straight-forward kind of *cynghanedd*.

Sixty-four *cywyddau* accepted as being by Dafydd ap Gwilym were printed by Professor Ifor Williams and Mr. Thomas Roberts,[1] but many more are attributed to Dafydd in the manuscripts of the fifteenth and sixteenth centuries and we now await the publication of the fruits of Professor Tom Parry's research into these.[2] Apart from a poem in praise of Ifor Hael, Dafydd's chief patron, four elegies on the death of bardic friends and a few poems in contemplation of his own life, the main body of his *cywydd* writing is divided almost equally between poems of love and of nature.

In the love poems two girls' names, Morfudd and Dyddgu, frequently appear, but the poet makes little pretence that his attentions were confined only to two. There may or may not have been an original Morfudd and Dyddgu, but in the poetry it becomes clear that Morfudd stands for any fair-haired and Dyddgu for any dark-haired girl the poet is in love with at the moment of writing, for they occur, like popular saints, in every part of Wales; they are sometimes married and sometimes virginal. Then there are many unnamed girls, including the pretty nuns whom Dafydd tried to entice away to the religion of the woods.

There is nothing romantic or spiritual or mysterious about Dafydd's love. It is physical love, the happy love of the body and the moment. Unlike some of his contemporaries, but like Shakespeare, he avoids detailed description of women. In his poem to Morfudd's arms he shows more interest in getting the arms about him than in the contours of the arms themselves. His pictures of women therefore have a pleasing vagueness, springing perhaps from the multiplicity of his love experiences, which enables the reader to imagine his own Morfudd as he does his own Juliet and Cordelia. This is how Dafydd describes Morfudd:—

[1] Cywyddau D. ap G. a'i Gyfoeswyr, Bangor, 1914.
[2] It has occurred since this book went to press.

Dy liw a wnaeth Duw Lywydd,
dy dal fal llygaid y dydd.
Duw a roddes it ruddaur;
dy wallt fal tafod o aur.
Dy fwnwgl yn dwf uniawn,
dy fronnau'n bellennau llawn.
Deurudd ysgarlad arael;
du Llundain, riain, yw'r ael.
Dy lygaid dau loewgae,
dy drwyn ar ddyn mwyn y mae.
Dy wên yw'r pum llawenydd,
dy gorff hardd a'm dwg o'r ffydd. [DGG. p. 36]

Your colour God made,
your forehead like the daisies.
God gave you red gold,
your hair a tongue of gold.
Your neck of straight growth,
your breasts full spheres.
Two scarlet sunny cheeks,
your brows of London black,[1]
your eyes bright enclosures,
your nose of a sweet girl.
Your smile the five delights,
your lovely body takes me from the faith.

Then we are told that she is slim, and that is all. A man during his lifetime is apt to make more than one attempt to find in women that of which he carries a vague apprehension from his childhood. Her nose may be of any tolerable shape as long as it is on a sweet girl. The main thing for Dafydd is to get her to the woods.

Dy deced, dyred i'r allt,
bid ein gwely fry ny fron
bedeiroes mewn bedw irion
ar fatras o ddail glas glyn
a'i ridens wych o redyn;
a chwrlid rhom a churlaw,
coed a ludd cawod o law. [DGG. pp. 36–7]

[1] This I take to be a fine black material by analogy with *llwyd Llundain*, London grey.

Beauty, come to the hillside,
our bed be high on the hill
four ages under fresh birches,
the mattress of green leaves
valanced with brilliant ferns;
a coverlet, against beating rain,
of trees that check the shower.

Things do not always follow that plan. The girl may prove difficult or her husband too watchful. The poet builds a house of boughs in the wood but the girl scorns it, requiring, quite naturally, a greater security; he has to wait, catching cold, under dripping eaves; the happiest moment arrives and there is a tremendous thunder-clap and the girl rushes off in fright. A high wave on the Dyfi prevents him from crossing over to a girl. Once he has almost got past the defences which Eiddig has set about his wife when a red dog leaps at him out of a pigsty and he has to escape in the midst of a great commotion. He is tormented by the face of a nun whom he has seen and another nun is too pious to surrender.

Er Duw, paid a'r bara a'r dwr,
a bwrw ar gasau'r berwr.
Paid, er Mair, a'r pader main
a chrefydd myneich Rhufain.
Na fydd leian y gwanwyn;
gwaeth yw lleianaeth na llwyn.
Dy grefydd, deg oreuferch,
y sydd wrthwyneb i serch.
Gwarant modrwy a mantell
a gwyrdd wisg a urddai well.
Dyred i'r fedw gadeiriog,
i grefydd y gwydd a'r gog,
ac yno ni'n gogenir
er ynnill nef ny llwyn ir.
A chadw i'th gof lyfr Ofydd,
a phaid a gormod o ffydd. [DGG. p. 10]

For God's sake, no more bread and water,
throw aside watercress.

For Mary's sake, cease your thin prayers,
the Roman monks' religion.
Don't be a nun in springtime,
worse is the nunnery than the grove.
Your faith, my pretty paragon,
sets its face against love.
The ring's warrant, a mantle
and a green garment ordain you better.
Come to the spreading birch,
the cuckoo's church in the woods;
no one will mock at us there
for winning heaven in a green grove.
Keep in mind Ovid's book
and, please, not too much faith.

Dafydd does not seem to have enjoyed much luck at Llanbadarn, the place where he was born. He tells us, in a very amusing poem to the girls of that place, how every Sunday finds him in church,

a'm wyneb at y fun goeth
a'm gwegil at Dduw gwiwgoeth. [DGG. p. 27]

my face towards the fine girl,
my back to the pure God.

The girls mock at his interest in them and predict his failure with them. They ask each other, and here is one of our pictures of the poet,

Y mab llwyd wyneb mursen
a gwallt ei chwaer am ei ben,
pa ddisgwyl ffol ei olwg?
Gwyr ei ddrem garu i ddrwg.

That pale fellow with the affected look
and his sister's hair on his head,
what does he expect, the silly ogler?
His looks are for bad loving.[1]

[1] A note in MS Gwyneddon 3 says that Dafydd ap Gwilym was tall and thin, with long curly yellow hair, full of silver clasps and rings. p. 84a.

Dafydd ap Gwilym makes great use of the love messenger (*y llatai*), a device we observed in twelfth century Welsh poetry, and, if he is far from the girl he loves, or if there is some obstacle to his reaching her side, he asks the wind, the lark, the seagull, the cock pheasant, the eagle, the swan, the blackcap, even the salmon in turn to carry his message of love to the girl of the moment.

If some of the poems attributed to Dafydd in the manuscripts are really his, then his expression of erotic experience went far beyond our present limits of printability. I find no difficulty in believing him capable of indecency, though the style of some of these poems seems to indicate fifteenth century composition, for there is nothing very nasty about them, only a bolder extension of the happy paganism we see in Dafydd's indubitable work, an extension within the limit of taste in that age, and, unhappily, beyond the limit of ours. It is the task of scholarship unhampered by nonconformist prejudice to estimate the authenticity of these poems whilst we hope for the advent of a cleaner social conscience to allow them to be made available to the general reader.

Every aspect of nature is reflected in the poetry of Dafydd ap Gwilym and no poet has better conveyed the sense of wonder at the varied manifestations that seasonal change brings about in the land of Britain. Like most of us he prefers summer to winter and he makes this clear in an ode which contrasts the months of January and May. After some storm-filled lines, the dull greyness of winter is depicted thus:—

Ac annog llanw ac annwyd
ac mewn naint llifeiriaint llwyd
a llawn son mewn afonydd
a llidiaw a digiaw dydd
ac wybren drymled ledoer
a'i lliw yn gorchuddiaw'r lloer. [DGG. p. 91]

Urging on tides and colds
and in the brooks a brown flood;
a turmoil fills the rivers,
day is angered and offended,
and the heavy, chilly sky
with its hue obscures the moon.

Summer brings magic and alchemy to the broom.

Pan ddel Mai a'i lifrai las
ar irddail i roi'r urddas,
aur a dyf ar edafedd
ar y llwyn er mwyn a'i medd.
Teg yw'r pren a gwyrennig
y tyf yr aur tew o'i frig.
Duw a roes, difai yw'r ail,
aur gawod ar y gwiail.
Bid llawen gwen bod llwyn gwydd
o baradwys i brydydd.
Blodau gorau a garwn;
barrug haf ydyw'r brig hwn. [DGG. p. 79]

When May comes in its green livery
with ordination for the fresh leaves,
then gold grows along the threads
of the bush for him who owns it.
Fair is the tree and lively,
from whose branches grows thick gold;
God gave, o faultless structure,
a shower of gold to its stalks.
Let my girl rejoice that a green grove
makes a paradise for a poet.
We love the loveliest flowers,
but these boughs are summer's frost.

He often personifies birds and beasts, he has a conversation with a woodcock, and the nightingale and the blackbird sing a mass in the woods. Here Dafydd's figurative use of religious ritual is charmingly, though perhaps for some shockingly, exemplified, for, if his religion is that of the cuckoo in the woods, the faith of Rome, with which he is clearly very familiar, finds continual echoes in the wild life of the countryside, as well as in his love-making.

The following lines are from a poem called *The Mass of the Cock Thrush and the Nightingale*. He is listening to the dawn chorus of birds in the woods on a May morning, and this is how they sing.

Mi a glywwn mewn gloewiaith
ddatganu, nid methu maith,
ddarllain i'r plwyf, nid rhwyf rhus,
efengyl yn ddifyngus.
Codi ar fryn yn yna
afrlladen o ddeilen dda.
Ac eos gain fain fangaw
o gwr y llwyn gar ei llaw,
clerwraig nant, i gant a gân
cloch aberth clau a chwiban
a dyrchafael yr aberth
hyd y nen uwchben y berth;
a chrefydd i'n Dofydd Dad
a charegl nwyf a chariad. [DGG. p. 62]

I heard, in polished language,
a chanting, free from tedious faults,
a reading to the parish, unhesitant,
of an unclouded gospel;
and on the hill the elevation
of the Host from the good leaves.
Then the fine slim nightingale
from the edge of a bush nearby,
poetess of the brook, sings to the many
the Sanctus bell in her whistling.
The sacrifice is raised
up to heaven above the hedge;
devotion to God the Father,
a chalice of liveliness and love.

Here, it seems to me, and in the use of ritual for love-making too, for that matter, there is no need to see blasphemy, but an apprehension of the immanence of God and of the universality of worship. Parody, topsiturvidom and the grotesque were an essential part of faith in the Middle Ages, but here there is something more. For Dafydd, as for many another, there could not be a faith which undervalued the song of a bird and the body of a girl.

Poems to Snow, to the Mist, to the Stars and the Moon all give Dafydd ap Gwilym scope for the art of which he is the greatest master, that of the accumulation of similitudes, known to Welsh poets as *dyfalu*. Subtly woven epithets follow each other for line after line, with little logical linking or progression, once more following the Celtic mode of even tracery rather than the centred composition of the Mediterranean tradition. Dafydd can convey the gloomier moods of nature in this way as well as the freshness of early summer. Here is his description of the mist which hindered his meeting with a girl.

Casul o'r awyr ddulwyd,
carthen anniben iawn wyd.
Gwrthban y glaw draw drymlyd,
gweuddu o bell a gudd y byd.
Mal tarth uffernbarth ffwrnbell,
mwg y byd yn magu o bell:
mwg ellyllдan o Annwn;
abid tew ar y byd hwn;
ucheldop adargopwe
fal gweilgi'n llenwi pob lle. [DGG. p. 67]

A cloak from the grey-black sky,
a very endless coverlet,
a blanket of distant heavy rain,
black weaving from far, hides the world,
an exhalation from the far oven of hell,
the smoke of the world from a far source,
goblin-fire smoke from the underworld,
a thick habit for this world;
a lofty weaving of spiders
filling each place like a sea.

Dafydd's *cywyddau* lamenting the death of his bardic friends Madog Benfras, Gruffudd Gryg and Gruffudd ap Adda have already been referred to. In praise of his patron Ifor Hael he wrote a poem which suggests that it was the poet who gave Ifor the title of *Hael* or the Generous and which ends with the following promise of immortality, comparable to those promises which the Elizabethan English sonneteers later made their patrons.

Hyd yr ymdaith dyn eithaf,
hyd y try hwyl hy haul haf,
hyd yr heuir y gwenith
a hyd y gwlych hoewdeg wlith,
hyd y gwyl golwg ddigust,
hydr yw, a hyd y clyw clust,
hyd y mae iaith Gymraeg
a hyd y tyf hadau teg,
hardd Ifor hoewryw ddefod,
hir dy gledd, heuir dy glod. [DGG. p. 104]

As far as man may travel,
whilst summer's sun runs its brave course,
as long as wheat is sown,
as long as the bright dew wets,
as long as a clear eye watches,
certain it is, and an ear hears,
as long as the Welsh tongue lasts,
as long as fair seeds grow,
splendid Ifor, o fine custom,
long of sword, your praise will be sown.

That Dafydd ap Gwilym did not go without criticism in his own day is made clear in his poems of controversy with Gruffudd Gryg, in which Gruffudd mocks at Dafydd for suffering so much from love's pains that the wonder is that he is alive. Gruffudd was a friend of his and other more conservative poets must have had harsher things to say about this mellifluous abandoner of the old, stiff, though dignified, gait of poetry.

I cannot resist one more quotation, even though it be from a poem not, I believe, generally accepted as by Dafydd. It is, however, attributed to him in at least one manuscript and it savours to me of the truest Dafydd vintage. The poet complains of the joylessness of Lent, and then, at last, Easter comes.

Yno daw in' y dydd
ai lonaid o lawenydd
a Mai a haf lle mae hon
a chogau fel merch Wgon
a phob bedwlwyn mewn manwallt
a phais wyrdd a phwys o wallt
ac ar ystryd o gyrs drain
sioppeu lawnd fal Sieb Lundain;

llysiau mewn garddau a gwlith,
grawn gwin a grynau gwenith,
wybr eglur a mor briglas
a llen glud yn y llwyn glas
a lle ynial a llanerch
a changen feinwen o ferch
a gorphen cwbl o'n penyd
a threio'r badd a throi'r byd
a rhoi ein melldith y rhawg
ar y Gwanwyn oer gwynnawg. [Ll. 133 p. 1066]

Then our day will come
with its plenitude of joy.
May will come and summer
and cuckoos like Gwgon's daughter.
The birchgrove in fine down,
a green skirt and a weight of hair,
and on the street of thorn stems
linen shops like London's Cheap.
Herbs and dew in the garden,
berries for wine, ridges of wheat,
a clear sky, a blue-capped sea,
a snug screen in the green grove,
an unfrequented glade
and a slim branch of a girl.
Then we'll end all our penance,
ebb out the bath and spin the world
and put our long damnation
on the chilly windy Spring.

It is unlikely that much more will ever be known of Dafydd ap Gwilym's life, though scholarship will without doubt succeed in delimiting more exactly the corpus of his work. This work, as I have already suggested, is more serious than it may at first appear, even for those who insist upon high seriousness only in great poetry. Dafydd's very abstention from politics, and his refusal to praise, as did Tudur Aled later, those who were beginning to turn towards Westminster for the satisfaction of their ambitions, were a protest against the situation in which his country found itself.

When a nation is defeated there are sensitive spirits for whom politics and religion cease to be serious concerns, who turn for their delight and consolation to the more immediate personal things, to friendship, to passing love and to the sweetness and grandeur of the world outside the towns. Dafydd ap Gwilym's attitude, and that of his friends Gruffudd ap Adda and Madog Benfras, to the new market towns cannot have been very different from that of the earlier bards to the towns the Romans established along the Welsh border to seduce the Western Britons to an urban docility. The cuckoo's church in the woods is still a temple resorted to in Wales, and the culture of Wales is still strongly anti-urban.

Whatever departures were made by Dafydd ap Gwilym from the strict line of bardic tradition, his great contemporary Iolo Goch, the dates of whose life are roughly 1320–1398, carried on completely enough the ancient functions of the poet in society. He wrote with detailed gratitude in thanks for his entertainment at the tables of the great, particularly that of Bishop Ieuan of St. Asaph and Owain Glyndwr's at Sycharth. There is more than conventional praise in these poems, for surely no one ever enjoyed good food and drink and the comfort of a well-appointed house more than Iolo Goch. This is how he describes Owain Glyndwr's hall at Sycharth.

Llyma y modd a'r llun y mae
mewn eurgylch dwfr mewn argae.
Pand da'r llys, pont ar y llyn,
ac unporth lle'r ai ganpyn?
Cyplau sydd, gwaith cwplws ynt,
cwpledig bob cwpl ydynt.
Clochdy Padrig, ffrengig ffrwyth,
cloystr Westmestr cloau ystwyth . . .
A'r pedair llofft o hoffter
yn gydgwplws lle cwsg cler . . .
Gwirodau bragodau brig,
pob llyn, bara gwyn a gwin,
a'i gig a'i dan i'w gegin . . .
Ni bydd eisieu budd oseb,
na gwall, na newyn, na gwarth,
na syched fyth yn Sycharth. [CIGE. pp. 36–8]

Here's the manner and form of its making,
closed in its girdle of golden water.
How good the hall, the bridge on the lake,
with its one gate for a hundred loads!
Couplings secure the rooftree,
each rafter safely coupled in,
like Patrick's belfry, fruit of France,
or the fine-linked cloister of Westminster . . .
Four sweet lofts joined together,
where travelling poets sleep . . .
Spirits and finest bragget,
all liquors, white bread and wine,
with meat and fire in the kitchen . . .
There'll be no lack of gifts,
no fault, no famine, no shame,
nor thirst ever in Sycharth.[1]

Similar entertainment and even greater gaiety was found by the poet in the hall of the Bishop of St. Asaph, and this is how Iolo describes a typical day at the Bishop's palace during the last decade of the fourteenth century.

Offeren fawr hoff eirian
a gawn, a hynny ar gân,
trebl, chwatrebl, awch atreg
a byrdwn cyson, tôn teg.
Ar ol Offeren yr awn
i'r neuadd gydladd goedlawn.
Peri fy rhoddi ar radd
iawn a wnai yn y neuadd,
i eistedd fry ar osteg
ar y ford dal, arfer teg.
Anrheg am anrheg unrhyw
a ddoi i'r arglwydd, Nudd yw.
Diod am ddiod a ddaw
o'i winllan im o'i wenllaw.
Cerdd dafawd ffraeth hiraethlawn,
cerdd dant, gogoniant a gawn;
cytgerdd ddiddan lân lonydd,
pibau, dawns a gawn pob dydd. [CIGE. p. 83]

[1] In Welsh this is the more effective for the similarity of the words *syched* (thirst) and Sycharth.

A grand sweet splendid Mass
we get, and that in song,
tenor and quatrible,[1] lively prolonging,
with a steady undersong of fair tone.
After the Mass we go together
to the well-timbered hall.
I am caused to be placed
correctly in this hall,[2]
to sit, when silence is proclaimed,
fine custom, at high table.
Gift for gift in its kind
comes to my lord, for he is Nudd.[3]
Drink for drink comes to me
from his vineyard, from his fair hand,
and poetry, eloquent of longing,
and music; we get glory.
A sweet fair quiet concert,
then pipes and dancing every day.

The noblemen of the fourteenth century liked to have their ancestry recorded in verse (this love of genealogies was the source of English jokes at the expense of the Welsh up to the eighteenth century) and Iolo Goch performs this office for Owain Glyndwr.[4] Iolo is one of the last to record the bloodiness of battle with the cruel delight that so many poets we have noticed seemed to take in the detail of slaughter and disaster. He speaks thus of the deeds of Sir Hywel of the Axe in France, for those Welshmen who loved fighting now found opportunities under the banner of the English king and Sir Hywel was knighted by the Black Prince after Poictiers, where he is said to have taken the King of France prisoner.

Pan rodded, trawsged rhwysgainc,
y ffrwyn ym mhen brenin Ffrainc;
barbwr fu fal mab Erbin
a gwayw a chledd, trymwedd trin;

[1] Above treble and one octave above the mean.
[2] Note Iolo's pleasure at being accorded the ancient honour.
[3] One of the three generous ones of the Island of Britain, and father to Gwyn, king of the fairies, lover of Cordelia.
[4] CIGE, pp. 31–2. *Achau Owain Glyndwr.*

eilliaw a'i law a'i allu
bennau a barfau y bu;
a gollwng gynta gallai
y gwaed tros draed—trist i rai. [CIGE. pp. 26–7]

When he put, what a check for pomp,
a bridle on the French King's head,
he was a barber like the son of Erbin,[1]
with lance and sword, both heavy in battle;
he shaved, with his hand and strength,
the heads and beards he met,
letting flow as fast as he could
blood over the feet, a grief for some.

Nothing symbolises the loss of Welsh independence more than that Iolo Goch should use the old conventions and craftsmanship to praise Edward III,[2] in poetry where once again martial exploits are brutally specified.

Dolurio rhai, dal eraill.
llusgo'r ieirll oll, llosgi'r lleill.
Curo a blif, ddylif ddelw,
cerrig Caer Ferwig furwelw. [CIGE. pp. 7–8]

Wounding some, capturing others,
dragging off the earls, burning the rest;
striking with catapult, image of a flood,
the stones of pale-walled Berwick.

This poet's range extended to a charming ode to a girl, an amusing dialogue between the poet and his beard, which scraped a girl when he was kissing her,[3] a poem to a ship, poems of asking and of thanks for granted requests, elegies to Dafydd ap Gwilym and to some of his patrons, poems to Saint Anne and Saint David, and a fine poem to the Twelve Apostles and Doomsday. Finally there is a *cywydd* in the form of a

[1] Geraint, son of Erbin, of Arthurian romance.
[2] Iolo died before Glyndwr's rebellion.
[3] There are two other poems on this subject which Mr. Henry Lewis has attributed to other poets, on internal evidence, but against the consistent testimony of the manuscripts.

dialogue between the Body and the Soul, in which the Soul advises the Body to make ready for burial in Strata Florida, where Dafydd ap Gwilym already lay.

Iolo Goch is a complete poet, a careful craftsman ready to turn to any aspect of life, grim, comic, lovely or glorious, for matter for his fine verse.

Gruffudd Gryg, who lived from about 1340 to 1412, said of himself that he was a disciple of Dafydd ap Gwilym.

> Disgybl wyf, ef a'm disgawdd,
> dysgawdr cywydd hyawdr hawdd. [DGG. p. 155]
>
> I am a disciple, he taught me,
> the teacher of the easy eloquent *cywydd*.

Gruffudd was called *Cryg* or hoarse because of an impediment in his speech, but he proudly claimed to have no impediment in his verse. In his early twenties he took up the cudgels, in a friendly enough way, against Dafydd ap Gwilym, an interesting controversy[1] in which he seems to have seriously disapproved of the triviality of the subject matter of Dafydd's great verse. The two poets wound up their duel by exchanging funeral odes. Gruffudd's ode to Dafydd ends thus:—

> Tristach weithian bob cantref,
> bellach naw digrifach nef. [DGG. p. 156]
>
> Sadder now is all the land,
> but heaven is nine times gayer.

After Dafydd's death, Gruffudd wrote a fine *cywydd* to the yew tree under which Dafydd lies in the graveyard of Strata Florida Abbey, where ancient yews are still to be seen. However much he may have scorned Dafydd's love-pinings, Gruffudd Gryg himself wrote racily enough of the beauty of girls and of his disappointments in love. A *cywydd* to a Faithless Girl begins thus:—

[1] For treatment of this see HLlG, p. 96.

Y fun uchel o fonedd
sy ymysg osai a medd,
bonheddig esgeiddig wyd
ac anwadal Gwen ydwyd.
Beth a dal anwadalu
wedi'r hen fargen a fu? [DGG. p. 134]

O girl of noble birth,
living amongst wine and mead,
courteous and graceful are you,
and fickle, Gwen, as well.
What's the use of fickleness
after the old bargain we made?

Like Dafydd, however, Gruffudd Gryg has won many kisses in the birch wood, but his description of the girl is apt to be more detailed than those of his master.

He too is a keen observer of nature. A vigorous poem to the Wave was probably occasioned by a sea journey on his pilgrimage to the shrine of Saint James of Compostella, a voyage which also inspired his poem to the Moon. He dislikes the pallor of the April moon and fears that she will cause storms for his journey.[1] He asks, as Shelley was later to ask, why she is so pale.

Cron drymlaw, crawen dremlwyd,
curiaw'dd wyf ai caru'dd wyd?
Clwt awyr, clod it dewi,
ai claf wyd, fursen? Clyw fi.
Pwy o'th genedl, rwystrchwedl restr,
a gollaist, fflwring gallestr? [DGG. p. 139]

Hold back heavy rain, o grey-faced crust;
I pine. Are you in love?
Rag of the sky, praised be your silence;
are you sick, wanton? Listen to me.
Which of your tribe, hindrances to a tale,
have you lost, you flinty florin?

[1] cf. Shakespeare, *Midsummer Night's Dream*, II.i.
Therefore the Moon (the governess of floods)
Pale in her anger, washes all the air.

Gruffudd wrote on the popular themes of mediæval allegory, Avarice, Death and the follies of this world. His *cywydd To God*, which has sometimes been attributed to Dafydd ap Gwilym, begins splendidly.

Pwy yw'r gwr piau'r goron,
Duw wyn, a'i frath dan ei fron . . . [DGG. p. 146]

Who is the man who owns the crown,
White God, with his wound under his breast . . .

Good specimens of the heaping up of similarities are to be found in Gruffudd's *cywydd* lamenting the death of Rhys ap Tudur, who took part in Owain Glyndwr's revolt, for in it he compares North Wales to a violin,[1] a bell and a harp, but a violin without strings, a bell without rope or tongue and a harp without hands to make it sing. These images return again in his statement of the deprivation of North Wales.

. . . y mae Gwynedd
heb gun Mon, heb gan mynych,
heb glain eglwys Dduw, heb glych,
heb law Dduw Naf, heb dafawd,
heb gerdd dant, heb ffyniant ffawd,
heb wledd, heb gyfanheddrwydd,
heb Rys ior hael, heb ras rhwydd,
heb oleubryd, heb loewbrim,
heb ddawn, heb urddas, heb ddim . . . [DGG. p. 153]

. . . Gwynedd is
without Mon's lord, without frequent song,
without the gem of God's church, without bells,
without the Lord God's hand, without a tongue,
without harp music, without good fortune,
without feast, without domesticity,
without Rhys, noble giver, without ready grace,
without bright face, without bright dawn,
without talent, without honour, without anything . . .[2]

[1] Not, strictly speaking, a violin but the old *crwth* or crowd.

[2] The temptation in translating this passage was to use *sans* for without, as Shakespeare did in *As You Like It*.

It is of this man that Dafydd ap Gwilym with justice said:—

Edn glwys ei baradwyslef,
ederyn oedd o dir nef.
O nef y doeth, goeth gethlydd,
i brydu gwawd i bryd gwydd.
Awen fardd awen winfaeth,
i nef, gwiw oedd ef, ydd aeth. [DGG. p. 114]

A bird of sweet paradisal cry,
a bird he was of heaven's country.
From heaven he came, fine singer,
to make a song of the woodland's face.
Poet of wine-nourished muse,
to heaven, and worthy of it, he went.

Llywelyn Goch, who wrote during the latter half of the fourteenth century and the first years of the fifteenth, seems to have been house poet at Nannau in Merioneth. The epithet *coch*, which means *red*, presumably refers to the colour of the poet's hair, for his full name was Llywelyn ap Meirig Hen. Distinguishing but not always flattering descriptive adjectives were a regular feature of the old Welsh nomenclature, and the traces remain in such modern names as Lloyd, Wynne, Vaughan, More, Tew, which mean, respectively, grey, white, little, big, fat.

Llywelyn Goch had other patrons besides the Nannau family and to them he wrote the usual poems of praise, but his poems are no stale following of a convention, for *cynghanedd* is a device which seems to make possible entirely fresh statements of old material. He gives thanks for hospitality.

Gwin o ffiolleu[1] gwynn a phali. [RBH. p. 1307]

Wine from white phials and silk.

Of two other patrons he says that they were good judges of a book of verse, that they loved harmony in music, and that they searched into the heart of a matter when dealing with a case in law.

[1] So in the MS, but should obviously be pronounced *ffioleu*.

Llywelyn Goch's best-known poem is his lament on the death of Lleucu Llwyd, wife to Dafydd Ddu of Cymer. He calls upon her to arise from her grave as though she were a girl lying in bed listening to her lover's aubade or serenade, a startling, original but in no way grotesque use of old conventions.

Nid oes yng Ngwynedd heddiw
na lloer, na llewych, na lliw,
er pan rodded, trwydded trwch,
dan lawr dygn dyn loer degwch.
Y ferch wen o'r dderw brennol,
arfaeth ddig yw'r fau i'th ol.
Cain ei llun, cannwyll Wynedd,
cyd bych o fewn caead bedd,
f'enaid, cyfod i fyny,
egor y ddaearddor ddu,
gwrthod wely tywod hir
a gwrtheb f'wyneb, feinir.
Mae yma hoewdra hydraul
uwch dy fedd, huanwedd haul,
wr prudd ei wyneb hebod,
Llywelyn Goch, cloch dy glod;
udfardd yn rhodio adfyd
ydwyf, gweinidog nwyf gwyd. [DGG. p. 167]

There is in Gwynedd today
neither moon, nor light, nor colour,
since was put, unlucky passing,
under hard earth the moon's beauty.
O girl in your oak chest,
a bitter destiny is mine without you.
Fine of form, candle of Gwynedd,
since you are closed within the grave,
my soul, bestir yourself,
open the black earth-door,
refuse the long bed of gravel
and rise to meet me, maiden.
There is here a brief brightness
above your grave, the shining sun,
and a sad-faced man who lacks you,
Llywelyn Goch, bell of your praise.
A wailing poet in adversity
am I, serving the strength of passion.

She has broken her promise to meet him and now her beauty is in earth. The poem ends:—

Gwae fi'r ferch wen o Bennal,
breuddwyd ddig ,briddo dy dâl;
clo dur derw, galarchwerw gael,
a daear, deg ei dwyael,
a thromgad ddor a thrymgae
a llawr maes rhof a'r lliw mae
a chlyd fur a chlo dur du
a chlicied,—yn iach, Leucu. [DGG. pp. 167–70]

Woe is me, o girl of Pennal,
hateful dream, that your forehead should be earthed;
a hard case of oak, bitter grief finding,
and earth, o fair of feature,
heavy door and heavy enclosure,
a floor of field between me and her form,
a secure wall, a black steel lock
and a latch,—goodbye, Lleucu.

Llywelyn Goch seems later in his life to have had feelings of shame about this *cywydd* for he refers to it as one of his transgressions in a confessional poem.[1] Some part of the story of Llywelyn's love for Lleucu Llwyd is given in a prose dream which occurs in an early seventeenth century manuscript, where, unfortunately, the copyist has cut out much of what he calls vanities.[2] In the dream Llywelyn dies on the road immediately after hearing of Lleucu's death and writing this poem. He had loved her for eighteen years.

Llywelyn Goch's *cywydd I'r Benglog*, To the Skull, is a poem striking in its grim simplicity. The poet talks to the skull and begs to be spared the contemplation of death and to be left to his poetry, but the skull goes on to reminiscence of its youth upon the earth, for, even in this most frightening *memento mori* which we have in mediæval Welsh poetry, the beauty of the world contrives to assert itself.

[1] *see* DGG, pp. xcix–x.

[2] The Dream occurs in several manuscripts and has been printed by Mr. D. Gwenallt Jones, *Yr Areithiau Pros*, Welsh University Press, 1934. An early translation of the poem to Lleucu occurs in MS Panton 7, pp. 7–13.

Gwallt gwinau modrwyau mân
a thal gwastadlaith hoywliw
a threm gwalch a thrumiau gwiw
a min gynefin ofeg
a mwyn gyfartal trwyn teg
a thyfu gweniaith hoywfaint
a thafod coeth doeth a daint
a chael ym goruwch hoywlawr
cred merch ar ddwyn cariad mawr
ac oed ym medw unoed man,
och Iesu Grist, a chusan. [DGG. p. 166]

Brown hair in little ringlets,
a fresh-hued, smooth, moist forehead,
a falcon's eye and fitting brows,
a lip familiar with speech,
a dear, shapely, fair nose,
fair words springing from neat gums,
a fine wise tongue, and teeth;
to have, above the trim ground,
a girl's faith in a great love,
a tryst in a copse of young birch trees,
Christ Jesus, and a kiss.

Sypyn Cyfeiliog was the nickname and bardic name of Dafydd Bach ap Madawg Wladaidd. He was a very little man and, if credit is to be given to a reference to him in a prose work,[1] a great drunkard, both of which notions are implied in the word *sypyn*, which means a little drop and is cognate with the English sop and sup. He flourished during the second half of the fourteenth century and was the author of one of the finest poems of praise written in a century of which one of the chief glories was poetry of this kind. In a poem which occurs in the *Red Book of Hergest* he sings the praise of the house of Bachelldref. It should be noted that the metre here is not the new *cywydd* metre in which so many of the poems referred to in this chapter were written but one of the older *awdl* metres used by the poets of the twelfth and thirteenth centuries. The line is known as *cyhydedd hir* (or long equivalence) and consists of

[1] D. Gwenallt Jones, *Yr Areithiau Pros*, p. 15.

nineteen syllables divided into three groups of five and one of four. The first three groups rhyme with each other whilst the fourth, or last, group carries the main rhyme, rhyming with the last group in the successive lines. Other internal links of rhyme, assonance and alliteration are permitted and may be observed in the passage quoted. This line is usually divided into two for convenience of printing, so that a couplet forms a four line stanza.

> Yn llwyr degwch nef yn llawr bachelldref
> y lle y byd dolef bob nydolic
> A llu ogereint allynn tramedweint
> allewychu breint bro hil meuric
> A llawer kerdawr allawengrythawr
> allewenyd mawr ywch llawr llithric
> A llef gan danneu a llif gwirodeu
> allauar gerdeu gordyfnedic. [RBH. p. 1255]

> Full fairness of heaven on the floor of Bachelldref
> where there is jollity every Christmas,
> a host of friends and great drunkenness,
> and shining honour of Meurig's homeland;
> many a minstrel and many a fiddler
> and great joy on the slippery floor;
> a cry from the harp-strings, flowing wine,
> the customary resounding songs.

The poem ends with a line that has become proverbial in the language as a statement of hospitality.

> Dyret pan vynnych kymer awelych
> agwedy delych tra vynnych tric.

> Come when you like, take what you see
> and once you have been, stay frequently.

Like most of his contemporaries of note, Sypyn Cyfeiliog wrote beautifully about girls. He laments his failure to win a girl whose eyes are as black as bilberries. In another *cywydd*, for Sypyn very properly turns to the new metre in his praise of girls, her hair is wine-coloured, her face the colour of the foam of the mill-race, her eyebrows like a blackbird's wing. She robs him of sleep, of the love of wine, of laughter, of song, of glory, of husbandry and of desire.

Whether his smallness and his drunkenness really brought him ill success in love or whether these poems of disappointed love are the poetic exercises of a normally happy man will never be known and is of no importance. Sypyn Cyfeiliog turned lines of unforgettable beauty, and when a woman is introduced with lines like the following we feel that we are in the presence of one of the beauties of this world.

> Fy lloer a'i gwallt fal lliw'r gwin
> a'i phryd fal ffrwd y felin. [CIGE. p. 31]

> My moon with hair the colour of wine
> and a skin like the mill-race.

At this point it may be well to turn to a type of verse we have not yet encountered in this survey, a grosser, often openly indecent type of invective in verse, such as we see in the work of two more poets of the fourteenth century, Madawg Dwygraig and Dafydd y Coed. Both these poets were masters of the traditional craft and wrote noble odes of praise to their patrons, but they will be noted here chiefly for their more rabelaisian work. This grosser kind of occasional verse must have been written by earlier poets and either not recorded or lost, but the fourteenth century brought at the same time more manuscript recording of poetry and a breakdown in the categories of poets and poetry, so that these cruder products of the poetic craft came to be written into the *Red Book of Hergest* together with the verse offerings to patrons, which were traditionally considered to be of a higher order. The boundary that separates the decent and the indecent, and one asks whether it really existed in the fourteenth century, was gaily crossed by Dafydd ap Gwilym, but Madawg Dwygraig and Dafydd y Coed, his contemporaries, take humour still further into the grotesque, one of the characteristic elements of mediæval art, and sometimes into the obscene.

In the *Red Book* there are poems representing every aspect of Madawg Dwygraig's work, one to Morgan ap Dafydd, whom he compares favourably with Rhydderch Hael, the stock Welsh example of generosity, and then a series of religious poems ending with the following quatrain.

Ner a anet y gret grym
nadolyc rac tremyc trwm
da vu ymaethlu methlem
duw eurvab a diweirvam. [RBH. p. 1280]

A Lord was born to a strong faith,
a Christmas against heavy scorn;
good was the nursing at Bethlehem,
God, child of gold, and the chaste Mother.

This quatrain is extremely interesting from a technical point of view. Outstanding is the type of rhyme used here, a half rhyme in which the consonant is repeated and the vowel differs. This is known in Welsh as *proest* and it is essential that the vowels in the rhyming syllables should all be of the same quantity.[1] Thus, to give examples in English, *loom* could rhyme with *seem* but not with *dim*. Devices already indicated in other quotations may also be observed in this passage, the initial linking consonants, the internal rhyme, the multiple alliteration and the assonance.

In the midst of all these more reputable poems comes a long and unpleasant diatribe against Mallt, Gruffudd Gryg's Irish mother, whom Iolo Goch also attacked. What the rival poet's mother had done to call forth this attack has long been forgotten, but nothing could be in worse taste, by our standards, than the unsavoury and often unprintable epithets which Madawg Dwygraig heaps upon her.

Another equally rabelaisian poem is written to an unnamed old hag, and is the pleasanter for the anonymity of its subject. It is something of a tour de force, for each line in this series of

[1] This is to be distinguished from the repetition of the vowel with differing consonants, a type of rhyme which Sir Ifor Williams has called Irish rhyme, because used by Irish poets, though he himself says that it is found in Welsh in the ninth century.

seven *englynion* begins with the word *gwrach* (old hag), and there is only one end rhyme in the whole series. This is one of the *englynion*.

Gwrach gallawdyr groenllawdyr gravellin—horawc
gwrach lechawc gwrach lychwin
gwrach abrec ynychegin
gwrach afylsur llywyadur llin. [RBH. p. 1274]

Stalk of an old hag, trouser-skinned, gravelly, swine-lousy,
rickety old hag, soiled old hag,
old hag with a blot on her kitchen,
sour-apple hag, a winder of string.

Dafydd y Coed presents us with a similar range of subjects. Here are some lines from his religious verses as recorded in the *Red Book of Hergest*.

Ytt y adolaf ti vd delweu—eur
vyggloewner wyt ar vygglinyeu
Om pedeiryeithdysc am padereu
am cu wrd seilmawl am kerd salmeu. [RBH. p. 1303]

I worship you, master of images of gold,
you are my bright lord, on my knees,
from my four-tongued learning and my prayers,
my loving, strong-based praise, my psalmody.

One imagines that the fourth tongue he claims to know was French, for the first three would obviously be Welsh, Latin and English.

Unlike Madawg Dwygraig, Dafydd y Coed turned the biting edge of his tongue on places rather than people, as when he gives himself the following advice in a stanza which affords another specimen of *proest* or half rhyme.

Dafyd y koet hoet hydyrsant
dyn wyt kerdlawn ratlawn rent
ffo r bore or brithle brwnt
ffi lan ymdyfri du vront. [RBH. p. 1361]

David of the Woods, (bold, pious grief),
you are full of song and gracious with goods;
flee in the morning this spotted place of dirt.
Fie on you, foul Llandovery!

The pleasantest application of this grotesque technique is to be found in Dafydd's poem to the waterfall at Rhayader in Central Wales, and, whilst it is remarkable enough that a poem should have been written to a waterfall in the fourteenth century, it is clear that the poet's attitude towards such a phenomenon is closer to that of Dr. Johnson than to that of Wordsworth.

Raeadyr oercri kadyr ar crwkedeu—bach
    bychin geinyawc wertheu:
rugyl ffugyl ffagyl magyl mwygyl refreu
regylwern i gwm uffern geu. [RBH. p. 1360]

Falls of mighty wailing with your little pails full,
    little pennyworths;
rattle, blow, blaze, snare of warm buttocks,[1]
swampy gutter leading to Hell's hollow vale.

The poet seems to have come near to losing his life here, though whether in satisfying the needs of nature or from the teeth of mastiffs is not quite clear, and so he curses the whole place.

Tristchwedyl vlin doet yr dinas
tanfflam drwy raeadr gwy gas.

May sad hard news come to the town,
a flame of fire through nasty Rhayader.

The poem's most important quality is its varied onomatopeia, the cold, thin clatter of the water in the first line, the rugged thunder of the falls in the third line, where, as we have seen, the words are linked more by sound than by sense, but linked in a subtly planned manner, to achieve an effect similar

[1] The meaning was not the poet's first concern in choosing these words, and it might well be better to disregard literal meaning in translating this line and attempt a similar effect, e.g. rattle, battle, blare, snare of warm buttocks.

ey Hopkins in such lines as this
Nature is a Heraclitean Fire:—

to squeezed dough, crust, dust;
stanches, starches.

ecency and piety is attributed to
One of her *cywyddau* complains
parts in their cataloguing of
n to make good the omissions
ther this and other similar
she and Dafydd ap Gwilym
r's private parts, which are
hardly be discussed and
d to be unprintable.
century a good deal of
oets came near enough
verse, in the effort to
ir metres, the sense
of parentheses,
forms or

Another nonsense englyn in the s
Lewis Môn, writing at the end of
closer to the pullulating flower I
Dutch painters of the seventeenth

> Postdrws biattws a byt
> ac adar a chlodd
> a bron las a breua
> a chnwd o lyffain

> A chapel doorpos
> and birds an
> a green hill, a
> a crop of toad

A number of good an
century have had to be r
was Gruffudd Llwyd w
of his poetic contemp
shine upon his love
to treat at great
in the

to those of Gerard Manl
from a poem entitled *That*

Squandering ooze

A comparable output of ind
the poetess Gwerfyl Mechain.
of the neglect by poets of certai
the beauties of the body and goes o
in the frankest possible way. Whe
poems are really hers, and whether
exchanged the *englynion* to each othe
still extant, are questions which ca
settled whilst the material is considere

From the fourteenth to the sixteent
nonsense verse was written in Welsh. P
to nonsense sometimes in their serious
meet the complicated requirements of the
having to be traced by a continual sidesteppin
so it is not surprising that in order to exemplify stanza
arrangements of *cynghanedd* the master poets and their apprentices should abandon the attempt to make sense and use words only for their phonetic value. It is lucky for us that some of these exercises in verse have been preserved, recorded perhaps in vague apprehension of the surrealist composition they often present. Here is a demonstration of an *englyn* form (the form known as *englyn unodl union*) with a nonsensical juxtaposition of objects which might have served Salvador Dali.

Ysgidie a bratie a brain—a chwthu
 a chathod o Rufain
a chelioc mawr a chelain
a lleian draw a llwyn drain. [M. 131, p. 45]

Boots and aprons and crows and a blowing
 and cats from Rome
and a great cock and a corpse
 and a nun over there and a thorn bush.

ame manner, attributed to
the fifteenth century, comes
pieces and still lives of the
century.

au—a gwdyn
iau
n lysiau
t a chnau. [M. 131, p. 45]

t, fishbaskets, a withie,
d hedges,
herb handmill,
s and nuts.

d interesting poets of the fourteenth neglected in such a survey as this. There ith his important mentioning of so many poraries[1] and his *cywydd* asking the sun to d Glamorgan;[2] and it has been difficult not ter length Gruffudd ap Maredudd, a fine poet aditional style, whose odes of praise are recorded in the *Red Book of Hergest*, and who was the author of a lovely series of *englynion* and half-rhymed stanzas to a lady called Gwenhwyfar (*Anglice* Guenivere). Here is one of these *englynion*, and with it we may fittingly and with regret take leave of the fourteenth century.

Lle bu ra a gwyrd, lle bu rud—aglas
  neut gloes angheu gystud
lle bu eur am y deurud
lle bu borffor kor ae kud. [RBH. p. 1318]

Where was vigour and green, where was red and blue,
  are pangs of death's grief;
where was gold about the forehead,
where was purple, the choir hides her.

[1] CIGE, pp. 116–18.
[2] CIGE, pp. 144–6.

Chapter VI

THE FIFTEENTH CENTURY

★

Practically nothing is known of the life of Sion Cent,[1] a poet whose work, composed during the first thirty years of the fifteenth century, differs very greatly from all that preceded it. In English his name is John Kent, and there seem to have been so many John Kents and John a Kents in South Wales and the border country during the fifteenth century, and the tradition concerning them has become so confused, that it is no longer possible to extricate any one of them with any certainty[2]. So famous did one of these become as a writer of religious verse that scores of poems of that kind, demonstrably not his, were attributed to him in the manuscripts of the fifteenth and sixteenth centuries.

The titles of some of the *cywyddau* now accepted as indubitably his will give an indication of the nature of his work: The Eight Punishments, To the Trinity, To the Great Judgment, The Vanity of Man's Boasting, The Vanity and Worthlessness of this World, Not to Anger God, The Way to Heaven, To the Miser, To Compare Man with a Day. How close these poems were in subject matter to poetry that was being written outside Wales will appear if the titles are compared with those of English lyrics written about the same time: The Day of Life, Night Comes Soon, Three Lessons to make ready for Death, The Rich Man's Farewell to the World, Wordly Joy is only Fantasy, The Rancour of this Wicked World.[3] Lydgate and

[1] Pronounced in English as Shawn Kent.
[2] *see* CIGE for treatment of this question, which is left open.
[3] Titles from Carleton Brown, *Religious Lyrics of the fifteenth century; see also* Chambers & Sidgwick, *Early English Religious Lyrics.*

Dunbar dwell upon the vanity of this world and the brevity of life, and all these matters had, of course, been dealt with in mediæval Latin verse.

There are also some similarities between Sion Cent and his homiletic English contemporaries in the treatment of their material. The grisly details in the frightening picture of death are much the same, and Sion Cent's trick of repeating a line as a kind of refrain at the end of sections of his *cywyddau* must have been learnt from English or Latin writing since it is entirely foreign to the *cywydd* and unhappily incongruous. But there are differences too. Whereas in the English lyrics of the time we observe the growing pains of English stanza form and a hesitation between alliteration and rhyme, with results sometimes clumsy, sometimes flashingly beautiful, Sion Cent's work is in an established metrical tradition which he confidently modifies to his own purposes. The impression one inevitably forms in reading Hoccleve and Lydgate alongside Sion Cent is that of passing from a new literature to an old one.

Sion Cent's language is much simpler than that of most Welsh poetry written before and even after him, for the vocabulary is that of everyday Welsh and there is a marked freedom from compound words and the conventional parentheses. He was a preacher in verse and he wanted to be understood. He wrote, therefore, so that all could understand him and a clarification of style results which is similar to that which occurred, for a comparable reason, that is the need for comprehensibility, in seventeenth century English prose. There was no more need to flatter princes with thought-twisting, half-apprehensible echoes of the heroic age, for the heroic age had passed and it was now time for penitence rather than pride. Sion Cent's message to the nobility of Wales was not of their greatness in this life but of their nothingness in death. He sounded the knell of the Welsh princely way of life, which had suffered its death pang in the failure of Owain Glyndwr's rebellion. Here is his picture of the dead nobleman.

Heddiw mewn pridd yn ddiddim
O'i dda nid oes iddo ddim.
Poen a leinw, pan el yno,
Mewn gorchfan graean a gro;
Rhy isel fydd ei wely,
A'i dâl wrth nenbren ei dŷ;
A'i rwymdost bais o'r amdo,
A'i brudd grud o bridd a gro;
A'i borthor uwch ei gorun,
O bridd du fal breuddwyd yn;
A'i ddewrgorff yn y dderwgist,
A'i drwyn yn rhy laswyn drist;
A'i gorsed yn ddaered ddu,
A'i rhidens wedi rhydu,
A'i bais o goed, hoed hydyn,
A'i grys heb lewys, heb lun,
A'i ddir hynt i'r ddaear hon,
A'i ddeufraich ar ei ddwyfron,
A llwybrau gwag lle bu'r gwin,
A'i gog yn gado'i gegin,
A'i gwn, yn y neuadd gau,
A'i emys yn ei amau;
A'i wraig, o'r winllad adail,
Gywir iawn yn gwra'r ail.
A'i neuadd fawrfalch galchbryd
Yn arch bach yn eiriach byd.
A da'r wlad yn ei adaw
I lawr heb dim yn ei law. [CIGE. pp. 288–9]

Today in earth he's nothing,
now all his goods are gone.
Pain's at its full when he goes there,
under that cover of gravel;
his bed will be too low,
his head will touch the rafter.
The shroud's his tight-bound kirtle,
his heavy cradle the earth.
The porter over his head
is black nightmarish earth,
his brave body in a box of oak,
his nose a dismal grey,
his corslet the dark soil,
its fringes now are rusted,
his tunic of wood, what longings,

his shirt without sleeve or shape,
his journey sure into this earth,
his arms across his breast.
The paths are empty where was wine
and his cook leaves his kitchen;
his dogs in the empty hall
and his stallions doubt him now.
From the wine-filled building, his faithful wife
now takes a second man;
his proud, lime-washed mansion,
a little coffin from the world.
The land's wealth lets him go
down with nothing in his hand.

In contrast to this terrible picture of the death of the ungodly, Sion Cent presents heaven as a land of Cockayne, but he is not so blind to the beauty of this world that he cannot regret the brevity of life and the passage of worldly glory, a mood which he expresses in lines where, in his own way, he asks the question —*Où sont les neiges d'antan?*

Alexander a dderyw,
Ector, Arthur, eglur yw.
Mae Gwenhwyfar, gwawn hoywwedd,
Merch Gogfran gawr, fawr a fedd,
A'r sidan, eres ydiw,
A'r gwallt llawn perles aur gwiw?
Mae Tegfedd ryfedd yrhawg
Coelferch Owain Cyfeiliawg?
Mae Firain, eurfain wryd,
O Ffrainc, oedd decaf ei phryd? [CIGE. p. 270]

Alexander has perished
and Hector and Arthur, that's clear.
Where's Guinevere, neat, gossamer-featured,
daughter of the rich giant Gogfran,
and the silk that was so marvellous
and the hair full of pearls of fitting gold?
Where's Tegfedd, for ever wonderful,
the girl of Owain Cyfeiliog's embrace?
Where's Vivien,[1] the slim golden chain
from France, whose face was fairest?

[1] There are many forms of this name in the MSS, not one recognisable, so that it is anyone's guess whom it represents. Vivien seems to me to qualify.

The only unconditional love Sion Cent expresses for anything in this world is for the shire and people of Brycheiniog (Brecon), where, as a poet, he has been given the best welcome, and it is in a *cywydd* to Brycheiniog that he comes nearest to the old traditional manner of praise.

One of the sources of satire is the union of moral purpose with keen observation, and this combination persists throughout Sion Cent's work, but one poem of his is pure satire without homiletic appendage, the *cywydd* to his Purse,[1] which he thanks for all the good things he has enjoyed in this life. This *cywydd* is divided, against all previous practice in the construction of poems in this form, into regular sections of eight and ten lines, each ending with the refrain:—

> Fy mhwrs, gormersi am hyn.
>
> My purse, gramercy for this.

Sion Cent is the first consistent preacher and moralist in Welsh poetry. A great deal of religious verse had been written but mostly of the penitential sort, and Sion Cent was the first writer since Gildas to attack the upper class on the grounds of the impiety and luxury of its way of life.

The work of Rhys Goch Eryri (Red Rhys of Snowdon), who flourished during the first half of the fifteenth century, at first appearance presents a conventional enough range of subject matter, poems of praise, a genealogy, elegies on the death of patrons and of a rival poet, a political prophecy, a saint's praise and a poem of *dyfaliad* (comparison making) to a dagger; but closer examination reveals peculiar and original features.

A *cywydd* on the genealogy of William Fychan (CIGE. page 307) is of special interest, as Sir Ifor Williams has pointed out, since it seems to have been written at a time when this William Fychan was applying to the King of England to be considered as an Englishman on the grounds of having an English mother and of his fidelity to the English crown. The

[1] CIGE, pp. 259–261. Sir Ifor Williams discusses the possibility that this poem is by Sir Philip Emlyn, *op. cit.*, pp. lxviii–lxix.

poet traces this unworthy person's ancestry back to Brutus, traditional founder of Britain, then through the Trojan worthies to the Greek gods, to Japhet and Noah and so to Adam, submitting every name in its turn to the device of *cynghanedd*. Surely the purpose must have been reproach, for in his elegy on the death of William Fychan's father, Rhys Goch asks pardon of his fellow poets, for he is praising an enemy of Owain Glyndwr and the father of a turncoat. He is old, he says, and for this song he will receive payment. The mercenary nature of this kind of writing is thus confessed but the poet's conscience is not appeased or silenced.

Rhys Goch has a charming poem in praise of the Celtic Saint Beuno in which he depicts the saint on his deathbed seeing the gates of heaven opening. The picture of heaven has the clarity and sweetness of mediæval miniature painting.

Gweles henwlad Baradwys
A'i chaerau glan a'i chor glwys,
A'r pedair afon, ton teg,
Rhydaer drwyddi yn rhedeg;
Gwin a llaeth, gwiw enau llew,
Mawl goel, a mel ac olew. [CIGE. pp. 322–3]

He saw the white homeland of Paradise
with its fair towers, its holy choir,
and the four rivers of sweet water
urgently running through it;
wine and milk, bright worthy mouths,
the song of faith, and honey and oil.

Unfortunately, Rhys Goch indulges too much in the trick of parenthesis for the sake of the *cynghanedd*, so that the main thread of what he has to say has to be picked out of the running, but not always immediately apt, commentary. This descant of comparison and padding tends often to overload the theme and one feels that the technical requirements of the metre have taken charge to the detriment of what is to be said and of the originality of the saying. It may be unfair to seize upon Rhys Goch only for a criticism of this kind, for the use of *trychiad* (parenthesis) and the occasional subordination of meaning to sense are characteristic of the *cywydd*, but, as the following passage shows, he is a notable exponent of a Celtic mode become mannerism.

> *Y seithfed dydd*, rhydd rhwyddlwyr,
> *Cyn y Pasg Gwyn* (pwy nis gwyr?)
> *Pan ydoedd*, ior farmor fedd,
> *Feuno*, feudwyaidd fonedd,
> Gwawr goeth gras doeth, *o'i groes dŷ*,
> Waladr, *yn ei glaf wely*. [CIGE. p. 321]

I have italicised the main statement, which means, "The seventh day before Easter, when Beuno was away from his church, in his sick bed." The rest is padding to bolster up rhyme and alliteration.

A great craftsman, in spite of this fault, Rhys Goch undoubtedly was and as a piece of virtuosity it is hard to find anything more successful than his *awdl* to the fox which killed his peacock. Here we have a great variety of metre and a vigorous, nervous, mouth-filling use of language in the tradition of Madawg Dwygraig and Dafydd y Coed. One may attempt to translate the following couplet:—

> Egroes-ffagl carddagl cerddawdd gwtterau
> y creigiau ai crygodd . . . [G. 3, p. 110]

> A skirt of flaming berries he walked the ditches,
> the rocks made him hoarse,

but, although the picture remains, the angry consonants are gone and the poem has to be read aloud in Welsh if one is to believe the story that this poem caused the death of the fox!

With the poetry of Llywelyn ap y Moel, who also lived and wrote during the first half of the fifteenth century, we are back again in the company of a poet who was, like Aneirin, Cynddelw and Owain Cyfeiliog, a man of action as well as a writer. In the fifteenth century there were two courses open to such a turbulent character as this, foreign war under the banner of the English king or outlawry, and it was the latter way which Llywelyn ap y Moel chose. His lair was Coed y Graig Lwyd, the Grey Rock Woods, in North Wales, and in a *cywydd* written to the woods he praises the outlaw's way of life, contrasting it in such a manner to the slavish acceptance of the new order in Wales that the poem becomes as much a criticism of Welsh society as any of Sion Cent's. He will no longer go on the traditional bard's journey from hall to hall.

Gwell o lawer no chlera
I ddyn a chwenycho dda,
Dwyn Sais a'i ddiharneisio
Dan dy frig, dien dy fro. [CIGE. p. 199]

Far better than wandering minstrelsy,
for him who covets the world's goods,
to take and unharness an Englishman
under your branches, o sweet spot.

Narrative verse is unhappily rare in Welsh but an amusing and exciting specimen is Llywelyn's *cywydd* on the Battle of Waun Caseg (CIGE. pp. 191–2). He describes how he and his friends met and prepared for the fray and swore not to yield however hard pressed they might be. Then suddenly they were attacked by more than a hundred horsemen, led by one with a face like an ape who sounded such a clarion call on his horn that they were dismayed and fled in disorder. The poet tells us that he was one of the first in the retreat and he swears that he will never make one of that company again. As Sir Ifor Williams says, only a brave man can talk about his own cowardice and Llywelyn ap y Moel was famous for his courage in a fight. In Guto'r Glyn's *cywydd* on Llywelyn's death his sword and his bravery are mentioned before his skill in poetry, and his rival, Rhys Goch, pays tribute to his martial prowess at the beginning of two *cywyddau* in their verse controversy.

Llywelyn ap y Moel wrote poems of praise to patrons and made famous the name of Euron as the girl to whom he addressed his love poetry, but even in the usual birch grove where he awaits his girl his imagery cannot quite get away from fighting, for the branches are as straight as arrows and the trees stand in order like the spears of Owain's best men.

Whilst wilder natures like Llywelyn ap y Moel found outlet in fighting, rebellion, outlawry and banditry, others, more scholarly, took advantage of the new conditions in the fifteenth century to study at one of the universities. It was probably to Oxford that Ieuan ap Rhydderch, a wealthy young gentleman of Cardiganshire, went to complete his education, and the account he gives of his learning and the academic terms he uses suggest that he must have stayed at the university long enough to take an M.A. if not a doctorate in law.

Ieuan ap Rhydderch, in his *cywydd* called *Y Fost* (The Boast), gives proof of familiarity with every branch of learning, and interesting features of the poem are the list the poet gives of his authorities and the evidence it affords of the acclimatisation of mediæval scientific terminology in Welsh. He is proud of his knowledge of French.

> Dysgais yr eang Ffrangeg;
> doeth yw ei dysg, da iaith deg. [CIGE. p. 228]

> I learnt the spacious French;
> wise is its teaching, good, fair tongue.

Nor has he neglected the learning of his own country for he has mastered the metres of poetry and read all the available chronicles and saints' lives. He claims to be something of a sportsman too, he can run, jump, swim and handle horses. He plays backgammon and chess.

In spite of his long sojourn in England and although he was more of a scholar than a soldier, it was out of Welsh patriotism that Ieuan ap Rhydderch took the Lancastrian side in the Wars of the Roses, for he saw in Jasper Tudor a possible avenger of the death of Llywelyn, last prince of Wales, a century and a half before, and he called on this Jasper Tudor not to sheathe the sword drawn by Owain Glyndwr.

> Dialwr tre Lywelyn
> ar Loegr balch yw'r gwalch gwyn. [CIGE. p. 234]

Avenger of Llywelyn's home
upon proud England is this white hawk.

These lines occur in a poem consciously written in the old tradition of political prophecy, though in the new *cywydd* form, for the poet mentions Taliesin and Myrddin, and calls to mind the old personifications of Welsh hopes, Owain, Cadwaladr and Cynan, whose place and immortal destiny Jasper Tudor is now called upon to take and fulfil.

Nor did Ieuan ap Rhydderch neglect the other two matters of poetry, love and religion. His poem in praise of a girl's hair is in the convention established by Dafydd ap Gwilym, that of the *cywydd dyfalu* or poem of comparisons, and consists of forty-eight lines of metaphor and description befitting a head of golden hair, each line beginning with the letter *d*. As a contrast to the involved jewellery of this poem is the simplicity of style and language in his *Conversation with a Ghost*, which must surely owe something to the influence of Sion Cent. The poet is at prayer in a church when he feels a trembling in the earth beneath him. He asks what is there, in the name of Christ and the Holy Ghost, and is answered by the spirit of a dead man who bitterly contrasts his fleshless state with the handsome lustiness of his manhood in life.

Darfu fy nghnawd, wawd oerfas,
Pregeth wyf i'r plwyf a'r plas;
Darfu fy nhrwyn a'm hwyneb,
Mud iawn wy, ni'm edwyn neb. [CIGE. p. 237]

My flesh has gone, cold swooning words,
I'm a sermon to parish and mansion;
my nose and face have gone,
I am dumb and no one knows me.

Ieuan ap Rhydderch wrote a fine *cywydd* to the Mass, another of a hundred and twenty-eight lines on the Life of Saint David, and, in a quite different metre, a long poem to the Virgin Mary. This *awdl* begins with a series of six-line stanzas in consonantal rhyme of which the following is the first.

Mair yw ein hyder rhag perigl
morwyn wyryf, myr un arogl,
mirain nefol fain fwnwgl
mawr yw i'n gael a miragl
gorph Duw glwys i'r eglwys rygl
gywrain a'i waed o garegl. [G. 3, p. 19a]

Mary is our trust against danger,
virgin maiden, all scent of myrrh,
comely, heavenly, slim of neck;
much it is to have by miracle
God's pure body for the wise worthy
church, and his blood from a chalice.

The metre then changes to the sixteen-syllable *rhupunt hir*, a line which is sometimes written as a couplet or as a four-line stanza.[1] The vocabulary becomes macaronic with occasional Latin words and then occurs a series of lines or stanzas where the first three sections are in Latin and the fourth, carrying the main rhyme, in Welsh.

O Maria
Virgo pia
recta via
  rhag tew feiau . . .

Mundi Rosa
preciosa
speciosa
  ysbys oessau.[2]

O Maria, pious virgin, the straight path from thick sins . . .
Rose of the world, precious, lovely, evident for ages.

This poet also translated into Welsh the Latin hymn *Te Deum Laudamus*, *Ti Dduw Addolwn*, (MS. Peniarth 53, p. 29).

[1] It is given this last form in MS Gwyneddon 3

[2] The cynghanedd in these two stanzas shows how the Latin words were pronounced by the poet, i.e. in the English way. The consonants of *recta via* are exactly reproduced in the Welsh words following, where the consonants are the modern English r, k, t and v sounds. Similarly the *c* in *speciosa* must have been pronounced as *s* in order to correspond with the final *s* in *ysbys*. In Welsh, g before t and b after s are altered to c and p respectively in pronunciation.

Ieuan ap Rhydderch was lucky in his life, for his poem *The Boast* gives thanks for what life has given him in honour and gifts from great men and in love from women, and ends with a request for burial at Llanddewi Brefi in his native Cardiganshire.

Wales was as divided as England during the Wars of the Roses, except when Henry Tudor, Earl of Richmond landed in Wales on his way to the victory which was to end the unhappy cleavage and Welshmen of both parties flocked patriotically to his banner. Guto'r Glyn favoured the Yorkists, sang in praise of Edward IV and of the Herbert family of Pembroke. He wrote an elegy to William Herbert, Earl of Pembroke and to his brother Thomas who were captured at the Battle of Banbury, where so many Welshmen died, and who were executed at Northampton on July 28th, 1469. The poet threatens on this occasion to become wild like Merlin as the result of a terrible slaughter and to live like him in the woods. He laments his patron thus:—

Doe ydd aeth dan y blaned ddu
drwy'r fal draw i ryfelu.
Ymddiried i'r dynged wann
a'i twyllodd o Went allan.
Och y finnau uwch fannyn
nad arhoe'n ei dir ei hun. [G. 3, p. 147b]

Yesterday he went under the black planet
through the hills yonder to fight;
trust in a feeble fate
tempted him out of Gwent.
Woe is me, above my grief,
that he did not stay in his own land.

The valley which gave Guto, a native of Llangollen, the descriptive part of his name was Valle Crucis (Glyn Egwestl in Welsh) and he was house poet to the Abbot of Valle Crucis Abbey. One of his works is a poem of asking on behalf of the Abbot, seeking to borrow for him a certain *Book of the Holy Grail* from Trahaearn of Trallwng.

Another poem of asking was a *cywydd* despatched to Robert ap Ieuan Fychan with the request for two greyhounds. After praising the owner of the dogs and his ancestry, Guto has some biting things to say about the Welsh gentry of his day.

> Eirchiaid yw'n pennaethiaid ni
> ni wnant orchwyl ond erchi.
> Clerwyr rhyadwyr ydynt
> clera nis gwnai'r gwyrda gynt.
> Erchi pob rhyw dywarchawr
> erchi meirch, erchi aur mawr. [G. 3, p. 108]

> Suppliants are all our chieftains
> and they do nothing but beg.
> The wandering poets are nobles;
> those of the past never sang for money.
> They beg each ploughing ox,
> they beg horses, they beg gold.

Then follow thirty lines of description of the greyhounds, the conventional *dyfaliad* or comparison heaping, and even their age and colour are not neglected in the detail of the specification.

> Blwydd a mwy yw bleiddiaid Môn,
> blomoniaid boliau meinion.

> A year old and more are these wolves of Anglesey,
> niggers with narrow bellies.

An amusing *cywydd*, printed in *Llên Cymru*, volume III, described Guto'r Glyn's experiences as a sheep drover, and nothing better indicates the declining position of the poet in society than that he and his rival, Tudur Penllyn, are forced into such occupations as this. The sheep lose their wool in the hedges, lambs are drowned in the rivers, and prices are low in the markets of Warwick, Coventry, Bidfield and Stafford. Never again will he go on such a journey or even as far as the Marches.

Guto'r Glyn records the death of a poetess, Gwerful Madog,

whom he praises for her generous hospitality as well as for her verse[1]. In his old age he thanks his unchanging patrons and looks back on his successful wanderings as a poet.

> Clera Môn, cael aur a medd
> gynt, a gwin Gwent a Gwynedd.
>
> A wandering poet in Anglesey, getting gold and mead
> once upon a time, and the wine of Gwent and Gwynedd.

A very funny elegy on the death of Guto was written whilst he was still alive by Llywelyn ab y Gutyn, the latter pretending that Guto had been drowned at sea. He has gone to heaven because he could not swim (*mae'n y nef am na nofiai*), his body lies in a mackerelly cradle, the men of Anglesey pack herrings in his boots and his brain-pan is the haunt of eels.

> Y kawell lle bu'r kywydd
> yn geudod llysywod sydd. [LlC. III, p. 44]
>
> The cradle where the poem lay
> is a hollowness for eels.

In reply to this Guto protests that he still lives and dreams that he sees rivers in flood carrying the drunken Llywelyn away to the sea and damnation.

As fine as any tribute to a dead poet is Guto'r Glyn's *cywydd* on the death of the outlaw poet Llywelyn ap y Moel, a poem which exemplifies the extraordinary freshness which such a poet could bring to conventional variations on a set of themes, for in such elegies girls regularly lament, the muse is widowed, burial is grimly pictured and the dead poet is imagined as singing in heaven. It is the *cynghanedd* that makes the unforgettable line and charms one away from criticism on the ground of conventionality. There is a power in the very first line which arises equally from the simplicity of the statement and the echo of the internal rhyme.

[1] *Y Flodeugerdd Newydd*, W. J. Gruffydd, p. 84.

Mae arch yn Ystrad Marchell. [CIGE. p. liv]

There is a coffin in Ystrad Marchell.

Of Llywelyn's death we are told:—

Aeth priawd cerdd dafawd hy
a'r awdurdod i'r derwdy.

The bold husband of the art of poetry
and its authority have gone to the oak-house.

Again if we analyse these lines we find that their effect springs equally from meaning and sound, the contrast between authority and the grave being rendered the more striking by the repetition of the consonants r d r d in the same order, whilst the second line is linked to the first by two rhymes, the internal *-awd* and the final *-y*.

In the last lines of the poem the poet goes to heaven, taking with him a new poem. God is the patron who now welcomes him and the patron's conventional gift to the wandering poet who has fulfilled his function at the feast in hall is this time the heavenly life.

Dafydd Nanmor, who flourished during the second half of the fifteenth century, was a North Walian who lived out his life in South Wales, but whether for some forgotten political reason or because of his famous love for Gwen o'r Ddol, another man's wife, is not known. He was buried at Whitland (Ty Gwyn ar Daf).

Dafydd Nanmor combined the writing of love poems with the usual other kinds, the praise of patrons and of God, but it was love poetry which gave him the greatest opportunity for the exercise of his fancy in the invention of comparisons, so that in fact the poem ceased to have much relation either to love or to the girl in question; this to a more obvious degree than is customary, though it may be asked how often good love poetry is really about either love or a particular woman. Good examples of this use of a girl for the purposes of art, a use more openly acknowledged by painters, are a *cywydd* to the hair of a girl called Llio Rhydderch and another to a kiss. Llio's hair has the brightness of lightning on a fine snowdrift, she is the primrose-haired girl, such hair falls on the breasts of mermaids, her hair is a mantle of the colour of the chalices of the knights, it is like ripe nuts, like a bush of broom, like a golden lattice, like an orange, like the tip of a flame, like two chains of yellow silk, like a sacrificial taper, like a golden smoke.

This is how he describes a girl's mouth:—

> Pand mwyn pennod ei minws
> Prennol i gadw per annerch
> Pantri rhwng seleri serch
> Per fal y pader myn Pedr
> Melysach na mel lessedr. [Ll. 133, p. 463]

> How mild the chapter of her mouth,
> a coffer for sweet greetings,
> a pantry between cellars of love,
> sweet as a prayer, by Peter,
> sweeter than a honey pot.

In a poem to the Peacock[1] he begs the bird to go and greet Gwen o'r Ddol and seek an opportunity to cause trouble between her and her husband. That is put into the first eight lines. Then follow twenty-five lines of *dyfaliad* in which the peacock's colours are conveyed in metaphor and simile. In the last four lines the poet remembers why he is addressing the peacock and asks it to steal Gwen and bring her back to her lover.

> A dyred fel adarwr
> a dwg Wenn o dŷ ei gwr.

> Come back like a bird-catcher
> bearing Gwen from her husband's house.

The extreme unlikeliness of this proposition is indication enough, if one was needed, of the true motivation of the poem. Mr. Saunders Lewis considers the love poems to be apprentice work, which may account for their air of unreality.

[1] *I'r Paun.* Works ed. by T. Roberts. Welsh University Press, 1923.

A much more real feeling and, for that reason perhaps, a more convincing inevitability of epithet are to be observed in Dafydd Nanmor's *cywydd* to lament the death of Gwen o'r Ddol (YFN. pp. 89–91), an elegy which recalls that of Llywelyn Goch to Lleucu Llwyd. He bewails the putting of her beauty in earth and their final separation by death.

O Dduw tad, o chuddiwyd hi
Nad oeddwn amdo iddi.

O Father God, if she was hidden away
why could I not be her shroud?

She died in the month of May and the cuckoo and the burgeoning trees are widowed for her. Like Lleucu Llwyd, she seems to the poet to be for the moment not beyond love.

Och un awr na chawn orwedd
Gyda bun dan gaead bedd.

O that I might lie one hour
with a girl under the grave's lid.

His mind turns to miraculous raisings from the dead, to Christ's raising of Lazarus, to the Celtic Saint Beuno's miracles, and so comes his final prayer for her return too.

Gwnaed Duw, am ddyn gannaid hir
A minnau, godi meinir.
Dulas ydwyf fal deilen
O frig yw am farw Gwen.
Hon fo'r wythfed ddiledryw
Bun fain a wnel Beuno'n fyw.

May God, for the sake of a tall white girl
and for me, raise this young woman.
Blue-black am I like the leaf
of a yew branch for Gwen's death.
May she be the eighth pure
slim girl for Beuno to restore to life.

A curious *cywydd To God and the Planet Saturn* shows less of the weaving of similitudes that one might expect than of puzzled enquiry into the nature of this heavenly body. Does any adventurer, any master of art or learned doctor, any teacher or magician know what the essence of this planet is and what path it follows through the sky? The riddle poem seems in this *cywydd* to take upon itself something of the air of modern scientific enquiry.

Dafydd Nanmor's greatest work was done in praise of national heroes and of his patrons, the chief of whom was Rhys ap Maredudd of Tywyn, and it was to him and to his family that some of the poet's best things are written. Of a high degree of craftsmanship is the *awdl* to Rhys which contains one of the loveliest of all englynion.

> Mal blodau prennau ymhob rhith, mal od,
> mal adar ar wenith,
> mal y daw y glaw a'r gwlith
> mae i undyn fy mhendith. [DN. p. 4]

> Like every kind of blossom from trees, like snow,
> like birds on wheat,
> as the rain comes and the dew
> is my blessing on one man.

Of greater historical interest are Dafydd Nanmor's poems to Jasper and Henry Tudor. His enthusiasm for Jasper, Earl of Pembroke takes him rather too far in a series of *englynion* which fore-shadow that hero as conqueror of Paris, Cologne, Venice, Friesland, Holland, Zeeland, Iceland, the castles of the Rhone and Rome. Later he comes nearer home and nearer to ful-fillable prophecy in his list of towns in England and Wales, some of which Jasper Tudor had already taken.

> Kaernarfon, Kaer Fon, Kaer Vanaw, Kaer Dyf,
> Kaer Dyvi, Kaer Lwdlaw,
> Kaer Gwyntri wen, Kaer Gaint traw,
> Kaer vawr Ystwyth, Kaer Vrystaw. [DN.. p. 38]

Caernarvon, Anglesey, Man and Cardiff,
Aberdyfi and Ludlow,
fair Coventry and far Canterbury,
great Aberystwyth and Bristol.

These towns, like the European cities in the previous stanzas, are very cunningly linked by *cynghanedd* and are a pleasure to read, but they provide conspicuous examples of the subjugation of sense to metrical requirement and neither the sequence of the places mentioned nor the descriptive adjective allotted to some of them is to be taken seriously or even thought about. No one in his senses would call Aberystwyth castle great in a list which gives the castles of Caernarvon, Ludlow and Cardiff without any adjective at all. This is poetry become incantation, which has to be read aloud for the sound to triumph over the sense, as then indeed it does.

Welsh literature is notably deficient in narrative verse, for from the beginnings prose must have been considered the proper medium for story telling. Dafydd Nanmor's *cywydd* which tells the story of Damon and Pythias in eighty-six lines was therefore something of an innovation in its day.[1] The story is told directly and economically with only occasional parentheses as a running commentary. Once the narrative is complete, one couplet only makes a general and final comment on the tale.

Chwerwa wedd, ni cheir heddyw
Eu bath yn unlle yn byw.

The bitterest aspect—nowhere today
will you find anyone like them alive.

An amiable and entertaining person, Dafydd Nanmor loved the good things of life as much as did Iolo Goch, and no Welsh poet shows a greater love of wine, for unlike others who were clearly glad to drink any sort of wine Dafydd Nanmor specifies the kind of wine brought out for his entertainment at great houses. Here are two of his tributes to generous hosts. The first is from the elegy on the death of Rhys ap Maredudd.

[1] YFN. pp. 96-9. The poem may be by the later Tomas Prys.

Ni bu glerwr yno heb glared
ni buom nifer na baem yn yfed
ni bu drai ossai neu ddowsedd—na chêl
ni bu nos uchel ar neb un syched. [DN. p. 17]

No poet there went without claret,
we were never assembled without drinking,
there was no ebb of Osey or Doucet[1]—no concealment,
and no high night with anyone thirsty.

And of his reception at the house of Sir Dafydd ap Thomas, priest of Maenawr:—

A gwely oedd danaf amgeledd dynion
vai'n abl i ddug o vanblu ddigon.
A llun wybr o waith yn llennau brithon
ar ucha ngwely val airchangylion. [DN. p. 55]

And a bed beneath me, refuge of men,
good enough for a duke, with plentiful down,
with a picture of the heavens worked into tapestry
above my bed like archangels.

Mr Saunders Lewis has drawn attention to the high proportion of indoor imagery in the work of this comfort-loving poet.

Lewys Glyn Cothi, who also flourished during the second half of the fifteenth century, took his bardic name from his birthplace in the lovely Cothi valley near the northern limits of Carmarthenshire and is said to have lived as a child in a house with the gloomy name of Pwlltinbyd, the Pit of the World's Backside. The situation of this house can hardly have been a happy one and Lewys Glyn Cothi, once he had left home, found a pleasanter and easier life in Anglesey. When outlawed he went to live in Chester, not, as one might expect, in the remote safety of the Carmarthenshire uplands. He came back to his native shire to die, not in the valley of his birth but in the gentle landscape of Abergwili.

More than most poets was Lewys Glyn Cothi involved, both as writer and man of action, in the confusion of the Wars of the

[1] Osey was a wine of Alsace and Doucet a sweet wine.

Roses in Wales. He is notable as a writer of the *cywydd brud* or chronicle poem of prophecy, but it is clear that his main concern is neither with the house of York nor of Lancaster, but with the triumph of prominent Welsh partisans in the struggle. He laments the death of Edmund Tudor, father of the Henry Tudor who became Henry VII, in an ode which shows his great mastery of the *awdl* measures, beginning, as became the custom during the fifteenth century, with *englynion*. He describes him as the "fleur delis" of kings and, by association with the heraldic beasts of the Tudor coat of arms, there enter into the poem some of the symbolic creatures which are a common feature of European mediæval political writing.

> Y tarw a'r ceiliog o'r tiroedd oll gynt
> a'r llew gwyn o'r gogledd
> a gwennol Owain Gwynedd
> o eitha'r byd aeth i'r bedd. [G. 3, pp. 144–6]

> The bull and the cock from all lands of the past,
> the white lion from the north
> and Owain Gwynedd's swallow
> from the ends of the earth have gone to death.

In lamenting the gap left by the death of this prince Lewys Glyn Cothi uses the old gnomic style as a rhetorical device. A land is empty without a ruler, a house is empty without a bed and children, so also are a town without great houses, a beach without water, a habitation without feasting, a church without a priest, a tower without a soldier and a hearth without smoke. This fine poem ends in despair and a note in the Gwyneddon 3 manuscript tells us that when it was written the poet did not know that Edmund Tudor's widow was pregnant with a son who was to be king of England.

Another *awdl* in a similar variety of measures praises Jasper Tudor, Earl of Pembroke, and his nephew Henry Richmond, the future king. A *cywydd* laments the death of Thomas ap Rotsier, lord of Herast, who died at Banbury in 1469 with so many other Welshmen, the battle which Lewys Glyn Cothi says was lost by a mistake.

An elegy on the death of Thomas ap Rhydderch, who seems to have died a more natural death in his bed, is in a more unusual form, for after opening the *awdl* with two *englynion*, a by now customary practice, the poet concludes with twelve four-line stanzas of the type known as *gwawdodyn byr*, except that each line has eight syllables instead of the usual nine. Lewys Glyn Cothi thus shows himself to be not only a master of the currently accepted metres but an innovator and experimenter within the narrow limits permitted.

A *cywydd* to Niclas ap Gruffudd of Oswestry is interesting on account of the different sources to which the poet goes for comparisons to suggest the handsomeness of his patron. This Nicholas has the body of Jason and should be portrayed on the long tapestried curtain side by side with the Arthurian Gwalchmai (Sir Gawayn). He is a brother to Moses and may be compared to Priam's three sons, to Adam and to Bran, son of Llyr. Is he any worse than they were, this big man with an eagle's might? The answer comes:—

> Gwell vydd gwasgwin no gwin gwan
> ac aur vydd well nog arian. [LlC. IV, p. 73]

> Gascon is better than weak wine
> and gold is better than silver.

Lewys Glyn Cothi got into trouble for prophesying the coming of Henry Tudor to the English throne and had to go into hiding. He had married a widow and chose to live quietly at Chester but the people of the town or its officers descended on his house and confiscated all his belongings. He himself escaped but, as he says in a *cywydd* asking for a coverlet, as naked as a salmon in a stream. No reference is made to the plight of his wife on this occasion. Another unfortunate contact he made with the English was when he offered his services as poet at a marriage feast amongst the English community of Flint. He began to sing an *awdl* of praise but was greeted with scorn and laughter, for those dealers in barley and wheat could do without his art. The company then called on William the Piper and there follows an amusing grotesque description of the playing of the pipes. Lewys is sent empty-handed away and curses Flint, the English and their piper, for no more than Dafydd ap Gwilym and William Llŷn did Lewys Glyn Cothi like the shape or the sound of the bagpipes. Suitably enough the miserable rewards handed out to Will the Piper are expressed in borrowings from the English language, *ffis* (fees) and *lardies* (largesse).

> Gwedi darfod, gwawd oerferch,
> gwichlais hon, gochelai serch,
> cael ffis o Wil y cawl ffa,
> lerdies nid o law wrda,
> ceiniogau lle cynigian
> ac weithiau dimeuau mân,
> a'm gollwng yn drablwng draw
> o'r goegwledd yn wr gwaglaw. [YFN p. 103 and G. 3, p. 136b]

The first couplet of the passage quoted here affords a good example of the grammar of the *cywydd*. The prose order of the words would be—*Gwedi darfod gwichlais hon, gwawd oerferch gochelai serch*. By a kind of development of the parenthesis it became possible for two parts of a sentence to proceed together, once more reminiscent of the parallel up and down movement of the stone tracery of Celtic crosses. The meaning in such a case is far easier to follow on the written or printed page than when the poem is recited or sung, unless the swing from one clause to another be expressed by modulation of the voice.

> When its squealing voice had done,
> words of a cold girl who would shun love,
> Will got his fees of bean soup,
> no largesse from a good man's hand,
> pennies where they were offered
> and sometimes little halfpennies;
> whilst I was sullenly sent forth
> from this false feast an empty-handed man.

Lewys Glyn Cothi loved his comforts and appreciated lavish hospitality as much as any of his predecessors in the profession of poetry and he seems to have received the best treatment in the island of Anglesey.

> Gwin grabs a gawn i a graens,
> gwin ac aur gwyn ac oraens,
> rhessing, cwrrens a fenswn
> rhost, nid er bost, adar y bwn . . .
> Gorddu yw brig Iwerddon
> gan fwg ceginau o Fôn. [YFN. p. 101]

> Wine from grapes I got and cardamon,
> white wine and gold and oranges,
> raisins, currants and venison
> roasted, I'm not boasting, bitterns . . .
> The trees of Ireland are blackened over
> by the smoke of the kitchens of Anglesey.

And when, after losing his goods at Chester, he begs a coverlet of Elen of Llwydiarth, no ordinary coverlet will serve his turn, for this lady, he imagines, will promptly send him an embroidered bed covering of many colours, with birds and deer worked into it and hundreds of leaves of different hue, with green as a background. This will keep him from cold till summer and will be nightly a green banner over his naked bed. Yet another *cywydd* to a bed testifies to Lewys Glyn Cothi's love of soft lying (*Llên Cymru* IV, pp. 77–8).

As a precautionary penance for such love of the things of this world Lewys Glyn Cothi composed a number of religious poems, and of all biblical characters he surprisingly chooses John the Baptist for especial praise in a *cywydd* in which he stresses the extreme simplicity of his way of life.

> Bwyd y maccwy meudwyaidd
> berwr hallt a bara o'r haidd.
> Yn ddiod gan ei ddewin
> dwfr a gai, nid seidr a gwin. [G 3, p. 70]

This youthful hermit's food
was salt cress and barley bread.
For drink in his foretelling
he got water, not cider or wine.

His most impressive religious poem is an unusually long *awdl* to the Trinity which runs to a hundred and twenty four-line stanzas, some of them *englynion*and others half-rhymed stanzas. Having dealt severally with the members of the Trinity and with the Catholic faith he ends with this statement of the unity and immanence of God.

Yn y Trwn y mae trwy ynni yn Un
yn y nef y mae'n dri:
yn yr haul yn yr heli
yn y ser myn fennioes i.

Yn y gwydd y bydd ym-hob âr drwy'r byd,
yn yr yd yn yr adar,
yn dduw y mae yn y ddaear
yn ddewin gwyn yn ddyn gwâr.

Yn eigion ym-hell, yn agos y mae,
yn y main, yn y rhos,
yn y dydd yn y diddos
yn y niwl ac yn y nos.

Yn egin y llin ger llaw yn y gwynt
yn y gwellt yn gwreiddiaw
yn y gwenith yn rhithiaw
yn y gwlith ac yn y glaw.

Yn fryn y dwyrain yn Frenin ieithoedd
yn eithaf gorllewin:
yng-ogledd anhunedd hin,
yn y deau un dewin.

Yn dec y mae ym-hob degwm,
ym-hob da oll ym-hob dim,
yno y mae Duw ynom,
yn Nuw er ioed, yno yr ym. [G 3, p. 201]

In the Circle through power he is One,
in heaven he is three;
in the sun, in the brine,
and, by my life, in the stars.

He is in the trees, in all the world's tilth,
in the corn, in the birds;
he is a god in the earth,
a white magician and a mild man.

He is far in the ocean, he is near,
in stones, in the moorland,
in the daylight and in shelter,
in the mist, in the night.

In flax seed nearby, in the wind,
in the rooting grass;
he appears in the wheat,
in the dew and in the rain.

The hill of the east, the king of tongues
in the far west,
in the north in stormy weather,
in the south a magician.

He is fair in every tithe;
in every good thing, in everything,
there God is in us,
Eternal God, and there are we.

With Dafydd ap Edmwnd we are back in the tradition of Dafydd ap Gwilym. Like the earlier Dafydd, Dafydd ap Edmwnd was of aristocratic birth and, like him, kept out of politics, a notable achievement for anyone writing in Wales during the Wars of the Roses.

Dafydd ap Edmwnd was a poet's poet and is one of the great names in the tormented history of Welsh prosody. He won the silver chair at the Carmarthen eisteddfod of 1451 for re-arranging the twenty-four metres and composing and reciting an example for each metre.[1] As Sir John Morris Jones points

[1] Specimens of some of these metres, including forms of the *englyn*, the *rhupunt hir*, the *cyhydedd hir* and the *cywydd* couplet, have already been indicated. For fuller treatment see the Appendix.

out, the purpose of this eisteddfod (the word originally means session) must have been to tighten up control of the bardic orders. The break-up of the bardic system which we have observed taking place with the changing social and political conditions in Wales had, by the middle of the fifteenth century, assumed alarming proportions and it was considered necessary to make the claim to the rank of *pencerdd* or chief poet more difficult to make good. Any poet seeking this grade had to compose an acceptable specimen of each of the twenty-four metres, and the more conservative poets must have thought that the surest way to preserve the standards of the poetic craft was to make these metres more difficult. This, then, was Dafydd ap Edmwnd's task and he set about it by heightening the difficulty of some of the old metres, insisting in some cases on double instead of simple rhymes, and by introducing two new metres of his own invention which are really, to translate Sir John Morris Jones, "old metres intertwisted to a degree of madness."[1]

We have seen in the work of Madog Dwygraig how easy it is for the requirements of *cynghanedd* to bring the meaning of a line to the verge of nonsense. Let us now consider these two new metres which represent the ultimate complication of alliteration and rhyme, and in one of which, the *cadwynfyr* or little chain, it has never been possible for anyone, including the inventor, to write anything which has much meaning at all!

The first of these is the *Gorchest Beirdd* or Poet's Bravado, an adaptation of the old *rhupunt hir* measure. Here is the best of the series of six stanzas the inventor wrote to exemplify this new torment for the apprentice in verse. I give it in Welsh only, for it is not worth translating, being a conventional tribute to a patron's hospitality distinguished by clumsy acrobatics of rhyme and alliteration, which may easily be picked out.

I'ch llys iach llawn, wiw Rys, yr awn
a gwys a gawn, agos ged;
a'th fudd, wyth fael, o gudd i'w gael,
aur rhudd, wr hael, rhwydd y rhed.

[1] *hen fesurau wedi eu lincloncio i ynfydrwydd, op. cit.*, p. 350.

At its best, therefore, this metre is a horrible jogtrot and it is fortunate that it has been neglected, for Sir John Morris Jones says that in all his reading he has not seen another sequence of stanzas in this form.

To exemplify the other invention, the *cadwynfyr*, Dafydd ap Edmwnd wrote the following stanza. It will be observed that the main feature is the repetition of one set of consonants three times in each line, the rhymes, both end rhyme and internal, occurring alternately.

Gwenfun gwynfau gainfun gynful
gariad gwervyl gyriad gorau
gwirfydd gyrfau gorfydd gwyrful
Gorwag eurul gwiw ragorau.[1]

This is cacophonous nonsense. The form was never intended as anything but an examination exercise, and as such it was confirmed, together with the rest, as an official measure at the eisteddfodau of 1523 and 1568 at Caerwys.

It may well be imagined that his contemporaries did not accept these modifications and additions to the old code without protest, and there is evidence of bitter controversy over the matter and strong opposition at the eisteddfod of Carmarthen, where the metres were accepted by the assembly of poets in spite of objections from South Wales. Gutyn Owain says of Dafydd ap Edmwnd:—

Gwraidd vu gyrrodd ai vin
ynghur beirdd yng nghaer vyrddin.

A root he was, driving his point
into the pain of poets at Carmarthen.

And Lewys Môn, speaking of the same occasion, says:—

trychant yn tario i ochel
trwy bawb i dug ynte'r bel.

[1] CD, p. 351 gives the earliest text from the hand of Gutyn Owain, 1455, but the above version from MS Peniarth 96 perhaps does greater visual justice to the rhymes.

Three hundred waiting on guard,
through them all he carried the ball.

The opposition was therefore considerable, and Dafydd ap Edmwnd's triumph is compared to that of the primitive rugby player who takes the ball through the mass of enemy parishioners to the goal of the church door.[1]

From these civil wars of poetry let us turn to Dafydd ap Edmwnd's achievement in the established *cywydd* form. After Dafydd ap Gwilym no poet has offered such metrical inducements to a girl to leave her father's or her husband's roof. *Cywyddau* follow one another to girl after girl, a tour de force to a cobbler's wife with one rhyme throughout and each line beginning with the same letter, poems to specific girls and unnamed girls, to an apple a girl gave him as a sign, to a kiss, several poems to lovely heads of hair. A yellow-haired girl of Maelawr carries her hair like a peacock's tail of broom flower from her head to her feet. For a century a girl's hair had been the most regularly used subject for the weaving of comparisons but Dafydd ap Edmwnd is not content with the tried similarities of broom flower and gold.

Eginodd gwaith y gwenyn
egin y tes o gnawd dyn,
  saffrwm ar lysiau effros,
  siriau o nef, ser y nos. [YFN. p. 113]

Labour of bees has ripened
  the seeds of warmth from a girl's flesh,
saffron on the herb eyebright,
cherries from heaven, the stars of night.

He asks whether a bush was ever so yellow, as though doubting the power of comparison. *A fu lwyn cyn felyned?*

Like all lovers he has good and bad luck. He throws out an enchanting promise.

[1] For a lively description of this old Welsh game see George Owen, *Description of Pembrokeshire*, 1603, Cymmrodorion Record Series, no. 1.

Angel bryd yngwely brwyn
ai gwrlid o vrig irlwyn
angylion bob ton in ty
angyles ar vyngwely
nid a om kof dameg gwen
down i vyd dan y fedwen
am enaid mi a meinir
a el i nef o lwyn ir. [C. 49, p. 6 and DE].

An angel face in a rush bed
with its coverlet of fresh branches;
in our house the angels of the lay land
and an angel on my bed.
I'll not forget Gwen's parable,
we'll come into a world under the birchtree,
and my soul and that of my girl
will rise to heaven from the green grove.

One *cywydd* is a serenade of forty-two lines, all beginning with the letter d. He has been foolish enough to walk the night and now he shivers under a girl's wall. His hair is wet with rain and his face soiled. Won't she hand out her mother's shawl to roof his head? Not even an Englishman would be so spiteful towards him. But he wants more than that.

. . . dy lety dy law ataf
dy dec gorff dywaid ai kaf
dy fwyn air er dy fonedd
dy fin fal diod o fedd. [DE. p 1 and YFN, p. 114]

Your lodging, your hand towards me,
your lovely body, say, shall I have it?
Your sweet word from your nobleness,
your lip like a drink of mead.

One girl refuses to say a word to him any more, not even a good night, for she seems to have gone dumb. Is there no sorceress to cure her of this affliction? Let her make offerings, an image of her lips at Llangynin; let her put an infusion of bugle (*llysiau Mair*—Mary's herb) to her mouth and offer a picture to Mary and a golden tongue to Saint Ithel. At St. Davids, if she makes the pilgrimage, the power of speech may return to her or Non, mother of David, may take pity on her and cure her there. Finally the poet begs Christ to make the mute one talk (YFN. pp. 116–18).

The nearest Dafydd ap Edmwnd came to expressing a political opinion, apart from implied dislike of the English, was in a *cywydd* written on the death of the harpist Sion Eos (*Anglice* John Nightingale). This is a more informative poem than most of its kind and tells how Sion was involved in a quarrel, and in the affray which resulted unintentionally killed a man. He was tried at Chirk and, although the jury were not unanimous, he was put to death for the offence. The poem is a strong plea against the death penalty in such a case and Dafydd ap Edmwnd asks why Sion was tried according to the cruel English law, and not according to that of Hywel Dda. Why, as the result of an accident, should two lives be lost and one of them such a precious life as that of the master harpist? In all Wales there is no one left like him. The magical harp of Teirtu, the obtaining of which was one of the tasks in the tale of *Culhwch and Olwen*, is broken and with it the school of descant, the measure of music's foot has been broken. How Dafydd ap Edmwnd must have loved this harpist and harp music to speak so warmly and beautifully of his playing! Nothing better has ever been said of the harp than the following couplet.

> Myfyrdawd rhwng bawd a bys,
> main a threbl mwyn a thribys. [YFN. p. 110]

> A meditation between thumb and finger,
> mean and sweet treble and three-fingered chord.

The first line is slow and haunting, the second alive with plucking consonants.

Dafydd ap Edmwnd wrote religious poems as well and with the same artistry, a *cywydd* to Mary and to God, and one with the arithmetical title, *Cywydd pedair merched y Tad, pump llawenydd Mair, a phump pryder Mair, a saith goruchafiaeth Mair*, a *cywydd* of the four daughters of the Father, the five joys of Mary, the five troubles of Mary and the seven triumphs of Mary. (BM Add. MS. 14967).

But this poet is remembered as the master of lovely words woven with the highest skill into praise of nature in springtime and the beauty of girls. The following couplet to a nun sums up his interests and his craftsmanship.

I leuad haf ail wyd di
a nos gudd yn wisg iddi.

You are like the moon of summer
with secret night as her garment.

In Tudur Aled's elegy Dafydd ap Edmwnd's death is associated with that of Dafydd Nanmor and Ieuan Deulwyn in a kind of *Lament for the Makers* and Gutyn Owain said of him:—

. . . gweddw byd am gerdd gwydd a bun
gwin oedd a ganai uddun
bwrrwyd addwyn brydyddiaeth
breuddwyd oer i bridd y daeth.

The world is widowed of song to the woods and girls;
what he sang to them was wine.
True poetry is struck,
cold dream, it's come to earth.

And Lewys Môn ends his final tribute to Dafydd ap Edmwnd with the couplet:—

. . . penn owdur yn penn ydoedd
poettri n iaith yn pattrwn oedd.[1]

Chief author, he was our head,
the poetry of our language, he was our pattern.

Once more poets have had to be neglected in this summary treatment, for the fifteenth century offers a score and more of versifiers of great interest and a high degree of technical skill,

[1] Peniarth MS 80, quoted from introduction, DE.

and I am likely to be taken to task for not dealing with Maredudd ap Rhys, Bedo Brwynllys, Llawdden, Ieuan Deulwyn, Gutyn Owain and Tudur Penllyn. Nor have I perhaps given sufficient space to the *cywyddau brud* or prophetic political poems which are such a prominent feature of the literature of this century.

An amusing story indicates what store was set by popular leaders on these prophetic poems in the fifteenth century, though there is likely to have been less of faith in the poet-prophet than a realisation of the value of the support of a reputed seer in the gathering together of an army. Henry Tudor, Earl of Richmond, on his way from Fishguard to Shrewsbury made a halt in the Dyfi valley to consult Dafydd Lwyd of Mathafarn, a renowned poet-seer, on the likelihood of the success of his bid for the English crown. Dafydd could not decide right off what judgment to give in the matter and said he would answer on the following morning. When Dafydd's wife heard of his hesitation she rounded on him furiously. "What! You a poet and a seer and you cannot answer such a question as that! Tell him confidently that he'll win the battle. If it turns out like that, your name will be held in high honour. If he loses the battle you may depend he'll never come back this way to accuse you of false prophecy." The poet followed his wife's advice, Henry Tudor went happily forward, won the battle and became Henry VII of England.

In the history of Welsh metrics the fifteenth century is notable for refinement and modification rather than innovation or change. The *englyn* was established as a regular constituent of the *awdl* and as such fit for the highest purposes of poetry. In the writing of the *cywydd* a development took place which is clearly foreshadowed in the work of Dafydd ap Gwilym, a tendency for the couplet to become more complete in itself, that is for the couplet rather than the phrase to become the unit of expression. Thus the old interlinking flow of Celtic tracery which we have observed as the main pattern of Welsh poetry came to be broken and sometimes entirely replaced by a series of almost self-contained epigrams. The difference between the *cywydd* metre of the fourteenth and fifteenth centuries is similar to that between the decasyllabic couplets of Marlowe and Pope. The effect on the *cywydd* was to make its texture more tightly knit and to make less necessary the use of the parentheses conventionally employed to sustain the *cynghanedd* in a passage of some length. As Professor Tom Parry says in his admirable history of Welsh Literature, it is possible for the *cywydd* couplet to become almost as tiring as the English heroic couplet, but the danger of this appears to be small in a poetic form which rarely achieves the length of a hundred lines. The victory of the couplet over the phrase facilitated quotation and provided an infinity of sweet sounding epigrams.

Cynghanedd was now insisted upon much more strictly than in the more easy-going fourteenth century and even, as we saw in considering Dafydd ap Edmwnd, tightened up to a pitch of craziness in some of the measures.

For this tightening up of the bardic tests at Carmarthen in 1451 to have been necessary there must have been a great increase in the number of inferior or careless practitioners of the craft of versification who laid claim to patronage. The system of patronage still worked moderately well, even if with the changed social conditions a landowner's support of a chief poet became less regular and permanent and the best poets took to the wandering ways which had earlier characterised lesser bardic orders. The fulsome traditions of conventional praise now became more transparently unjustified and Sion Cent sums up this realisation in the couplet:—

> Haeru bod gwin teuluaidd
> a medd lle nid oedd ond maidd.
>
> To claim that there was family wine
> and mead where there was only whey.

Although it is difficult to doubt that Lewys Glyn Cothi actually drank the wine he so carefully names, there must have been a decline in lordly hospitality during this century and correspondingly less reason for the kind of praise which Cynddelw and, quite probably Iolo Goch, had every reason for bestowing.

The Welsh poets of the fifteenth century showed no interest in the important new developments taking place in Italy, though, as Professor Tom Parry points out (*Hanes Llenyddiaeth Gymraeg*, p. 120), Humphrey, Duke of Gloucester, one of the great book-collectors and propagandists of the new movement and a student of Dante, Petrarch and Boccaccio, spent a great deal of time in Wales. It was a great friend of the "good" Duke Humphrey, Gruffudd ap Nicolas of Dinefor, who sponsored the Carmarthen eisteddfod of 1451, at which it was not the new learning but the old rules that interested the assembly of writers. This, however, should surprise no one familiar with the literary history of England and Scotland during the fifteenth and early sixteenth centuries, for there too poetry showed a similar slowness in reacting to the new movement. Professor Atkins says, "Nor again can it be said that Humanistic activities did much to further an understanding, still less an appreciation, of literature . . . Classical studies were in the main pursued for utilitarian ends by men who cultivated a correct Latinity for ecclesiastical and diplomatic purposes. The wider intellectual effects of Italian scholarship were thus to some extent missed, the prevailing interests being centred, not on imaginative literature, but on works of theology, philosophy, medicine, and the like."[1]

English poetry was therefore very little affected by what was happening abroad until the innovations of Wyatt and Surrey well on in the sixteenth century. Carleton Brown sums up the situation thus. "Even a casual reading of these fifteenth century lyrics is sufficiency to demonstrate that no real line of cleavage exists between the fourteenth and fifteenth centuries . . . the lyrics of the century, if studied attentively, supply evidence of a development from the fifteenth to the sixteenth century almost as constant as that traceable from the fourteenth to the fifteenth."[2]

In Scotland the situation was much the same. Mr. John

[1] J. W. H. Atkins, *English Literary Criticism, The Renascence*, p. 36, Methuen 1947.
[2] Carleton Brown, *Religious Lyrics of the Fifteenth Century*, OUP 1939, p. xxxi.

Speirs says, "The Scots poetry of the fifteenth, and the beginning of the sixteenth century is still mediæval."[1] Later in his excellent book on the Scots Literary Tradition Mr. Speirs refers to the Scots poetry of the sixteenth century as "in general moribund in the mediæval modes."[2]

If therefore the English and Scottish poets of the fifteenth century, struggling to emerge from a chaotic mediæval tradition and not even able, in England at least, to appreciate the technical achievements of Chaucer, failed to benefit from the new experiments made overseas, how understandable it is that Welsh poets writing at the peak of a movement, when a slowly developed technique of versification had achieved the ultimate perfection, should have thought it absurd, if they thought of it at all, to fiddle with any foreign tricks of stanza construction. There is an indication of an awareness on the part of the poets that a culmination had been reached, in the need felt to classify definitively the metres and devices permissible to the poet. Some metres, as has already been seen, are as old as the *Gododdin* and the Juvencus *englynion*. Einion Offeiriad and Dafydd Ddu in the fourteenth century made the metrical forms up to the neat number of twenty-four, and since Dafydd ap Edmwnd's revision of these twenty-four metres in 1451 they have remained unchanged until today. The term *mesurau rhyddion* (free metres) was first used in the sixteenth century and is a convenient one for any form used in the writing of poetry outside the official twenty-four. A treatment of the twenty-four measures and their history, as well as of alliteration and rhyme in Welsh verse, will be found in the Appendix on versification at the end of this book.

[1] & [2] John Speirs, *The Scots Literary Tradition*. Chatto and Windus 1940, pp. 4 & 83.

Chapter VII

THE SIXTEENTH CENTURY

★

The sixteenth century is the last during which every reputable Welsh poet was a master of the classical metres, and the century which witnessed the decline of an impulse whose finest manifestations we have seen in poetry written between 1350 and 1450. No literary movement or tradition or style goes on for ever. It weakens and dies a natural and organic death, for a movement or tradition exists in so far as we observe inter-dependency in the work of individual and changing poets. There were factors external to poetry which must have speeded up the process of decline as there are to all organic structures. The order of bards had clung to its traditional ways by denying the new economic, political and legal circumstances, but now, at the beginning of the sixteenth century, is observable a regular affluence of Welshmen to the Tudor court which is to continue throughout the age of Elizabeth.

The Act of Union of England and Wales in 1535 marked the final imposition of English law upon Wales. Welsh gentry had more recourse to Westminster and the policy of the Tudor monarchs was opposed to the perpetuation of the Welsh language and culture. The system of patronage declined and, in spite of two eisteddfodau organised by the bards under royal licence, the grades defining the practitioners of poetry were clearly falling to pieces.

The work of Tudur Aled links the fifteenth and sixteenth centuries and he was as careful a craftsman in the traditional metres as any of his predecessors, amongst whom Dafydd ap Gwilym, Dafydd ap Edmwnd and Guto'r Glyn were those to whom he was most indebted. An amusing story, told of Tudur Aled's encounter with a fishwife, shows how familiar his tongue was with the terminology of his craft (*Cymru Fu*, p. 185).

There used to sit at Chester market a fishwife famous for her Billingsgate Welsh whom Tudur Aled delighted in talking to. One day he mentioned her to a friend, who said, "Yes, she'd even silence a poet's mouth." "You think so, "answered Tudur. "Let's go and see. I'll wager a gallon of metheglin that I'll shut her up in five minutes."

The encounter opened with the poet asking the price of the mackerel and qualifying them as skinny, red-eyed, gaping, stinking abortions. "Good enough for a stiff-bellied poet who knows nothing about mackerel," returned the fishwife. Then Tudur set to work with his terms of grammar and prosody. He called the protesting goodwife all kinds of stanza forms and rhetorical devices, heaping *unodl crwca*, *rhupunt byr*, *cyhydedd nawban* on her head. He had seen her with a *proest* under each arm. She had drunk three pints of *toddeidiau* and had had to be carried home in an indicative verb. She threatened the law on him for his slanders but a final sequence of mouth-filling terms reduced her to inarticulate moaning.

Tudur Aled's society was one which still disliked the English but which perforce turned its eyes to London. For many of his patrons new ambitions and new careers were opening under government from Westminster and some of those whose praise he sang were successful in the new offices and the new ways.[1] A revolution in upper class Welsh life is thus reflected in the work of Tudur Aled. Even in the praise of these followers of the Tudor fortunes, however, it was ancestry rather than recent success that he found the more admirable, for he laid great store by accuracy in the tracing of genealogies in a century which is distinguished by the widespread invention of family trees in the interest of new-made gentry and nobility.

The malaise of Tudur Aled under these new social conditions is particularly noticeable in a *cywydd* he wrote to patch up a quarrel between Humphrey ap Hywel of Ynys Maengwyn

[1] v. Saunders Lewis, *Efrydiau Catholig*, vol. i for treatment of this point.

and some of his relatives. The poet refers to the famous family feuds of the past and to the disastrous battles, Goddeu, Camlan and Arderydd, fought for such trivial reasons.

A oes heddyw am swyddau
Megis hyn yn ymgashau?
Ni chredir yn wir i neb
Ond i un a dau wyneb. [YFN. p. 158]

Today, for the sake of office,
do people hate each other like this?
No one is now believed
unless he be two faced.

The good of the country is squandered by this selfish, office-seeking generation.

Cymry yn waeth caem o'r noethi,
Lloegr yn well o'n llygru ni. [YFN. p. 158]

Wales has been worse for this denuding
and England thrives on corrupting us.

He shows how peace breeds wealth, wealth breeds the pride that leads to war, war breeds wretchedness and poverty leads to anger. Haughty triumph is not secure, for decline is all about it. To strengthen his homily the poet suggests that human behaviour really controls fortune's wheel, for he gives Humphrey this advice.

Heddychu heddyw uchod
a wna parhau'n nhop y rhod. [G 3, p. 121a]

Peace-making in today's eminence
will keep you at the top of the wheel.

After all this moralising there comes a warmer appeal, an appeal to the blood, with a moving play upon the images of frozen blood, of water under ice, and of fire melting the blood back to its perfumed sweetness.

Tynn y rhew i'r tân yrhawg
tawdd dy lid hydd dyledawg. [G 3, p. 121b]

Draw the frost to the fire for the future,
melt your anger, noble stag.

Tudur Aled weaves a good deal of traditional wisdom into memorable arrangements of alliteration and rhyme.

Gwae a wnai gaer ne wal
ag ar wendid y growndwal. [Pen. 76, p. 79]

Woe to him who builds castle or wall
with the groundwall on weakness.

It is thus that he begins a *cywydd* which reproaches a girl for breaking faith with him.

An *awdl* in praise of John Gray, Lord of Powys, gives Tudur Aled an opportunity to show his skill at stanza forms such as the *tawddgyrch cadwynog* and the *hir a thoddaid*, and never has the difficult *cyhydedd hir* been used with such tenderness as in his elegy on the death of Jane Stradling, wife of Sir William Gruffydd of Penrhyn.

Iesu wylasom, Iesu gwaeddasom,
Iesu gwybuasom wasgu bysedd;
yma y rhed môr hallt o'm bron don hyd allt,
ymdynnu o'm gwallt a'm dwyn o'm gwedd.

Ni ddeil calon ddur, ni chwardd bardd yn bur,
nid kur nod dolur ond dialedd;
nid dydd dydd o'i dwyn, nid gwin gwin gwenwyn,
nid cwyn cwyn wrth gŵyn araith Gwynedd.

Arch Sian ferch Sioned, wen vun, anvoned
at Dduw gogoned, Tegau Gwynedd;
daearwyd orau dan vur doe'r vorau;
dod i wraig orau, Duw, drugaredd. [LlC. IV, p. 22]

Jesus, we wept, Jesus, we cried,
Jesus, we knew the squeezing of fingers;
here flows a salt wave from my breast down the hillside,
my hair is torn and my looks are gone.

No heart stands steel, no bard laughs freely,
no pain is the mark of grief but a doom;
the day of her taking is no day, wine no wine but poison,
moaning no moaning compared to the moaning of
Gwynedd.

May the coffin of Jane, daughter of Janet, be sent
to glorious God, this jewel of Gwynedd;
Yesterday morning the best was earthed under a wall;
God, grant mercy to this best of women.

In a lament on the death of an unnamed girl, whom the poet loved and with whom he had exchanged promises, there is exaggeration of the sort indulged in by the Elizabethan English sonneteers, but, as from their loves, literary and conventional though we sometimes suspect them to be, unforgettable lines are born from the over-statement.

Os marw bun, oes mwy o'r byd?
Mae'r haf wedi marw hefyd. [YFN. p. 154]

If the girl is dead, is anything left of the world?
Summer has died as well.

In translation the thought withers like a cut flower, as does the softness and anguish of another couplet which suggests the extent of a girl's grief for a dead lover.

Y gwr marw, e gar morwyn
ddaear dy fedd er dy fwyn.

O dead man, a girl will love
your grave's earth for your sake.

Tudur Aled's rather gloomy view of life seems to persist in his love poetry, which is mostly of unrequited love, but it must be remembered that the unwilling girl has always provided poets with more usable poetic material than she who responds too easily. He begins a *cywydd* thus:—

Serch a rois ar chwaer Essyllt
sy waeth ym no saeth wyllt . . . [Pen. 76, p. 203]

I set my heart on a sister to Iseult,
worse for me than a stray arrow.

She fills and makes empty his world.

Duw ni welais dyn wylwych
llan ni bai wag lle ni bych.

God! I never saw, shy bright girl,
any church not empty with you not there.

Would that her arms were over him like angels above his bed. He is sleepless or he sleeps like a fish lying in a stormy sea.

Tudur Aled is at his best in his *cywyddau* of asking, for when he writes about animals his lines have a quick, clean vigour and nervousness, the fruit of his keen observation, incomparable in Welsh poetry. A good example of this is a poem to ask for a stallion. Having offered the customary praise for the generous hospitality which he has in the past received, the poet describes the animal he desires.

Llygaid fal dwy ellygen
llymion byw'n llamu'n ei ben;
dwyglust feinion aflonydd,
dail saets wrth ei dâl y sydd.
Trwsio fal goleuo glain
y bu wydrwr ei bedrain . . .
Ei flew fal sidan newydd
a'i rawn ar liw gwawn y gwydd . . . [YFN, p. 145]

Eyes that are like two pears,
lively and keen, they leap from his head;
two slim and restless ears
like sage leaves at his forehead.
A trimming like gem-polishing
the glazier's given to his hooves . . .
His coat is like new silk,
his tail might be tree gossamer.

He goes on then to speak of the movement of the horse.

Ser neu fellt ar sarn a fydd,
ar godiad yr egwydydd.
Bwrw naid i'r wybr a wnai,
ar hyder yr ehedai . . .
Ail y carw, olwg gorwyllt,
a'i draed yn gwau drwy dân gwyllt.

On the road there'll be stars or lightning
at the lifting of his fetlocks.
He throws a leap into the sky,
he flies in confidence.
Like a stag with fierce gaze,
his feet weave through wild fire.

It is on such a steed that the poet hopes to carry off an unmarried girl who awaits him.

Testimony to Tudur Aled's mastery of the *englyn* is the frequency with which his name appears in anthologies of this most continuously popular of all the old metres. Here is one of which the final couplet has become proverbial.

Mae'n wir y gwelir argoelyn difai
wrth dyfiad y brigyn;
hysbys y dengys y dyn
o ba radd y bo'i wreiddyn. [YGG. p. 44]

True it is that a certain sign may be seen
in the growth of a bough;
for man clearly displays
of what rank his root is.

Another *englyn* is written in the old vituperative manner.

Caws du Llan Bendu mal hen badell grach
a gwrych ar ei dafell;
caws yr ast o Drecastell;
caseg a wnai caws gwyn well. [YGG. p. 36]

Black cheese of Llan Bendu like an old scabbed pail
with bristles in each slice;
the bitch's cheese from Trecastell;
a mare would make better white cheese.

To indicate the completeness of Tudur Aled's range of subject matter as well as of metrical form, reference may be made to the *cywydd* that tells the story of Gwenfrewi. This virtuous young girl is compared to the eleven hundred virgins of Saint Ursula in that she is:—

> Cynnyrch nef cyn oeri o'i chnawd
> am wirionder morwyndawd. [YFN. p. 141]
>
> A product of heaven, before her flesh chilled,
> for the innocence of her maidenhood.

The cutting off of her head by her persecutor, Caradog, is a memory of early opposition to Christianity, traces of which are to be observed in the *Black Book of Carmarthen*, in the adventures of the Irish Suibhne Geilt, and in Gildas' attack on the British chieftains; and from the spot where her head fell Saint Beuno caused a stream to run which cured ills of the body and of the mind. The cures are described with the vivid briskness characteristic of this poet.

> Blin a thrwm heb law na throed
> a ddaw adre ar ddeudroed—
> bwrw dwyffon i'w hafon hi
> bwrw naid gar ei bron wedi.
>
> The weary, heavy man without use of his limbs
> will come home on his feet;
> he'll fling his crutches into her stream,
> then fling a leap before her.

On his death bed Tudur Aled composed the following *englyn*, his final poem of asking.

> Er ffrydiau gweliau gloywon yr Iesu
> er ei ysig ddwyfron,
> er gwaed ei holl archollion,
> na bwy'n hir yn y boen hon. [YGG. p. 59]
>
> By the clear flow of Jesus' wounds,
> by his bruised sides,
> by the blood of his each gash,
> may I not live long in this pain!

He is said to have become a Franciscan before his death and to have been buried at Cwrt y Brodyr, Carmarthen, near Sir Rhys ap Thomas, hero of Bosworth.

Wiliam Llŷn was a pupil of that great transmitter of the bardic tradition, Gruffydd Hiraethog.[1] He is said to have taken an M.A. and to have been a priest at Oswestry, where he died at the age of forty-five. He won the chair at the eisteddfod held under Queen Elizabeth's commission at Caerwys in 1568.

Wiliam Llŷn is outstanding in his age not for originality, a quality more suspect then than admired,[2] but for his mastery of the poetic craft and his upholding of the functions of the poet in a society that was rapidly changing. It was inevitable therefore that his work should be fuller of echoes of past writing than of new directions. Sion Cent is echoed in a funeral *awdl* to Huw ap Sion ap Hywel;

Mae'r medd ellynedd? mae'r llawnion seigiau?
Mae'r byrddau? mae'r beirddion? [CLl. p. 34]

Where is last year's mead? Where are the full dishes?
Where are the tables? Where are the poets?

and in a poem of praise to a member of the Thelwall family his debt to Dafydd Nanmor comes close to plagiary.

Val rhif dail gwiail mewn dol gaead
Val daw y glaw ar goleuad
Val gwlith ne wenith ar enyniad . . .
Vy mendith yw plith . . . [WLl. p. 185]

In number like leaves on twigs in a meadow hedge,
as rain falls and light comes,
as dew or wheat on a hot place,
my blessing amongst them . . .

[1] Who also taught Sion Tudor, Bishop Davies, Wiliam Cynwal and Simwnt Fychan, and was the compiler of a collection of Welsh proverbs which, with an introduction by William Salesbury, became one of the first printed Welsh books—*Oll Synnwyr Pen Kembero ygyd*. 1547. The extraordinary spelling of Cymro is typical of Salesbury's weird orthography.

Gruffydd Hiraethog was graded as chief bard in 1546.

[2] cf. James Sutherland, *Introduction to 18th century Poetry*. The study of the poetry and critical theory of the Restoration and Augustan periods affords an interesting parallel to the situation in Wales in the fifteenth and sixteenth centuries.

Another feature of this backward looking approach to writing is the frequent anachronism, such as the epithet *aur-dorchog*, gold-torqued, applied to sixteenth century landowners. In the many poems he wrote to Welsh gentry Wiliam Llŷn regularly stresses the ancestry and hospitality of his patrons, for he seems in spite of his clerical duties to have done the rounds like any professional poet, and in praising these virtues, for these had been the main themes of Welsh poetry for centuries, could not fail to fall into clichés. One comes to expect them and one ceases to be impressed by such similes as *fal Nudd*, like Nudd, one of the three famous generous ones of the Island of Britain, whenever a patron has to be flattered.

Even so, signs of the new times are to be found everywhere in the work of this very conservative poet. In his titles we meet the new nomenclature imposed by the renegade Tudors upon the Welsh and by means of which a Sion ap Dafydd Lwyd dwindled into John Davies or John Lloyd. One of his poems of asking is for a gun, and everywhere in his work we come upon words borrowed from English, words which the gentry had learnt in London, in their contacts with the new judicial system, and in fighting in France and the Low Countries. Here are some such words which I have picked at random out of his poems: *pasiwn* (passion), *nasiwn* (nation), *ffortuniad* (fortune), *mastr* (master), *cwestiwn* (question), *cronicl* (chronicle), *ystori* (story), *parc* (park), *tast* (taste), *wrsib* (worship), *sesiwn* (session), *braens* (branch), *emprwr* (emperor), *garsiwn* (garrison), *power*, *gosawg* (goshawk), *mendio* (to mend), *gown ffwr* (fur gown), *fflicht* (flight), and *rwymedi* (remedy). Less than half the above words, fortunately, settled in the Welsh language, and this tendency towards unnecessary borrowing seems to have been checked by the end of the sixteenth century. The temptation such new words held out to the prolific poet, always desperately in search of new consonantal and rhyme arrangements, can easily be imagined, and the justification for Wiliam Llŷn's employment of them is that they must have been current in the written and spoken language of many good Welsh users in his day.

Yet another sign of the times is evidence of the belated impact of the Renaissance on Welsh writing, the result of the closer contact with London under the Tudors, for alongside the traditional Welsh heroes we now find Jason, Achilles, Hector, Tros and the French Roland pressed into the service of flattering comparison.

Wiliam Llŷn's skill in the official metres is demonstrated in an *awdl* to an unnamed girl in which he uses each of the twenty-four metrical forms in turn. The purpose of such a demonstration can hardly have been other than the display of virtuosity or the achievement of success in a bardic examination, but it is remarkable that the *awdl* form and not the *cywydd* should be used for such a subject. Equally remarkable is the poet's approximation to a meaning in the more complicated forms of *gorchest y beirdd* and *cadwynfyr*. There is little else that is new in the poem, for what we get is a slightly differentiated and charming enough pattern employing the old motifs. Representative of the poem is the following couplet in the metre known as *Cywydd deuair hirion*.

Gwridog groywdon
gloyw teg liw ton.

Blushing, clear wave;
bright, fair, wave-coloured.

Nearly all Wiliam Llŷn's work was written in praise of patrons or to lament the death of some relative of a patron, but, in spite of his preoccupation with the long tradition behind him, sometimes simplicity of diction allied to the old magic of *cynghanedd* achieves a pleasing mellifluity, as in this final stanza (a *gwawdodyn*) of his *awdl* in praise of Owen ap Sion of Caer Gai.

Trafo kadw gair trafo koed a gwydd
Trafo twr a haul trafo tir rrydd
Trafo nant a ffant a ffydd—y Drindod
Na bom awr hebod vy hynod hydd. [WLl. p. 139]

Whilst a promise is kept, whilst trees grow,
whilst there's a tower and sun and free land,
whilst there's a brook and a valley and faith in the Trinity,
let's not be without you, my notable stag.

An *awdl* on the death of Huw ap Risiart ends with the memorable couplet:—

A fu a ddarfu a fydd—yn ddiau
Angau ac arfau ing ai gorfydd. [WLl. p. 222]

Who was, who has perished, who will be, without doubt
death and the weapons of agony master them.

In the *cywydd* on the death of his teacher Gruffydd Hiraethog he makes the dead bard say:—

Minnau nid oes im annedd
o'r byd ond fy hyd o'r bedd. [CLl. p. 103]

For me there is no dwelling
in this world but my length of grave.

Another *cywydd* on the death of a lady called Sian Mostyn begins in this telling way:—

Anwadal yw anwydau
y bywyd brwnt a'r byd brau;
od oeres y wlad araul
a gwlaw sydd lle gwelais haul. [CLl. p. 116]

Fickle are the qualities
of this foul life, this brittle world;
if the sunny land has grown cold
and there's rain where I saw sunshine.

It is thus, with simple, short, everyday words, which contrast pleasantly with the mouth-straining epithets of the older masters, that Wiliam Llŷn gets his best effects.

The *cywydd* on the death of Gruffydd Hiraethog is based on

one of Wiliam Llŷn's favourite devices, the dialogue, in this case between the poet and his dead master. In a *cywydd* on the death of the Lady Bagnol the conversation is between the poet and a swan which he asks to fly over to Ireland for news of the lady. The swan, however, appears not only to be better informed than the poet in the family history of this lady but more up to date in his news of her, for he tells the poet that she is dead and draws the date of her death into the metrical scheme of the poem. The versification of dates, chiefly into *englynion*, was a favourite exercise of sixteenth century poets.

Most interesting of all the death poems is one to the memory of another cleric-poet, Syr Owain ap Gwilym, curate of Tal-y-llyn, whom the poem shows to have been an old companion of Wiliam Llŷn. Once more the *cywydd* takes the form of a dialogue in which the poet first of all accuses his friend of having broken an appointment they had made to go together on a tour of patrons. He has called at Tal-y-llyn but failed to find Syr Owain. Has he gone off to the North or the South and what family is it that keeps him from his appointment. Syr Owain replies that death has caught him by the hands and fcct.

Y knawd gwynn megis knwd gwar
Y mae n duo mewn dayar
Y genau fu n klymu klod
Y mae n tewi mewn twod . . . [WLl. p. 133]

The white flesh, like a gentle harvest,
now blackens in the earth;
and the mouth that knotted praise
grows silent in the gravel.

The poet then at length laments the loss to society and to nature occasioned by his friend's death.

Wiliam Llŷn has also left us some very well turned *englynion.* A good epigram is his *englyn* to *Pipers*, which reveals a detestation of the bagpipes comparable to that of Dafydd ap Gwilym and Dafydd ap Edmwnd.

Pob llais a gerais, pob gwirion, pob hen,
pob heini gerddorion,
pob celfyddyd byd lle bon,
pob addysg ond pibyddion. [BE. p. 11]

Every voice I have loved, innocent and old,
all lively musicians,
all arts wherever they are in the world,
all knowledge save that of pipers.

Two of his *englynion* echo epigrams of the Alexandrian pessimist, Palladas, a late Greek writer of about the end of the fourth century A.D., whose work is to be found in the Greek Anthology.

Noeth bychan a gwan y genir dyn byw,
dyna beth a welir;
a gwan a noeth, gwn yn wir,
a diddim y diweddir. [BE. p. 49]

Naked, little and weak, the living man is born,
that is to be seen;
and weak and naked, I know,
he ends in nothingness.

Compare this with A. J. Butler's translation of the epigram of Palladas.

Naked I reached the world at birth;
Naked I pass beneath the earth:
Why toil I then, in vain distress,
Seeing the end is nakedness?[1]

Another *englyn* strongly reminiscent of another epigram by Palladas tells how life is whittled away by each day and night.

Oriau amserau y sydd diamau
yn mynd ymaith beunydd
einioes y dyn nos a dydd
yn ddiorfod a dderfydd. [CLl. p. 146]

[1] *Oxford Book of Greek Verse in Translation*, Higham and Bowra, no. 637.

Here is a translation by Sir Robert Furness of the epigram of which I am reminded by this *englyn.*

> From day to day we are born, as each night wanes,
> And nothing of our former life remains.
> The alien course of yesterday is run;
> What life we have this morning is begun.
> Say not, old man, that you are rich in age:
> Of years gone by you keep no heritage.[1]

Wiliam Llŷn produced some notable *englyn* sequences, to the Nightingale, to the Grave of the poet Rhys Goch, and, in ten *englynion*, a metrical version of the Ten Commandments.

We see in the work of this poet a determined clinging to the old traditions of the bardic craft, a melancholy perhaps induced by the changes taking place around him, and an occasional directness and simplicity of the kind that was already beginning to distinguish poetry in the free metres and which enabled him to make his most original contribution to Welsh poetry.

Sion Tudur of Llanelwy, who died in 1602, though like Wiliam Llŷn a pupil of Gruffydd Hiraethog, is much more clearly aware of decadence and change, and of the absurdity of the bardic convention of praising Elizabethan patrons as though they were the generous chieftains of the thirteenth century. He was a considerable master of the old technique of versification and, in quest of a living, he wrote many poems to patrons and elegies to their dead (one of the latter being in Wiliam Llŷn's favourite form of a dialogue with the dead man), but his sense of reality and his keen sense of humour impelled him to mockery of poets and of official poetry, and to the adopting of freer metres outside the classical twenty-four.

In a very interesting and well-turned *cywydd* of attack upon the poets, *Cywydd i Lhadd ar y Beirdd* (MS Mostyn 147), Sion Tudur shows his full awareness of the position of the poet in his

[1] Higham and Bowra, *op. cit.*, no. 641. The thought in the Greek and the Welsh poems belongs to no age or land and has been beautifully expressed in our own day by Aragon in *Au Biseau des Baisers.*

day. He begins by complaining that there is no longer any honour attached to the office of bard. He gives a list of the old themes of poetry, the praise of God, the flattery of chieftains, the honouring of courage and of learning. It is right that a poet should spend his praise on a soldier, he says,

herwydd nas gwnai ddyhirin
fentro ei oes o fewn trin.

because the worthless fellow
wouldn't risk his own life in a fray.

Then he speaks of the behaviour of the professional poets of his own day.

Ninnau'r beirdd a wnawn, rai bas,
o arddwyr wŷr o urddas,
a rhoi achau rhy wychion
a mawl i Siac mal i Sion;
pob chwit chwat yn lledrata
penillion prydyddion da,
a'i troi i iangwyr truan,
poen trwy freib, fal paentio'r fran;
asgell o bob edn wisgwych
ar fron a wna'r fran yn wych. [LlC IV. p. 31]

We poets make, o base ones,
of gardeners men of honour!
We grant too bright a lineage
and praise Jack as we do John;
each prattler borrowing
the verses of good poets,
fitting them to poor commoners,
labour of bribery, painting the crow.
A feather from each bright-plumed bird
on his breast makes the crow brilliant.[1]

The new gentry have enriched themselves through extortion and usury, and now require the poet's support in the bolstering up of their social position.

[1] A favourite image of that time; Cf. Greene's "upstart crow beautified in our feathers".

Cerd o law bardd a'i harddai,
llawer bardd a llawer bai;
dwyn achau ac arfau gant
oddiar rywiog i ddrewiant . . .

A chart from a poet's hand beautifies him,
many a poet and many a wrong;
to take lineage and a hundred arms
from the gentle for the stinking.

Ar frys arfau a roesom—
arfau'i daid a fu ryw dom;
os chwilir y gwir, nid gau,
serfyll fydd ei bais arfau.

We hastened to grant arms,
the arms of his dunghill forefathers;
if the truth be sought, not the false,
dubious will be his heraldry.

But Sion Tudur warns these upstart gentlemen that there is no security in their doubtfully won gentility.

Chwilen a hed uwch heolydd
ac yn y dom cyn y dydd.

The beetle flies over the roads
and is in the mire by daybreak.

He then begs the poets, for the honour of their craft, not to praise the unworthy any more, to leave the commoner as commoner, the crow as crow, distinguishing them from the true nobleman and the eagle. He ends with his own resolution.

Ni welir, er a wnelon,
mwy o aur siwrl yn mhwrs Sion.

No more shall be seen, do what they will,
a churl's gold in Sion's purse.

Sion Tudur was as deeply concerned as his contemporary William Shakespeare that "the age is grown so picked, that the toe of the peasant comes so near the heel of the courtier, he galls his kibe." (*Hamlet* V. i).

Sion Tudur's parody on the literature of praise, a *cywydd*, hardly goes beyond many of the exaggerated offerings to the worthy and unworthy which occur too frequently in the work of the fifteenth and sixteenth centuries. As often happens where a clever burlesque only slightly enhances the absurdity of the original model, this *cywydd* was taken to be a seriously meant poem of praise by at least one reader, for in one manuscript a later hand has annotated it with the remark, "This poem was written by a liar!" Here is a passage from it.

Bwrw maen o lwyth wyth ychen,
neu farr ar nas tynnai fenn;
mae'n dwyn mewn deau ynys
grym pump o gewri mhob bys;
od ai i'r nef mewn dur noeth
e ddoi drin ar dduw drannoeth.
Ni thynn fodfedd o'i gleddau
ond i ddwyn enaid neu ddau;
ni bu waith na bai o'i wain,
ni bydd gwyl heb ddwy gelain. [LlC IV, p. 25]

He throws a stone, load for eight oxen,
or a bar which a cart couldn't pull;
he carries, in the land's right hand,
five giants' might in every finger;
if he went to heaven in naked armour
God would have a battle to fight the next day.
He draws no inch of his sword
but to take a soul or two;
there's no battle without its unsheathing,
no festival without two corpses.

Once more it is to Shakespeare that one turns for similar mockery, for this is very close to Prince Hal's laughter at the expense of Harry Percy, "the Hotspur of the North, he that kills me some six or seven dozen of Scots at a breakfast, washes his hands, and says to his wife, fie upon this quiet life, I want work." (*Henry* IV, part I, II, v.)

Ridiculously far-flung success abroad is prophesied for this paragon of violence, such as was promised to Jasper Tudor by his enthusiasts a century before.

Rhyd creigiau mae d'olau di
ar oror yr Eryri;
muriau kestyll mawr kostfawr
drylliaist a llywiaist i'r llawr;
trwy'r mor er ynnill tir Maen,
trwy'r eilmor hyd tir Almaen;
odid tref hyd at Rufain
heb eich rhoi'n fwbach i'r rhain;
tarw a llew torr y lleuad
tir y Twrk fydd it tre tad;
ti elli, am ein twyllaw,
torri klust y Twrk i'w law.

Your light is along the rocks
of the skirts of Snowdon;
walls of great costly castles
you've split and brought to the ground;
through the seas to conquer Maine,[1]
through a second sea to Germany;
no town as far as Rome
but holds you as a bogey;
a bull and a lion to the crescent,
the Turk's land will be your home;
you'll be able, since he deceived us,
to cut the Turk's ear down to his hand.[2]

If Sion Tudur was hard upon his fellow poets and their patrons, he was equally capable of laughing at himself, and this he does in a *cywydd* which consists of a dialogue between the poet and his horse, one of our best pictures of the wandering professional poet. The bard is in a hurry to get beyond Carmarthen to Abergwili, where he looks confidently forward to rich entertainment at the palace of the Bishop of St. David's, but the horse disdains the flattering epithets intended to urge him on and protests against the treatment he has received.

[1] A Province in N. W. France.
[2] It is not certain but probable that this poem is by Sion Tudur.

Caut ti win ym min a medd,
cawn innau cnoi fy nannedd. [LlC III, p. 55]

You get wine and mead to your mouth,
whilst I just grind my teeth.

The horse insists on the truth of his appearance in reply to the flattery of the poet.

Wyf gwympus dripiadus drwm
a phendrist a chyffondrwm;
achwynaf fyth na chawn fwyd
na phedol, anhoff ydwyd;
os cul wyf—eisieu cael yd,
eisieu gwair a seguryd . . .
d'ysbardun, wyd was burdcw,
swmbwl oedd drwy f'ais a'm blew;
torraist ar gledr fy mhedrain
wyth glawdd byw a'th gledd heb wain.

I fall, I stumble, I'm heavy,
sad-headed and heavy-tailed;
I complain I get no food
nor shoes, you're so unloving.
If I'm narrow, it's lack of oats,
lack of hay and leisure . . .
Your spur, you're a tubby fellow,
has gone like a goad through my coat and ribs;
you've cut on my hind quarters
eight live trenches with your sheathless sword.

The horse begs to be taken back to Gwydir where, for a song, Sion Tudur will be given a young horse by the generous landowner.

In another *cywydd*, one of a series he exchanged with Sion Phylip in a poetic war for the patronage of the Bishop of St. Asaph (Llanelwy in Welsh), Sion Tudur describes how his rival, on his way home from Llanelwy, lost his way in a snowstorm on the mountain and fell into an icy stream. The buzzards took the bread and cheese from his satchel and his hat was carried off to make a nest.

Mwydodd ac oerodd ei geg,
mwydodd ei lyfr gramadeg;
a'i lyfr croen hyfr anhyfryd,
gradd y gwr a'i gerddi i gyd;
a phwrs dill o ledr ffris du,
kryw bach, wedi krybychu,
ac yn hwn ugain hannerch
o arwyddion mwynion merch. [LlC III, p. 77]

It soaked and chilled his mouth
and soaked his grammar book;
and his ugly goatskin book,
with his rank and all his poems;
and his woven purse, of black napped skin,
shrunk to a little sliver,
with its twenty addresses
of the sweet signs in a girl.

Sion Phylip's reply to this attack was equally forceful and fanciful.

Sion Tudur displays the expected proficiency in the *englyn* form and here again it is his comic vision which delights us most. In the rabclaisian tradition of Madog Dwygraig and Tudur Aled he writes two *englynion* on a slut who makes dirty butter in filthy vessels. Here is the first *englyn*.

Ffei garnast filiast fowlyd ei menyn
    bras enllyn briwsionllyd
yn frych ni wna fawr iechyd
fal gwer ag yn flew i gyd. [M. 131, p. 15]

Fie, arrant greyhound bitch whose butter's filthy,
    coarse, crumby fat,
spotted and hardly health-giving,
like candle-grease and full of hair.

Then there are several *englynion* to the Nightingale, so many of which occur amongst the works of the later mediæval poets that it becomes obvious that the bird was a set subject given to apprentice poets by their bardic teachers. One of these (M 131,

p. 25) embodies a striking contrast of harshness and softness, whereas another is one of the sweetest things in the language.

> Mesurol garol dan geyrydd—glasberth
> gogleisbwnc llawenydd,
> miwsig mwyn ymysg manwydd,
> eos hyd y nos tan wydd. [BE, p. 30]

> A measured carol under the green hedge towers,
> a tickling theme of joy,
> sweet music amidst the shrubs,
> a nightingale a night's length under trees.

The gentlemen of Wales, however, in spite of all this sustained skill and ready singing, must have begun to expect from the travelling poets they entertained something lighter and more immediately comprehensible than the old conventional matter and metre, something closer to what was being written in England at the end of the sixteenth century, and Sion Tudur was resilient enough to supply this demand copiously, the more readily since this gave further scope to his satiric spirit. In a parody of the popular prognostication poem which he calls *Prognosticasiwn Dr. Powel*, a poem of over three hundred lines, written mostly in a simple four-line stanza unhampered by the rules of *cynghanedd*, Sion Tudur gives a gently mocking picture of the world of men about him. He prophesies that women will be proud and eager for new clothes, and that young men will be lazy. The planets will exert a poisonous influence and there will be rain, fair weather, frost, snow, spring and summer.

> Vo vydd llawer gweinidoc
> yn govyn bwyd a chyfloc
> ac yn vwy i vryd wyl a gwaith
> ar i vol nac ar i waith . . .

> Mae'r byd yn dechre methu
> kas gan blant vynd i ddysgu
> ni chaiff y kwn mor kysgu
> lle bo'r merched yn karu. [CRhC, p. 189]

There'll be many a minister
will ask for food and wages
with his mind both feast and work day
less on his work than on his belly.

The world begins to fail,
children hate to go to school
and for dogs there'll be no sleeping
where the girls are courting.

We are told what food will be eaten in Lent.

A Duw mercher y lludw
vo roir y kig i gadw
ac eir i vwytta kennin
a physgod hallt a chregin,

pottes pys a hen ymenyn
gidac ambell benhwigyn
ar nawed dydd o Ebrill
vo vydd llawen kael brithill.

On Ash Wednesday
the meat will be put by;
leeks will now be eaten
and salt fish and shell fish,

pease pottage and old butter
and sometimes a herring;
on the ninth day of April
a trout will be good eating.

Most aspects of life are touched upon, the rapacity of physicians and landlords, and the flattery of the poets.

Dyma vlwyddyn i brydyddion
i ganu kelwydd ddigon
a theuru ar wr bonheddic
i vod yn gythrel ffyrnic
A doedyd arno ladd
bedwar igain yn ymladd
a thorri kant o gestyll
ai dryllio yn vil o gandryll.

This is a year for poets
to sing a pack of lies
and swear that a gentleman
is a ferocious devil,
and say that he has killed
four score in fighting,
destroyed a hundred castles
and shattered them to fragments.

Women are not forgotten for long and they provide the most constantly recurring matter for mockery, but at the same time the pleasure the poet takes in their company is reflected in one charming stanza.

A lle bytho llankesse
vo vydd kanu dyrie
ac ar ddiwedd pob dyri
hai lwlian hai lwli.

And where there are girls
there songs will be sung,
and at each song's end
hey lully, hey lully.

Sion Tudur's most amusing parody is of the so-called *Englynion y Misoedd*, or Stanzas of the Months, a series of stanzas of uncertain date of composition and often similar to the gnomic verse in the *Black Book of Carmarthen* and the *Red Book of Hergest*. These stanzas are frequently attributed to Aneirin but any possible connection with him has been attenuated by centuries of re-shaping. Their popularity in Sion Tudur's day is indicated by their inclusion in a large number of manuscripts of the sixteenth and seventeenth centuries, and everyone therefore would be able to enjoy or be shocked at Sion Tudur's fun at their expense. Here are two of his stanzas in parody, using, as in all twelve, the form and first line of the old verses and a similar blend of proverb with observation of life and nature, the difference being in the facetiousness and indecency of Sion Tudur.

Mis ebrill wybraidd gorthir
da fydd kwrw gwell fydd bir
pan ddel dail ar y koedtir
llawer morwyn a gnuchir
ar draws meingkiau os neidir
llawer crimoc a dorir
gwell fydd morwyn ystlysir
no rryw hen wrach gedorir
knawd gwenith lle bo kleidir
gwaetha dyn yw dyn kowir. [CRhC, pp. 247–8]

Month of April, misty the uplands,
ale will be good, beer better;
when the leaves come to the woodlands
many a maid will be enjoyed.
If benches are jumped over
many a shin will be destroyed.
Better a long-flanked girl for a lover
than an ancient hag all hairy.
Wheat will grow where there are clay lands;
of the accurate man be chary.

More of the pleasures of life are incorporated into his July parody.

Mis gorffenaf hyglyd gwair
odid morwyn yn ddiwair
knawd tanllwyth lle bo kludair
gwych yw eiste mewn kadair
a chael telyn rawn gowair
a rroi'r march mewn llyffethair
a thwymnor traed ar esgair
a chanu kowydd deuair
a godart ar dy gyfair
a gweddio duw a mair.

Month of July, hay's fit to carry
and the girl who's chaste is rare;
you get a blaze from a heaped fire;
what a fine thing to sit in a chair
with a tunéd harp of hair!

On your horse a fetter put;
on a leg you'll warm your foot.
Sing a song in a short measure
with a tankard for your pleasure
and a prayer to God and Mary.[1]

Another very interesting poem in a free metre is *Hanes y Trwstan, The Story of the Unlucky One* (CRhC. pp. 410–21), a narrative of over five hundred lines in short, jerky couplets, which gives the life history of a prodigal. As a boy he refuses a good education and the chance of entering the church, becomes a lackey, inherits land when his parents die and goes up to Court, where he dissipates his inheritance in four years of rich living. At this point English terms enter in some profusion. Then follow months of poverty in London, a return to Wales and farming at which he is unsuccessful and is cheated and robbed to such a degree that he ends as a beggar. The poet seems to have felt some shame at abandoning the twenty-four metres in this poem, for the version in MS Peniarth 65 ends thus:—

Nyd yw hyn onid ffoledd
heb fesyr achanghanedd.

This is only nonsense
without measure or *cynghanedd*.

Sion Tudur was an accurate observer of life, fully aware of what was going on about him in society, respectful of the old traditions yet adventurous enough to follow new ways. In a literature not rich in social satire or narrative verse he assumes a perhaps exaggerated stature.

Consideration of the work of two more of Gruffydd Hiraethog's accomplished pupils, Wiliam Cynwal and Simwnt Fychan, as well as that of Sion Tudur's sturdy rival, Sion Phylip, must be set aside to allow space for the work of some representatives of a growing body of amateur practitioners in

[1] For a treatment of *Englynion y Misoedd* v. CRhC, 244–5 and Jackson. EWGP Introd.

verse, though reference will later be made to Simwnt Fychan's book on the practice of poetry. It was, of course, no new thing for chieftains and noblemen to master the art of poetry for their own pleasure, as Owain Cyfeiliog and Hywel ap Owain Gwynedd had done in the twelfth century, but from the beginning of the sixteenth century the number of occasional and non-professional poets increases in proportion and in relation to the decline in the status of the professional poet.

With the breaking down of the bardic categories came a greater slackness in the choice of pupils and in the handing on of the poets' lore, and when books on the art of poetry came to be published a teacher might no longer be thought necessary, although these early books are by no means complete compendia of the bardic teaching. More people certainly wrote verse and we have on record work in the old metres from such varied hands as those of young women, parsons, soldiers and sailors.

Cynrig Hanmer, of a family long associated with Welsh literature, whilst on one of Henry VIII's expeditions to France, turns a neat *englyn* to express his nostalgia.

Ffarwel i Dwrne ffairwych—a Therwyn
ni tharia mwy wrthych
mi af adre i edrych
am wenn a edewais en wych.[1]

Farewell to Tournai of the splendid fair, Therouanne
no more I'll tarry;
I'm going home to find
a bright girl I left behind.

Nor were girls, it seems, less able to express their feelings in verse for in the Mostyn Manuscript 131 there is attributed to three unnamed young ladies of Denbighshire a series of charming *englynion* addressed collectively to the men they loved. Here are a few of these stanzas.

[1] MS Mostyn 131, p. 103. Tournai and Therouanne are associated in Elis Gruffydd's MS as places old campaigners talked about in 1549, v. M. B. Davies, Fuad I Univ. Bull. vol. XII, p. 75.

Vy nydd vy newydd fy nos—vy meddwl
vy madde rwyt agos
a minne sydd war yn daros
ag od ei yn elyn ym, dos.

Pob mwynder ofer afiaith—pob meddwl
pob moddol gydymaith
a phob peth yn wir ond hiraeth
yn gynnar iawn oddi genny yraeth.

Mae afon a bronn a brig—y koedydd
yn kadw tair ewig
a heddiw ni wyr bonheddig
nai kael na phrofi moi kig.

Nid a chwn y mae i chwi—ei hela
nid hwylus mo reini
gore yt fynghar bwyntmannu
mewn koed heb illwng un ki. [M 131, p. 9]

My day, my news, my night, my mind,
my forgiveness, you're near me,
and I am waiting meekly;
go if you'd be my enemy.

All empty joy, all jollity, all thought,
all mannerly meeting,
everything indeed but longing
has quickly gone away from me.

There's a river, a hillside and boughs of trees
that hide three hinds;
today no hunter finds
them or makes proof of their flesh.

Not with dogs, should you decide to hunt them,
that won't be luckiest;
better for you, my love, to tryst
under trees with your dogs tied.

Another poetess, this time a witty satirist, was Alis, daughter of Gruffydd ap Ieuan of the Vale of Clwyd, who wrote towards the end of the sixteenth century. Parts of her *cywydd* on the Drunkard have been printed from MS Mostyn 147 in *Llên Cymru* III, p. 59, and further testimony to the quickness of her wit as well as to her mastery of *cynghanedd* is afforded by a rather improper extempore *englyn* composed in collaboration with her father, who was himself a poet as well as a landowner. Gruffydd ap Ieuan's miller had come into the hall and had spread his legs to warm over the fire. The father saw his daughter laughing and asked her in the first two lines (the *paladr* or shaft) of an *englyn* why she was laughing at his miller. Alis completed the *englyn* by explaining her laughter frankly enough in two more lines (the *esgyll* or wings of the *englyn*) (Mostyn 131, p. 98).

Another interesting amateur excursion into the classical metres was that of William Midleton of Llansannan, who was educated at Oxford. Midleton became a captain in Queen Elizabeth's fleet and distinguished himself in the fighting against the Spaniards in the West Indies in 1591. He is possibly, though not certainly, the Midleton who commanded the famous pinnace sent by Clifford to observe the Spanish preparations and to warn Howard, when Grenville, in spite of Midleton's entreaties, remained to fight in the *Revenge*. In his *Report* Raleigh spoke of this Midleton as "a verie good sailer."

Midleton's translations of the Psalms of David[1], though ably done, were not suitable for congregational singing, and translations by Edmwnd Prys and others into the freer metres became more popular; for Midleton did them, as Thomas Salesbury says in his presentation of the book to the reader, "in all sorts of meeters that ever were used in the Brytish tongue." Above each translation he gives the name of each metre he uses, and it soon becomes clear that his favourites are the *englyn unodl union* and the *cywydd deuair hirion*. Here are examples of his renderings. Reference to the *Psalms of David* will provide an English equivalent.

[1] These translations were published by Thomas Salesbury in quarto form in London, 1603, with the title: *Psalmæ y Brenhinol Brophwyd Dafydh, gwedi i cynghaneddu mewn mesurau cymreig*. Midleton himself notes that they were completed in the West Indies in January 1595, "apud Scutum insulam occidentalium Indorum."

Psalm CXLIX, englyn unodl union

Cenwch i'r Arglwydd caniad o newydd
Mewn awel o gariad
Bid i fawl rheidiawl yn rhad
Ymysg y saint gymysgiad.

Psalm CXLV, cywydd deuair hirion

Moliannaf medhaf a'm min
Mawr enwog dhuw fy mrenin:
A bendithiaf mwyaf mawl
Gwiwdhuw dy enw tragwyddhawl.

A skilful *awdl* on the death of his "lady mistress" the Countess of Pembroke[1], follows the conventional lines of praise, except that the lady is compared not to Non but to Lucrece, Dido and Claudia, thus reflecting the new interests of the age, though, since the lady died in 1575, the poem is likely to have been written long before Shakespeare, Marlowe and the translators of Catullus popularised the three classical ladies mentioned. Another interesting feature of this poem is the description of the coats of arms prepared for the Countess' funeral, with English heraldic terms woven into the alliterative system.

Yet another notable sailor poet was Captain Tomas Prys, a friend of William Midleton. He was a rich landowner in North Wales whose adventurous spirit impelled him to a life of action as a soldier and a sailor. He was at Tilbury in 1588, when Elizabeth inspected her troops and he fought in Ireland, Scotland, France and Spain. Later, with friends and relatives, he took to buccaneering and had to be warned by the Queen's government. With Captain Midleton and a certain Captain Koet, Prys is said to have been the first to smoke tobacco in a London street and he told the story in a poem. References to the smoking, or sucking of tobacco occur in several of his poems

[1] MS Gwyneddon 3, pp. 169–71.
This lady was not the famous Mary Herbert, Sir Philip Sidney's sister, third wife of the Earl, but Catherine, daughter of the Earl of Shrewsbury, second wife of the Earl of Pembroke. She died childless in 1575. Queen Elizabeth was much attached to her and visited her twice at Baynard's Castle during her fatal illness. This Earl of Pembroke was one of the focal points in the meeting of English and Welsh culture during Elizabeth's reign.

and his picture of the wild life of Welsh gentlemen in London is detailed and lively. He himself shows a gloomy familiarity with the prisons of London, which he lists with skilful *cynghanedd*.

One of the most successful of Elizabethan sea pieces is Tomas Prys' account of his failure to take a prize at sea. The conversation in this poem, the terms of command and the cries of despair are all in English, not only because English was the language of the ship, but because Prys took pleasure in the exercise of fitting these English phrases into his alliterative scheme. Here are the opening lines, followed by a passage in which the battle turns against him.

Dylynais diwael enyd
y dwr i Sbaen ar draws byd
tybio ond mudo ir mor
y trowswn wrth bob trysor . . .
ffeight ffor stor and lef sorow
ffear not shiwt the weild ffeir now
lay her a bwrd er dwrdiaw
now enter drwy fenter draw
Ag wrth ymladd gwarth amlwg
wee lost owr men ar lestr a mwg
gif bak lest all be taken
oes modd ffor to saf sym men
we twk wnffortunat day
wee ffeynd wee meynd this mynday
krio iownlef kur anlwk
o lord hear is to hard lwk
ffowk hari labi libin
is drownd pan oedd wres y drin
Brown Robin awstin withal
is dead and so is dwdal
wenfford Rowland and winffild
Wiliam and Kobam is kild . . . [M 122, p. 289]

I followed, o splendid season,
the water over the world to Spain,
thinking that taking to the sea
I should come by all treasure . . .

"Fight for store and leave sorrow,
fear not, shoot the wildfire now.
Lay her aboard!" In all the din;
"Now venture; enter yonder in."
And in fighting, open discredit,
we lost our men in the ship's smoke.
"Give back lest all be taken.
Is there a means to save some men?"
We took an unlucky day,
we find we mind this Monday;
loudly crying luck's onslaught,
"O Lord, this is too dearly bought!
Foulk Harry, gawky stripling,
is drowned in the battle's din;
Brown Robin Austin withal
is dead and so is Duddal;
Wenford, Rowland and Winfield,
William and Cobham are killed."

Although he was away a good deal in London and at sea, Prys did not neglect his life in Wales, for he built himself a house on Bardsey Island out of the ruins of a monastery, a wild, westward facing place where the wind carried sea spray to his mouth every day.

A life of such varied experiences produced poetry of great variety, for Tomas Prys' scope is wide and he is always fresh and interesting. In a *cywydd* on the death of a woman he loved he shows his acquaintance with the old conventions of such writing, with, for instance similar poems by Llywelyn Goch and Dafydd Nanmor, but there is nothing stale or hackneyed in his late handling of the usual material.

Od yw f'anwylyd ifanc
yn y bedd o dan y banc,
Duw na bawn, kawn le kynnwys,
dan ei phen yn dwyn ei phwys.
Os yw ei grudd is y gro
yn y tir yma'n tario,
och na bawn, ni chawn boeni,
ar frys wrth ei hystlys hi.

O rhoed Gwen mewn gweryd gudd
a derw ynghylch ei deurudd,
gofid na bawn yn gyfion
yn y pwll wrth wyneb hon;
od aeth mewn man a llannerch
y graean mân ar groen merch,
Duw'n bridd na bawn dan y bryn
yn ei harch fain ei herchwyn. [LlC IV, p. 13]

If my youthful darling
is in the grave under the hill,
God! that I might in that snug place
support the weight of her head.
If her cheek beneath the gravel
now lingers in the ground,
o that I were, no pain for me,
rapidly at her side!
If she's been put in the hidden grave
with oak about her cheeks,
o grief, that I'm not equally
face to face with her in that pit.
If in a certain clearing
there's fine grit on a girl's skin,
God! that I were earth under the hill,
her guard in her narrow coffin.

In his old age Tomas Prys wrote a *cywydd* of advice to his son Sion into which he packed his experience and knowledge of London, the court, government officials, lawyers and attorneys, drovers, taverns, soldiers and girls.

Gwylia swyddog, ail Suddas,
a berrau ci a bair cas;
ni all swyddog, fradog frest,
fadyn wên, fod yn onest;
na chred ith frawd llwyrgnawd llog
os yw heddyw yn swyddog. [LlC IV, p. 43]

Beware the official, second Judas,
his dog's shanks and his evil ways.
No official, treacherous breast,
with his foxy smile can be honest.
Don't trust your blood brother with a loan
if today he's an official.

He warns his son not to go to law unless he is forced to, for attorneys, the ravens of grey London, shear away castles and woodlands. He should avoid fickle, low loves but find a sweet-hearted bed-fellow. If he must trust a man, let him trust a soldier, and let him be generous to brave men.

Captain Tomas Prys brought a breezy, independent spirit to conventions that were stiffening with inertia and, since he wrote for his own pleasure and for that of his friends, he could afford to take liberties with the established rules which a professional poet, however much in touch he might be with the new trends of his age, might yet be unwilling to risk.[1]

Even when country parsons gave up touring the great houses in the manner of wandering poets, the Anglican Church continued to harbour poets until the muse seemed to depart from it with the Methodist revival, so that today the rhyming parson is a great rarity, whilst Baptist, Independent and Methodist versifiers are as frequent as poachers in the country-side.

One of these clerical poets, Sir David Johns, of Llanfair Dyffryn Clwyd, a conventional moralist in his verse, was one of the antiquarians who preserved much older poetry from disappearance by their industrious copying. Many possessors of manuscripts and those with access to old texts must have taken to heart William Salesbury's admonition in his introduction to the printing of Gruffydd Hiraethog's proverbs, "*I ba beth y gedwch ich llyfreu mewn coggleu, a phryfedu mewn ciste, – darguddio rac gweled o neb, a nid chwychwy ech hunain?*" "Why do you leave your books in corners and to get worm-eaten in chests, hiding them from the sight of everyone except yourselves?"

Another parson, Sir Rhys Cadwaladr of Llanfairfechan, writing about the middle of the seventeenth century, freely translated Horace, Petronius and Seneca into the *cywydd* form with considerable success, versions which stand out in a literature lacking in good translations and reluctant to accept

[1] For a sympathetic appreciation of the character and work of Prys v. Sir Idris Bell, DWP, pp. 104–5.

foreign influence. Three of these translations are printed in *Llên Cymru*, volume III.

Reference has already been made to some books on the art of poetry. Here is a list of such works up to the end of the sixteenth century, based on the list in Sir John Morris-Jones' *Cerdd Dafod.*

1. *Cerddwriaeth Cerdd Dafawd.* This is said to have been written by Einion Offeiriad (Einion the Priest) during the first half of the fourteenth century and enlarged by Dafydd Ddu Athro. There are versions of this work in the late fourteenth century *Red Book of Hergest* and other manuscripts.
2. *Cyfrinach Beirdd Ynys Prydain.* (The Secret of the Bards of the Island of Britain.) This is by the poet Gutyn Owain, and the Llanstephan 28 manuscript version is in his own hand, 1455.
2. *Pump Llyfr Cerddwriaeth.* (The Five Books of Minstrelsy.) This work by the poet Simwnt Fychan is the best treatment of *cynghanedd* within our period and was written some time before 1575. The original manuscript belongs to Jesus College, Oxford, which also owns the *Red Book of Hergest.*
4. *Cambrobrytannicæ Cymræcæve Linguæ Institutones et Rudimenta . . .* This Latin work (intended therefore for European study) is by Sion Dafydd Rhys, who had already published at Siena books on the Latin and Italian languages, and was printed in London in 1592. It deals incidentally with Welsh prosody, but this scholar was a better grammarian than a poet and his examples in verse are not always accurately chosen.
5. *Bardhoniaeth neu brydydhiaeth, y llyfr cyntaf, trwy fyfyrdawd,* Capten William Midleton, London, 1593. This appears to be a synopsis of the metrical section of the previous book, but it is fairly certain that Sion Dafydd Rhys, even though his book was printed first, owed a great deal to William Midleton.

Since pre-Roman times it had been contrary to the practice of the master poets of Britain to put the secrets of their craft into writing, but now once the bardic categories began to fall to pieces there were occasional practitioners who were prepared to record their knowledge in this way. Not enough of them, however, were willing to do this and Sion Dafydd Rhys, in his Welsh preface to the *Grammar*, roundly swinges them for their selfishness and secretiveness, which, he says, had endangered the continuity of the craft of versification. In a spirited passage he foresees how their carefully guarded manuscripts, after their death, will fall into the hands of destructive children, or of shop dames to wrap up their groceries, or into the hands of tailors to be cut up for patterns. "*A phann fei meirw y Prydyddion hynny, yna yr aei y tegwch hynny igyd i'r pridd, ynn y lle ny bei byth sôn am dano.*" "And when these poets die, then this beauty will all go into the earth, where it will never be heard of."

It will have been noticed that three of the books listed above date from the latter half of the sixteenth century, the period when grammar, orthography, meanings and style for the first time in Wales became matters for serious consideration. The discussion of these problems arose mainly out of the necessities of prose, not of verse, for whilst verse had its long tradition and established practices, prose had, since the loss of Welsh independence, been neglected in so far as written records went. Elis Gruffydd's vigorous and racy account of his wartime experiences on the continent[1] reminds us forcibly of what has been lost with the letters and records that have disappeared for ever. When the new Protestant Church felt the need for propaganda in Wales and when the time came for the Bible to be translated into Welsh, prose style became the passionate concern of such men as William Salesbury, Morus Kyffin, Gruffydd Robert and William Morgan, and experiments and enquiries were made comparable to those of Lyly, Elyot, Wilson and others in England.

[1] MS Mostyn 158. This has never been printed but translations of considerable parts of it by Professor M. Bryn Davies have appeared in the Faculty of Arts Bulletin, Fuad I University Cairo.

Apart from Simwnt Fychan's work it is doubtful whether any one of the treatises on poetry would be of much use to an aspirant poet without the personal tutelage of a master, any more than the better books of today can take the place of a university education. Some notion of the methods employed by master poets in their instruction of the apprentice writer may be formed from the *Areithiau*, exercises in prose which have been preserved in manuscripts. Mr. Gwenallt Jones, in his excellent book on this subject, relates the word *araith* to the old rhetorical term *oratio* and to a tradition which goes back to the Roman occupation of Britain. The purpose of the study of this branch of rhetoric in Welsh was the extension of vocabulary, the decoration of style and practice in *dyfaliad* or comparison-making. Aristotle had noted as a conspicuous device of rhetoric the formation of compound words, and it is clear that the invention and heaping together of such words was recommended to the disciple in the composition of his *araith* or *declamatio*. Such a teaching tended to divorce language from its main purposes and to give words an absolute value, with a beauty, strength, ugliness of their own without reference to exact requirements of communication, to develop art for art's sake. The interest of these *areithiau* as prose works does not concern us here.

The patriotic scholars whose treatises have been referred to believed that the Welsh language was bound up with the bardic tradition, that both language and tradition were dying at the end of the sixteenth century, and that to assure continuity in the one was to preserve the other. Happily, there was no justification for this gloomy view, for lively spirits were already turning away from the fossilizing old traditions not to the culture and language of England but to freer ways of expression in forms and idiom closer to the everyday life of the common people of Wales.

The twenty-four measures continued to be studied and employed, refreshed by revivals in the eighteenth, nineteenth and present centuries. The competition for the chair at this year's eisteddfod, Llanrwst 1951, requires a poem of not more than three hundred lines in full *cynghanedd* employing any number of Dafydd ap Edmwnd's measures, including at least one *awdl* measure, and the winner may well be a shepherd, a postman, a preacher or a journalist.

Chapter VIII

THE SIXTEENTH CENTURY; POETRY IN THE FREE METRES

★

Opinions differ whether the *clerwyr*, associated etymologically if not otherwise with the continental *clerici vagantes*, were the third or minstrel order of bards (the other two being the *pencerdd* and *bardd teulu* or chief poet and house poet), or whether *y glêr* was a term applied generally to all professional poets. Loose forms of some of the official metres, the *rhupunt* and *cywydd deuair fyrion*, are said to have been used by the minstrels, and the lowest order of bards must have continued from the fourteenth century onwards to sing in the freer modes which were permissible before the full evolution of *cynghanedd* in that century. The old *awdl-gywydd* measure, for instance, was deposed by the *cywydd deuair hirion*, whilst the *englyn cyrch* passed into popular poetry as the *mesur triban*.

It was in these freer measures that the songs sung by the whole nation had been written, the lullabies, words to dance music, game songs, love songs and holiday songs. The tradition is as old as the lovely, simple *Pais Dinogad* song which occurs in the *Book of Aneirin*, for lyrics of this sort are as old as poetry, even though in Welsh they were rarely recorded before the sixteenth century. Some Welsh brothers to Autolycus must have sold or taught girls the songs they are said to have been fond of singing in the sixteenth century. Sion Tudur, in the stanzas translated in chapter VII, says that wherever girls gather then songs are sung, with refrains such as *hai lwli hai lwlian*, and John Jones, Gelli Lyfdy, writes in the first decade of the seventeenth century that years before, during a feast in Wales, he heard men sing *cywyddau* and *awdlau* whilst girls sang songs and carols (*karole a dyrie*).[1]

The harp, the horn and the *crwth* (the crowd or early fiddle had in all probability been long established in Wales by the tenth century, but were not used apart from the singing o chanting voice until the twelfth century. Some indication o how these instruments were used as accompaniment to the voice may be gathered from the traditional manner of singing *penillion* or stanzas to harp music, which is still practised today The harpist plays a known air and the singer breaks in with hi stanza in a kind of descant, not even following the rhythm o the music but meeting it occasionally, and (this is essential ending his words with the last note of the melody. There are indications that the earliest harp music, played by the reciting poet himself, provided a simple, rhythmical background o chords whilst he chanted his verse. The banjo, guitar and ukulele are used much in the same way by singers of folk songs today. As the poet ceased to accompany himself, or as music came to be played without words the background music became more tuneful and independent, and airs were evolved which are known today as folk tunes. Words written to fit these tunes exactly, without complicated descanting, were alone within the scope of ordinary, untrained singers, and they became the literature of the common people, preserved in what we call *hên benillion*. By the eighteenth century, therefore, many folk tunes could either be sung with the simple, usually four-line stanzas which fitted them, or could be used as background music for the descanting of the more complicated *cywydd* and *englyn* sequences.

Church music too provided forms of melody which required words in the free measures. The English condut (Latin *conductus*), a motet or processional song sung as the priest went up to the altar, appeared in the Middle Ages in Welsh as the *cwndid*, and the *coundutes of kryst-masse* of *Syr Gawayne and the*

[1] Ir ystalm pan oeddem i yn gwilio ynghapel Mair o Bylltyn ir oedd gwyr wrth gerdd yn kanu kywydde ac odle a merched yn kanu karole a dyrie . . . quoted from CRhC, p. xvii.

Grene Knight very naturally became carols.[1] The blatantly pre-Christian nature of the Mari Lwyd ritual, with its British totemic horse, suggests that carols of some sort were much older than this and were associated rather with the mid-winter feast that preceded Christmas and became merged in it, just as the stone circle of Ysbyty Cynfyn became the churchyard wall.

But whilst there was thus already in Wales an ancient tradition of song in simple stanza measures, there is an indubitable English influence on writing in the free measures to be observed in the sixteenth century. It has been said that, in the lyrical outpouring of Tudor England, the musicians led the way by composing music that required words to match, thereby imposing upon the poets regular and varied forms and the need for mellifluity in diction. The same airs which charmed such lovely words from Shakespeare and Peele may equally well have evoked lyrics from Welshmen, and the Stationers' Registers for 1587 record the publication of a broadsheet, of which unfortunately no copy is known, entitled *A Sonett or a synners solace made by Hughe Gryffythe prisoner, both in Welche and Englishe.* In support of the claim of the English origin of some Welsh lyrical forms it has been pointed out that many of the airs popular in Wales from the sixteenth to the eighteenth century have English names like *Aboute the Banck of Elicon*, *Adew my pretie pussie*, *Heartes Ease*, *Sweet Richard.*[2] The objection has also been made that many of these English-named songs do not seem to be known in England, so that the sixteenth century Welsh minstrels may well have imposed on their public by giving the fashionable English names to what were in fact Welsh airs or airs of their own composition, just as pseudo negro blues or South American rumbas may today be written in London or Paris.

This whole matter is extremely complex, but there is no doubt that English example at least, if not wholesale borrowing

[1] Most of the religious *cwndidau* seem to have come from Glamorgan, the only remaining home of the Mari Lwyd procession.

[2] v. BBCS, vol. VIII, and Richard Morris' list of the songs he can play, *Llawysgrif Richard Morris o Gerddi*, ed. T. H. Parry-Williams, Welsh University Press, 1931, pp. 80–81.

of English tunes, gave great encouragement to writers to feel less ashamed of writing and recording verse outside the twenty-four official metres. One of the main effects of the Renaissance and of the impact of English culture on Wales in the sixteenth century was to make poetry in the free measures more respectable and more popular amongst educated people. It is significant that Gruffydd Robert, who, in his Welsh grammar published in Milan in 1567, makes the first recorded use of the term *mesurau rhyddion* (free measures), should also point out to his more insular compatriots that these are the sort of measures that the Italians use.

It does not surprise us, therefore, that educated amateur writers, with such reports coming from Italy, or having, like Cynrig Hanmer, been to France, having, too, the example of Skelton, Wyatt and Surrey before them in the Tudor court, should the more boldly have composed and recorded verse within the freer traditions of their own culture as well as in forms which are of foreign origin. Most of the verse we have in the free metres, that is the recorded verse, is obviously by educated writers, as is shown by the absence of any considerable dialectal difference between work done in the North and in the South. The more popular songs connected with childhood, play and work were more rarely recorded and must have shown a closer linking to regional ways of speech.

One result of this breakaway from the strict discipline of bardic teaching was a confusion in terms applied to the new versification. As Professor Tom Parry says, a *toddaid* or an *englyn unodl union* could mean only one thing, whereas a lyric might now be called *araith*, *baled*, *carol*, *dyriau*, *penillion* or even *awdl* without making much apparent difference. A similar confusion is to be observed in the Elizabethan English use of the term *sonnet* which took some time to settle down to the fourteen ten-syllable lines.

Satire, always considered in Wales as inferior material for poetry, found healthy new ground in the free measures of the sixteenth century and one of the earliest and most interesting of such experiments is a long and delightful poem called *Araith ddichan ir Gwragedd*, a Satire on Women, printed in *Canu Rhydd Cynnar*. The two hundred and sixty three lines of this poem are divided into sections of varying length, each section with one rhyme. This form is, of course, as old as the *Gododdin*, but the rhythm of the lines and the poet's fondness for abstract nouns and for adjectives as rhyming words remind me very strongly of the English poet Skelton, and I am tempted to dub the poem an essay by an anonymous author in Welsh Skeltonics. The earliest manuscript in which it is found is thought to date from about 1550 and, since Skelton was writing this sort of verse during the early decades of the century, this poem was probably composed during the second quarter of the sixteenth century, but long enough before 1550 for it to have become sufficiently esteemed to include in a manuscript collection of verse. The poem begins thus:—

Rryw i wraig o naturiaeth
fod yn rrwym i wassaniaeth
yn falch yn greulon odiaeth
ni wyr resswm na chyfraeth
na rrol nag iawn lywodraeth
gwneuthyr bost oi chenysgaeth
eskluso pob ffordd berffaith
a dilyn llwybrau diffaeth.

Ni wna ddim yn ei amser
ni cheidw gymhedrolder
ond gorwedd pan ei llocher
a neidio pann gynhyrfer
naws tan gwnias pan lidier
naws yr ia pan dristaer
ni wna ddim pann ddamuner
ond gwrando geirie over.

Woman is by aptitude
destined to servitude;
extremely cruel and proud,
she's by no reason bowed,
by law nor governance cowed;
of her dowry boastful,
of each good way neglectful,
of idle paths she's heedful.

She'll do nothing in its day,
observes no middle way;
she lies down if she's stroked
and leaps up if provoked;
a white hot flame in ferment,
like ice in disappointment;
she'll do no wanted thing,
she's storm without ending.

All the dangerous tricks and qualities of universal woman are listed in this gay doggerel (or should one employ Keats' pun, bitcherel?), and then, to support his case, the poet turns to antiquity for specimens of monstrosity in feminine behaviour, giving us lively descriptions of the crimes and immodesties of Tarpeia, Medea, Helen, Myrrha, Pasiphae and half a dozen more including Eve, the worst wife that ever was. A great point he makes is that no woman has ever yet returned permanently from the underworld, and he refers to Eurydice and Proserpina, whilst Aeneas, Orpheus, Hercules, Theseus, the Dioscuri and Christ have all achieved this return.

Towards the end of the poem the anonymous author works up to a fine rhetorical frenzy.

Yr hain yw yr anghenfiloedd
a pheryglon y moroedd
y sydd yn difa yr bobloedd
nid oes na mann na lleoedd
na themlau na mynwennoedd
na gwledydd nag ynyssoedd
na meysydd na mynyddoedd
na mor na man ar diroedd
na bu ddrwg gwraig yn gyhoedd.

For they are the sea monsters,
they are the deep sea dangers,
the ubiquitous destroyers;
for there's no town or city,
temple or cemetery,
no island and no country,
no meadow or mountain side,
no land or ocean wide
but there bad girls abide.[1] [CRhC pp. 108–19]

[1] For translation at length see my *Rent that's Due to Love*, Poetry London, 1950.

The *Satire on Women* was written in a mood common to Western Europe and related to *Les Quinze Joyes de Mariage* and *The Schole House of Women*, but another vituperative poem, on the Woods of Glyn Cynon, written later in the century, is more specific and local, for it attacks the English who have cut down the trees for their ironworks. These woods have been the haunt of birds, red deer, lovers and fugitives, and the poet laments on their behalf the passing of the trees. The ordinary citizen will suffer too, for no more will the Vale of Cynon provide wood for the building of bridges, houses and churches. Here are a few of the thirteen stanzas of this lively poem.

O bay gwr ar drafael dro
   ag arno ffo rhag estron
fo gae gen eos lettu iroed
   yn fforest koed glyn kynon

llawer bedwen glas i chlog
   ynghrog i bytho r sayson
sydd yn danllwyth mawr o dan
   gen wyr yr hayarn duon . . .

myna i wnythyr arnyn gwest
   o adar onest ddigon
ar ddyllyan dan i nod
   a fyna i fod yn hangmon

ag o daw gofyn pwy a naeth
   hyn o araeth greylon
dyn a fy gynt yn kadw oed
   dan fforest koed glyn kynon. [CRhC pp. 399–401]

If a man in sudden plight
   took to flight from foe,
for guest-house to the nightingale
   in Cynon Vale he'd go.

Many a birchtree green of cloak
   (I'd like to choke the Saxon!)
is now a flaming heap of fire
   where ironworkers blacken . . .

I'd like to call on them a quest
  of every honest bird,
where the owl, worthiest in the wood,
  as hangman would be heard.

If there's a question who rehearsed
  in verse this bitter tale,
it's one who many a tryst has kept
  in the depth of Cynon Vale.

Characteristic of these "carols" of the sixteenth century are the question and the veiled reference to the author in the final stanza. Equally characteristic is the metre, which may be here examined in some detail. For those unprepared to spell through the Welsh I have attempted to reproduce the form as exactly as possible without serious injury to the meaning and it will be observed that the first and third lines rhyme with words in the middle of the second and fourth lines. The second and fourth lines have an end rhyme which is common to all the stanzas of the poem, but this last feature I have failed to achieve in the English version. There are four stresses in the first and third lines and three in the second and fourth. With this stanza form in mind let us consider an old verse form in use before the full evolution of *cynghanedd* in the fourteenth century, the form known as the *awdl-gywydd*. Here is a specimen of this measure given by Einion Offeiriad in the fourteenth century.

O gwrthody, liw ewyn,
Was di felyn gudynneu
Yn diwladaidd da i len
A'i awen yn i lyfreu
Cael it filein aradrgaeth
Yn waethwaeth i gyneddfeu . . . [CD p. 327]

It will be seen that this is exactly the metre of the *Glyn Cynon* poem. All that was necessary was to separate two couplets to form a *pennill* or stanza of four lines. The *awdl-gywydd* measure was kept as one of the official twenty-four, but its use by the highest grades of bard required full *cynghanedd*, whereas there can be no doubt that it continued to be used by poets of a lower order even though their work was not thought worthy of recording. One of the most popular of the new free verse forms of the sixteenth century is therefore indubitably traceable to an old Welsh measure.[1]

Another charming carol in this same metre is one to the holly tree, again more suggestive of paganism than Christianity, which stresses its evergreen superiority to other trees.

Pan ddel rhew ac eira mawr
  i blagio llawr y vedwen
kewch i weled ymhob plas
  vraint ir las Gelynen. [CRhC. p. 402]

When come frost and a great snow
  to plague below the birchtree
every mansion will confer
  honour on the green holly.

Late in this same century the free metres were used to teach the Lord's Prayer, the Ten Commandments and the Credo to the common people of Wales, as part of the movement which produced translations and prose works of religious education, whilst Richard White, the Catholic matryr, used them to attack the Protestant church. A *cwndid*, obviously written soon after 1553, rejoices in the coming of the Catholic Queen Mary to the throne of England.

Rhoddi dy Fam Wyry fry
  Yn ben llu gweryddon;
Mari ein hynys ninnau sy
  Heddy yn dwyn y goron.
Y mae'n ei dwyn o dad a mam
  Nid oedd gam, ond cyfion,
Fe roed iddi wrth ei bodd
  Ac o anfodd Saeson. [HLlG. p. 137]

[1] Consideration of the possibility of the ultimate origin of some of these old measures in late Latin forms is beyond the scope of this study.

Your Maiden Mother, raised above,
heads the host of virgins,
whilst the Mary of our island
wears the crown today.
From father and mother it comes to her
conferred by right, not wrong;
and she takes it happily,
against the English will.

Mary's royal descent on both sides of her family tree is thus emphasised in contrast to that of Elizabeth, and the Catholic faith becomes a new cause of patriotic dislike of the English. Later come a large number of lyrics in praise of Elizabeth who, in the allegorical manner of the age, is referred to in Welsh as Sidanen, the silky one. Lodowick Lloyd, who wrote a Sidanen poem in Welsh, introduced the pseudonym into English verse too.

Sydanen conquers kyngs wythe quyll
Sydanen governs stars at will
Sydanen scars her fooes with penne
wythe peace Sydanen conquers men . . .
Sydanen feade on pallas pappe
Sydanen lulled on Junos lappe
Sydanen taght yn vestes towre
Sydanen nurste in venus bowre . . .
right wher she is pansophia stawlde,
yn Wales she is Sydanen cald. [CRhC notes]

Reference has already been made to Captain Midleton's version of the psalms in the classical metres. Towards the end of the sixteenth century Edward Kyffin was at work on another version, but it was yet another, that of the Archdeacon Edmwnd Prys, which became most popular in Wales. He too employed the old *cwndid* or carol measure of the *awdl-gywydd* and his arrangement of this measure into four-line stanzas came to be known as the *mesur salm*, since most of his translations of the Psalms are in this form. It was in this way that the old *awdl-gywydd* measure entered into hymnology and thus into the popular music and literature of modern Wales, for Edmwnd Prys' psalm measure is one of the most frequently sung of all hymn tune forms and his words are still familiar to Nonconformist as well as Anglican congregations. Here is one of his best-known hymns as it appears in the Welsh Methodist hymnal of today.

Disgwyliaf o'r mynyddoedd draw
  Lle daw im help wyllysgar;
Yr Arglwydd rydd im gymorth gref,
  Yr hwn wnaeth nef a daear.

Dy droed i lithro Ef nis gad,
  A'th Geidwad sydd heb huno;
O gwel dy Geidwad, Israel lân,
  Heb hun na hepian arno.

Ar dy law ddeheu mae dy Dduw,
  Yr Arglwydd yw dy Geidwad;
Dy lygru ni chaiff haul y dydd,
  A'r nos ni'th rydd i'r lleuad.

Yr Ion a geidw rhag pob drwg
  A rhag pob cilwg anfad;
Cei fynd a dyfod byth yn rhwydd,
  Yr Arglwydd yw dy Geidwad.

This is close enough to Psalm number CXXI, *I will lift up mine eyes unto the hills*, not to require translation. Williams Pantycelyn subsequently used this same stanza in hymn writing.

In a secular poem, on the other hand, Edmwnd Prys went boldly beyond traditional Welsh forms in an attempt to bring Welsh writing into line with contemporary English lyrical practice in an experiment which he called *Balett gymræg ar fesur aboute the banck of Elicon*, a Welsh ballad to the measure of *About the Bank of Helicon*. His reference to the air to which the words are intended to be sung is a clear indication of the way in which music conditioned lyrical form, and his use of the word *balett* shows that he is consciously introducing a foreign poetic form into Welsh versification. Here is the second stanza of this very charming poem, which follows a tribute to the linnet, the nightingale, the thrush, the blackbird and the lark as the master poets of the grove.

Llwyn nid pell nodau heb pallu
llwyn Ebrillaidd llawn byrriallu
  lle gward teg a llygaid tydd
Glyn a meillion glanme am allu
a gwyrdd ddillad gwir ddiwallu
  yn llenwi llywenydd
ar blode ar drwyne yr drain
ar fedwen fain ar glasddail
gwiw ywr ffynon glan ywr man
mae yn kodi tan y gwiail
  y gloiwddwr
  y kroiwddwr
  lle teg llwiddiant
  lle i gysgu
  lle i ddysgu
  holl glymau o ddesgant. [CRhC. p. 397]

A nearby grove with notes increasing,
an April grove and primrose-full,
  place of sweet song and daisies;
a dale full of spring clover
and the green dress of true delight
  filling with happiness;
with flowers on the thorn points,
the slim birch and the fresh leaves;
a worthy fountain in a sweet spot
rises from under the boughs,
  the clear water,
  the fresh water;
fair, lucky place,
a place to study
all the couplets of descanting.

As will be seen by reference to the Welsh, Edmwnd Prys incorporated *cynghanedd* into this metrical innovation and pointed the way to the ingenious mellifluity of Huw Morus some decades later.

Once more in the old *awdl-gywydd* measure adapted to a four-line stanza is a poem of longing for home (*hiraeth*), a favourite theme of Welsh poets, written by Sir Sion Gruffydd, chaplain to Mr. William Thomas, whilst they were in Flanders, to express his longing for Caernarvon.

Dyn wy'n byw drwy nerth y Tad
 ymhell o'i wlad yn estron
wyf ofalus a phaham
 o hiraeth am Gaernarvon. [CRhC. p. 408]

I'm a man living, through God's power
 a stranger to his nation;
the cause of all my sorrowing
 is longing for Caernarvon.

And so on for fourteen simple but deeply felt stanzas.

Other more extraverted travellers are more prepared to speak about their adventures and such a poem, written again in the *awdl-gywydd* stanza by Lieutenant William Peilyn in 1570, is a *Conversation between a Man and a Pelican* (CRhC p. 384). A note in the manuscript says that it is the tale of a group of Welshmen who went at Queen Elizabeth's command to harry the Spaniards in the West Indies. The poet asks the pelican to take a course due east and to fly the seven thousand miles to London with an account of their exploits, charging the bird to greet the Queen and Sir Roger Williams, the famous soldier, on their behalf. The account given to the pelican is lively and circumstantial, and at one point the metre dramatically changes under the stress of excitement.

Gwedi ni ddyfod ir Tir hwnn
Fe ddaeth yn grwnn i'n herbyn blaid
Gwyr Noethion yn rhwyfo au crwyn wedi Paintio
Bwaue'n eu Dwylo fal diawlaid.

And when we came unto this land
a compact band against us rose
of naked men rowing, their painted skins showing,
like devils all holding their bows.

Later comes a good description of a grim advance.

Rhai o'n hôl, a rhai o'n blaen
A Rhai yn Drayn o'n deutu
Fo fu rhyngom ymladd mawr
Do bedair awr or un tu

Hwynthwy'n danfon yn ei Dig
Grymm mawr, wenwynig Saetheu
A Ninneu'r Bwlets Plwm iw crwyn
Yn talu'r Echwyn adreu

Ni fuom felly ddwy Lêg hir
Yn ynill Tir wrth arfe,
Cin cael tynnu saeth o gig
Ein gwyr briwedig ninne.

Some behind and some before
and some like thorns about us
in this battle in one day
for four hours they fought us.

They in their malice send at us
their grievous poisoned arrows;
we send lead bullets to their skin,
each paying what he borrows.

And this for two long leagues went on,
with arms we won our ground,
ere from the flesh we pulled the darts
that smarted in the wound.

Adventures at home are recorded by the wandering minstrel Robin Clidro, mostly written in the essentially comic metre named after him the *mesur Clidro*, which again seems to be a form adapted from the old *cyhydedd* or *rhupunt hir* measures. Robin Clidro, who met his death at the hands of a highway robber in South Wales, reveals himself in his picaresque poems as a very Autolycus. One of these tells the story of his attempt to practise his craft at Ludlow, where he was no better received than was Guto'r Glyn at Chester. Another lively "*awdl*" in the same measure describes a fishing excursion in Cardigan Bay, with flat-bottomed boats from Barmouth, Mochres, Llanbadarn and Aber Rheidiol.

Yno i gwelech i slettene
yn kodi i moel dine
ag yn neidio rhyche
  fal geifr yn rhechain. [CRhC. p. 162]

There you'd see flat-bottomed boats
lifting their backsides
and leaping over troughs
just like farting goats.

In a satire on a stingy parson Robin Clidro employs a line of four stresses and ten or eleven syllables, with one rhyme throughout most of the poem, a metre rare in Welsh.[1] The minstrel would like to go to the Bishop and have the priest deprived of his rents.

ai rwymo yn ei garchar a chwain iw gyrchu
a chwn iw gyfarth pan el i gysgu
a llygod yn silio gwellt ei wely
ar cryd ar ddanoed am dano'n ymdynny . . .

and bind him in prison with fleas to seek him,
and dogs to bark when he goes to sleep,
and mice to breed in his bed's straw,
with fever and toothache growing upon him.
[CRhC. p. 165]

With equal freedom does this poet handle the *cywydd* form in a poem which protests against the cutting down of another wood and which is called a *Cywydd on behalf of the squirrels who went to London to file and make an affidavit on the bill for the cutting down of Marchan Wood near Rhuthyn* (Ll.C III, p. 69). As T. Gwynn Jones has said, Robin Clidro had a fair notion of *cynghanedd* and, when he wanted to, he came close enough to the official poets who consistently made fun of him. He used his eyes too, and this wood for him is peopled with more than the conventional nightingale and red deer.

nid oes fry o goed y fron
ond lludw y derw llwydion;
does gipyll heb ei gipio
na nyth brân byth yn ein bro;
mae'r tylluanod yn udo
am y koed, yn gyrru plant o'u ko;
gwae'r tylluan rhag annwyd,
oer ei lle am y keubren llwyd;

[1] The metre is similar to that employed by Gruffud Robert in rendering the scrap from Ennius in his translation of Cicero's *De Senectute*.

gwae'r geifr am ei koed a'u kyll
a pherchen hwch a pherchyll;
gwae galon hwch folgoch hen,
dduwsul, am le i gael mesen;
kadair y kathod koedion,
mi wn y ty llosgwyd hon . . .

Up there remains of the hill's trees
only grey ash of oak trees;
there's not a stump unsnatched
and no crow's nest left in our part.
The owls complain for the trees
and frighten all the children;
the poor owl catches cold,
left cold without her hollow trunk.
Woe to the goats without boughs and saplings,
and to the keeper of sow and piglets;
pity an old red-bellied sow's heart
on a Sunday when she gets no acorn!
The chair of the wild cats,
I know the house where that was burnt.

Another outstanding poet in the free measures was Richard Hughes of Cefn Llanfair, better known in Wales as Dic Huws, footman extraordinary or *pedis sequus* to Queen Elizabeth and one of the five hundred and fifty Welshmen who went on the spectacular Cadiz Voyage of 1596.

There is evidence that Dic Huws was a student of the old versification and a number of his *englynion* have been preserved. In Coriat's *Crudities*, where he is described as Richardus Hughes, Cambro-Britannus, Regi a Pedibus, he has the place of honour at the end of the series of Panegyric Verses addressed to the author, with the following *englyn*.

I Candish a Drâk i gwendid lhywiaist
    Mewn llawer aflendid
Dyscaist fwy mewn dwy eskid
Yr hên gorph, na rhain i gyd.

For Cavendish and Drake you pictured their weakness
    in many an uncleanness;
in two shoes you learnt more,
old body, than did these together.

He wrote an *englyn* to express his dismay at an illness of the Queen and his series of *englynion* on the occasion of the Gunpowder Plot are well known.

But it was in the free metres that Dic Huws was happiest and it is in them that he made his important contribution to Welsh literature, for he has some claim to be considered its first lyric poet. It is frequently stated that his poems show the influence of the contemporary English lyric, but, as the following quotations will demonstrate, the influence was not so much on the form of his verse, which derives from the old free measures, as on the feeling and the imagery. Here are the final stanzas of a conversation between the poet and his love.

Y mab madde ag mi a ddawa
kyn diweddiad mis gorffena
o chai amser modd a chyfle
er mwyn fenaid mi wna yngore.

Ir glas lwyni kyll tan irddail
lle mae'r knau'n brigdrymu'r gwiail
tyrd a hel or knau gweskia
a chadw dair heb dori'n gyfa.

O gyfynir pwy ai canodd
dic a merch erioed a garodd
rwy fel indeg yn ynfydu
na allai henwi i chael nai chelu. [CRhC. p. 3]

The girl speaks:—

I'll promise you if you'll forgive me
before July is past,
if time and means and luck permit me
for my soul's sake to do my best.

The poet concludes:—

To the green hazel grove's fresh leaves
where the nuts weigh down the boughs
come and pick the ripest nuts
and break none of your vows.

If it's asked who sang this song,
Dic and a girl, his only love.
I'm a madman going crazy
because I can't name her nor hide nor have.

The four-line stanza of this poem, with four stresses in each line, is the commonest metre of the *penillion telyn*, the traditional verses sung to the harp which form the main body of Welsh folk poetry. Sir John Morris-Jones has pointed out that this is an ancient form in folk poetry all over the world and he finds the four-beat line in the Sanskrit *Rigveda*, the Finnish *Kalevala*, and in Hebrew, Assyriac and Old English poetry. There is little question of borrowing here, nor is it difficult to imagine how such a line arose spontaneously in different parts of the world. Early poetry is associated with dancing and, since men and women have two feet, two steps one way and two another give the four beats which constitute the basis of this line and of so many dance patterns. The association of the movement of the line with that of the dance is preserved in the English use of the word *foot* in the measuring of verse.

In another carol to his love Dic Huws employs a four-line stanza which we have already met, that which is made up of two *awdl-gywydd* couplets.

O wir drymder kanu it wy
nid o nwy na maswedd
ond yn modd yr alarch gwyn
yn chwynfan cyn i diwedd. [CRhC. p. 3]

I sing out of true heaviness,
not wantonness or spirit,
like the white swan's lamenting breath
when death is close upon it.

Here it is permissible to detect an English influence, for the dying swan was a favourite image of the Elizabethans, and in another carol where the lover and the nightingale converse and the nightingale refuses to carry the poet's message in case the jealous husband mistakes her for a cuckoo, the meaning is in line with the popular Elizabethan linking of the cuckoo with warnings of cuckoldry. Dafydd ap Gwilym was unaware of this meaning of the cuckoo's song, though cuckoos and jealous husbands abound in his poems. In this same poem Dic Huws makes use of one of the most pleasant of the Elizabethan lyrical devices, the echo, and his use of it is as haunting as any in English.

Pwy, pwy, pwy, och pwy a ddial
fy llwyr gam am gorthrwm ofal
helped, helped, duw, duw, duw,
hi attabe duw yn ddiatal.

Yno i gelwais inne or un modd
ar y ddiwies bert am nychodd
a gai fy wyllys ai na chai
ar gais na chai hi attebodd.

Yr eos bach beth a wnaf
o gariad gwraig rwy yn glaf, glaf,
ni cha i yn ddifarn garu mo hon
casau lliwr ton nis gallaf. [CRhC. p. 14]

Who, who, oh who'll repay
my utter wrong and great injury?
Help me, help me, God, God, God;
she answered 'God' without delay.

And then besought I equally
the pretty goddess who vexes me;
shall I have my wish or be refused?
And 'be refused' she answered me.

Oh nightingale, what shall I do?
I'm sick, sick for the one I woo;
She will hardly capitulate
and I can't hate her wavelike hue.

Yet another of the old pre-*cynghanedd* forms is employed in this poem, that of the *englyn cyrch*, which Einion Offeiriad had considered too easy a measure for a master poet to descend to.

In another poem of pleading for love a note of bitterness is sounded, together with an echo of the Palladas epigram previously referred to.

Doudwch imi yn ddiomedd
ai ych da, ai ych prud, ai ych bonedd
ai ych rinwedd dai liwr od
syn peri i chwi fod mor rhyfedd.

Os ych koweth blode yr teirgwlad
syn peri i chwi ysglyso ych cariad
noeth y douthoch noeth ir ewch
ar dda na newch adeilad.

Pryd yr unferch lana ynghymru
er bod pawb mewn chwant oi charu
oedran dolur clais ne friw
a bair ir lliw ddiwlanu. [CRhC. p. 18]

Tell me now without omission
is it your wealth or looks or station
or your virtue, colour of the snow,
makes you show such aversion?

If it's wealth, flower of three nations,
that makes you careless of your passions,
naked you came, naked you'll go,
you'll build no future on possessions.

The face of Wales' prettiest maid
though each man's court to her is paid,
age, bruises, injury and ache
will make its colours fade.

Richard Hughes may owe a great deal to Renaissance culture but he delights us most with simple images from his own experience, and it is such a picture that we get in a carol of advice from an old man to a young soldier, who is warned that when the wars are over he will be thrown aside with no future but begging.

Pen droyr chwi allan mewn awr bach
ir ewch i'n gleiriach issig
megis keffyl hen pan droyr
i borfa oer fynyddig.

You'll be turned out in a short while
a vile and broken creature
like a horse when he is old
to the cold mountain pasture.

Dic Huws' loveliest lyric and the closest in spirit to the Elizabethan song lyric is the sequence of stanzas to Boreuddydd, the girl called Break of Day.[1] This poem exemplifies perhaps best of all the interweaving of the old Welsh traditions and memories of Welsh landscape with the new European mood of the love song. Again the form is old, but the smoothness of the rhythm, the regularity of the stanzas and the clarity of the diction testify to the poet's indebtedness to the musical achievement of his age.

The treatment of what little remains of Welsh Mystery and Morality plays has been outside the scope of this work, but reference at this point to a tragedy of Troilus and Cressida (*Troelus a Chressyd*), written probably about 1600, may be justified by the interest of the verse forms in which the play is written. The anonymous author shows close familiarity with all the previous versions of this story which had suffered so many modifications over two centuries, and he may have known Shakespeare's play. Parts of the work, particularly the prologue, are a close translation of Chaucer and Pandarus is still in the Welsh play a type of faithful friend, not having degenerated into the leering pander of Shakespeare's terrible view of the story. The play, never yet printed or translated, is in the Peniarth 106 manuscript.

Compared with the contemporary English drama *Troelus a Chressyd* is stiff, heavy and mediæval in its manner, for it is rhymed from start to finish and its different stanza forms do not allow the quick exchange of reaction which blank verse,

[1] v. my translation in *The Rent that's Due to Love.*

handled in the free Shakespearean manner, made possible. The grief of Troilus and the penitence of Cressida must therefore fall into set forms, but even so there is nothing quite so heavy or so long as the speeches of the Greek leaders in Shakespeare's play, with their winding out of Elizabethan political commonplaces.

Here are some specimens of the verse forms in which *Troelus a Chressyd* is written. The first occurs in the debate of the Trojan leaders on what is to be done with Cressida, whose father has gone over to the Greeks. After proposals ranging from mild to brutal, Troilus pleads for her and a stage direction here states: *ag ar hynn mae yn syrthio mewn kariad*, and at this point he falls in love.

Rho fy einioes drosti
   o bu honn un drygioni
Nac er moed yn arfer
   a thwyll ne ffalster
Ir ydym yn adolwc i chwi
   rhoi maddeuant iddi
Ac or awr honn allan
   yr wy vi Troelws vy hunan
Yn kaethiwo vy rhydid
   dros gowirdeb Kressyd.

I will give my life for her
   if she is evil
or ever conversant
   with deceit and falseness.
We beg of you
   to give her pardon
and from this hour forward
   I Troilus myself
will pledge my freedom
   for Cressid's honesty.

Pandarus is praising Troilus to Cressida by making him equal with his brother Hector, and here another stanza form is used, which looks like an adaptation of Chaucer's rime royal.

Yn siwr y mae i vrenin Priamws
ddau o veibion glan diniwed
y rhain yw Hector a Throelws
nid oes neb ar a aned
odd i wrth ddrygioni cyn belled
    Pawb a wyddys oddi wrtho
    y drwc ar da sydd arno.

Certainly King Priamus
has two fine innocent sons,
these are Hector and Troilus
and there is no one born
so far from wickedness.
    Everyone knows from him
    the evil and good that are upon him.

Finally, when Troilus has seen the brooch in the captured cloak of Diomedes and knows that Cressida has played the whore with him, he reproaches her at a distance in yet another stanza form.

O Kresyd o f'anwylyd o f'arglwyddes eurbleth
ple mae'r owran ych addewid na phle mae'r krediniaeth
ple mae'r kariad ple mae'r gwirionedd Kresyd
Diomedes sydd yr owran yn kael arnoch chwi ei wnvyd
    Hynn a ddygasswn
    a hynn drossod a dyngasswn
    er doedyd honod anwir
    na biessit byth anghowir.

O Cressida, my darling, my golden-woven lady,
where is now your promise and where now is faith;
where is the love, where is the truth, O Cressida?
Diomedes now takes his heaven on you.
    This I once wore,
    this many times I swore
    that though you told a lie
    you would never be false.

Halting and broken in rhythm though the lines may often sound, and though the meaning may be too forcibly locked into the metrical scheme, the tragedy has great dignity and pathos and would probably read and act well in the slower manner of Greek drama.

The end of the sixteenth century is as good a point as any at which to divide the old from modern Welsh poetry, but it would be wrong to make it too definite an end to one period and a beginning of another. The main change to be observed is the passing of the great houses and the independent leaders, and with them the justification for poems of praise, the writing of which since pre-Roman times had been the first duty of the chief poet. House poets kept on after this time were museum pieces rather than an integral part of a living society.

Nor should the centuries from the sixteenth to the present day be thought of as the period of writing in the free metres. It has been made clear, I hope, that the difference between academic and popular verse in Wales has always been distinct and is so still today. With the decay of the aristocratic society of Wales the recording of the more trivial and everyday poetry in the unofficial measures became more and more permissible, and many more copies are today sold of volumes of the simpler lyric than of the eisteddfod poetry in the twenty-four metres. Hardly anyone, in fact, today writes an *awdl* except for an eisteddfod competition, but mastery of these classical measures may be found in any section of society.

Something may have been done during the course of this study to set right a misconception for which the Romans were originally responsible, but which was fostered by Gray and Macpherson in the eighteenth century, by Matthew Arnold in the nineteenth, and condoned by Lady Gregory and Yeats in their protest against materialism, the view that Celtic poetry consists of the frenzied and extempore out-pourings of long-haired bards against a background of twilight tremulous with inchoate beings of another world. This is perhaps what a critic of today means when he applies the adjective "bardic" to the work of Mr. Dylan Thomas, the painstaking pattern of whose verse is now beginning to be appreciated. The discipline of Welsh poetry is the strictest in the known world of literature and it is beyond human ability to rave in an ecstasy whilst observing the requirements of a complicated alliterative system, with end rhymes and internal rhymes to find, and whilst paying due attention to stresses and to the exact number of syllables.

Welsh versification is a meticulous craft and Welsh poetry, with almost the sole exception of the mysterious transformations and knowledge associated with Taliesin, is essentially social. It has formed a part of social life comparable to the growing of wheat, the making of pottery and the breeding of children, and the Welsh poet has rarely felt himself to be alone in an alien society. The characteristics of Welsh poetry are not a misty, vague imaginativeness, but clarity of image, closeness to the physical world and a high degree of skill in the craft of word-using, with, it must be confessed, a recurring tendency towards repetition or variation within narrow limits in the conventions of epithet and form.

Appendix A

WELSH VERSIFICATION

★

All early Welsh poetry is rhymed. The word *awdl*, used for the work of a chief bard, is the same as *odl* meaning rhyme, and an *awdl* was rhymed speech.

The twenty-four measures permitted to the official poet, established in the fourteenth century and modified in the fifteenth, were a regularization of forms which had been evolved through the practice of poets from at least as far back as the sixth century. These twenty-four measures are divided into three groups, the *englyn*, the *cywydd* and the *awdl* measures proper. Whilst the *awdl* since the fourteenth century may employ *englyn* and *cywydd* forms as well as specific *awdl* measures, the *englyn* and *cywydd* have most frequently been used alone, though generally for purposes considered less noble than those for which the *awdl* measures were required.

Here are the old twenty-four measures as laid down by Einion Offeiriad and edited by Dafydd Ddu Athro in the fourteenth century. The term *cynghanedd*, which will occur in the notes on these verse forms, will be explained later.

Group A. Englynion

1. *Englyn penfyr* (short-ended *englyn*).

This is a stanza of three lines, of ten, seven and seven syllables, with one main rhyme. One, two or three syllables occur at the end of the first line after the main rhyme (these are known as the *gair cyrch*) and these are echoed by alliteration or rhyme in syllables in the first half of the second line. There is an example of this form in the *Gododdin* (XCIX) and the *Stavell Gyndylan* poem of the Heledd sequence in the *Red Book of Hergest* is in this measure. Here is the final *englyn* of this poem.

Stavell Gyndylan am erwan—pob awr
  gwedy mawr ymgyvyrdan
  a welais ar dy bentan.

The *englyn penfyr* is sometimes known as *englyn o'r hen ganiad* or *englyn* in the old style.

2. *Englyn milwr* (the soldier's *englyn*).

The *baglan brenn* sequence in Llywarch Hen's complaint is in this old form, which consists of three seven-syllable lines with one rhyme.

Baglan brenn neut kyntevin
neut ryd rych neut crych egin
etlit ym edrych ith ylvin.

The *englyn milwr* too is used in the *Gododdin* (XLVII) and in the *Englynion y Clyweit.*

The two above *englyn* forms are to be found in the earliest recorded Welsh poetry, the *Juvencus englynion.* They are traditionally associated with primitive Britain and were out of fashion by the twelfth century.

3. *Englyn unodl union* (the straight one-rhymed *englyn*).

This *englyn* consists of four lines of ten, six, seven and seven syllables respectively, with one main rhyme. It was evolved either by adding a line to the *englyn penfyr* or by combining a *toddaid byr* with a *cywydd deuair hirion* couplet. These terms are to be exemplified later. This has remained until today by far the most popular of *englyn* forms; indeed it is rare for any other kind of *englyn* to be written today. The first two lines are known as the *paladr* or shaft and the third and fourth as the *esgyll* or wings.

Cei fynwes gynes geni—cu fwynwalch
  cei f'einioes os mynni;
cei fy llaw yn dy law di,
cei fy nerth cyfan wrthi. [Anon.]

It will be noticed that the *gair cyrch* which follows the main rhyme in the first line is linked by alliteration with the first half of the second line. Each line has some form of *cynghanedd.*

4. *Englyn unodl crwca* (the crooked one-rhymed *englyn*).

This reverses the arrangement of the previous *englyn* for the wings come first and the shaft second. Here is Einion's example of this form.

Kyt ymwnel kywyt, bryt brys,
yn llawen llewych ystlys,
lletryt kallon donn ef ai dengys—grud
lliw blaen gruc Generys.

5. *Englyn cyrch.*

In this four-line stanza the first, second and fourth lines rhyme, whilst the third line rhymes with the middle of the fourth line. It is a linking of two couplets, the first a *cywydd deuair hirion*, the second an *awdl gywydd.*

Einion's example of this form is the following.

Hunys hirloyn y hystlys
gwymp y llun yn y llaesgrys
gwnlliw owyn gwendonn iawn
O dwfyn eigiawn pan dyurys.

This measure became very popular and many songs and *penillion* were written in it. For this reason probably it came to be scorned by the stricter craftsmen in verse as beneath their attention, but when employed as one of the twenty-four official measures it required an unaccented rhyme (as in sing-failing) in the first couplet. Thus the first couplet of Dafydd Nanmor's example runs:—

Deng mil o filoedd oeddyn
draw dri llu hyd ar dir Lŷln.

As a popular form it came to be known as the *mesur triban* and here is an old *pennill* in this metre.

Fel y cuddia'r llwyni gleision
ddolennog grwydriad Cynon
dymunwn innau lechu'r ferch
enynnodd serch fy nghalon.

The next three forms (6, 7 and 8) are the *englynion proest* or half-rhymed *englyn*, which follow the rules of *proest* rhyming to be explained in the section on rhyme. All three forms consist of four seven-syllable lines.

6. *Englyn proest dalgron.* This has rhymes formed of vowels of the same length or such vowels followed by a consonant or by the vowel *w*. Short-vowel half-rhymes would be *gwiwder*, *mynor*, *galar; dolur;* long vowel half-rhymes, *llên*, *gwin*, *tân*, *cwn.* Here is Einion's specimen.

Agharat hoen leuat liw
yghiyeth lewychweith law
wyf o'th garyat, glwyfgat glew,
ynvyt drwy benyt y'm byw

7. In the *Englyn lleddfbroest* the rhymes must be the four dipthongs ae, oe, wy and ei, to which the modern spelling of Welsh has added ai.

The example in Einion's *Grammar*, attributed in one manuscript to Dafydd Ddu, is the following.

Llawen dan glaerwen len laes,
lleddf olwg gloyn amlwg glwys,
llathrlun manol a foleis,
llarieidd foneddigeidd foes.

8. *Englyn proest gadwynog.* The word *cadwyn* means chain and here the rhymes occur alternatively. Each line half-rhymes with the next and rhymes fully with the next but one. There are two examples of this in Einion's *Grammar* but Sir John Morris-Jones (*Cerdd Dafod*, p. 326) says that he has failed to find any fourteenth century example. From then on examples are plentiful. The following is from the work of Dafydd Nanmor.

Kael or warr koler euraid
Karw Edwart mewn kaer ydwyd
Kael o ebolion lonaid
Kann ystabl yt, kwnstabl wyd.

The *Cywydd* measures

9. The *awdl gywydd*.

The unit in this measure is a couplet of seven-syllable lines, the first line rhyming with a word at the pause near the middle of the second line. The last syllable of the second line then carries the main rhyme. Einion's example has already been quoted in Chapter VIII[1] during the course of remarks on the origin of the free metres. After the elaboration of *cynghanedd* in the fourteenth century this form was very rarely used for *cywydd* construction, being replaced by the *deuair hirion* couplet. But the lesser orders of poets went on using it and it has thus passed into the popular poetry and hymnology of modern Wales. Two *awdl gywydd* couplets made a convenient four-line stanza and this measure was much used by later poets in the free metres. Here is an example from a lyric by the Elizabethan Dic Huws.

gwrandewch ganmol brig y don,
iraidd wynion ddeurudd;
gorlliw ewyn ymlaen lli,
fe'i gelwir hi Boreuddydd.

10. *Cywydd deuair hirion*, or long-lined couplet. The unit here is again the seven-syllable couplet but this time the rhyme is final and unaccented (as in dress-brightness). Dafydd ap Gwilym wrote his *cywyddau* in this measure and since his time it has been the regular *cywydd* measure. In Dafydd's work the first line of the couplet often has no *cynghanedd* but here is an example with a different kind of *cynghanedd* in each line.

Saith gywydd i Forfudd fain
syth hoywgorff a saith ugain.

The first line has *cynghanedd sain* and the second *cynghanedd groes*.

[1] p. 214.

In the rhyme the accent falls on *fain* but on the first syllable of *ugain*.

11. *Cywydd deuair fyrion* or short-lined couplet. This couplet of four-syllable lines has been very rarely used and is not often met with outside manuals of versification. Einion's example is the following.

> Hardec riein
> Hydwf glwysgein
> Hoywliw gwenic
> Huan debic
> Hawd dy garu
> Heul yn llethru.

This measure is charming enough but not tolerable for long.

12. *Cywydd llosgyrnog*. The unit here is usually three lines, two of eight syllables and one of seven. The first two lines rhyme with the middle of the third line, which carries the main rhyme with the sixth line. The Welsh poets are thought to have learnt this measure from a common mediæval Latin hymn form (v. *Cerdd Dafod*, p. 330). Dafydd ap Edmwnd wrote a whole *cywydd* in this metre, the following being the first six lines.

> Y mae goroff a garaf
> O gof aelaw ag a folaf
>   O choeliaf gael i chalon;
> Am na welais i myn Elien
> O Lanurful i lyn Aerfen
>   wawr mor wen o'r morynion.

The *Awdl* measures

13. *Rhupunt*. The *rhupunt* is a line of three, four or five sections of four syllables each. The first two, three or four sections rhyme with each other, whilst the final section carries the main rhyme. The *rhupunt* is as old as Welsh poetry and occurs in the *Black Book of Carmarthen* and in Aneirin's *Gododdin*. A *rhupunt* may be written out as one line or each of its divisions may be taken as a line .The following example is from the *Gododdin* (LXIII A).

Angor dewr daen
sarph seri raen
sengi wrymgaen
e mlaen bedin.

A couplet by Iorwerth ab y Cyriawg, given as a specimen by Gutyn Owain, runs thus.

Mi a baraf i'm gwenn araf gann a garaf gain o gerydd
am lyvassu, vy niflassu a'm lliassu, em lliossydd.

It will be noted here that whereas the first three sections are linked by rhyme, the third and fourth in each line are linked by *cynghanedd groes* or cross alliteration, *g*, *n*, *g*, *r* in the first line and *m*, *ll*, *s* in the second.

Dafydd Nanmor has a *rhupunt* of twelve syllables followed by one of sixteen, and this measure was one of those tightened up by Dafydd ap Edmwnd in 1451.

14. *Cyhydedd fer* or short equivalence.

This is a rhymed couplet of eight-syllable lines, which occurs in the *Gododdin* and in the *Book of Taliesin.* In twelfth century poetry long sequences of these couplets have the same rhyme. Sir John Morris-Jones quotes the following Taliesin couplet as an early specimen.

Ni roddes na maes na choedydd
achles i ormes pan ddyfydd.

15. *Byr a thoddaid.* This measure is a combination of the *cyhydedd fer* with the *toddaid byr*. The *toddaid byr* is a couplet also of sixteen syllables, but divided into lines of ten and six syllables. One, two or three syllables come after the main rhyme in the first line and these syllables must be linked by alliteration or assonance with the first syllables of the second line. When the *toddaid byr* is mingled with the *cyhydedd fer* the effect is to give variety to the eight-syllable couplet by a break in rhythm.

In the following example from Einion the *toddaid* comes first and the *cyhydedd* couplet second.

Thomas a Roppert rwyd par—gwersyllic
  Rwyf ryfyc ryuelgar
Ruthur Arthur areithraw essgar
Reithion gawr rwythawr llawr llachar.

16. *Clogyrnach.* This measure is associated with the name of Cynddelw. Once more a couplet of the *cyhydedd fer* is taken and to it is added something rather like a long *rhupunt* except that here the sections measure 5, 5, 3 and 3 syllables, the first three sections rhyming together and the fourth carrying the main rhyme of the *cyhydedd fer* couplet. The specimen which follows comes from the work of Dafydd Nanmor.[1]

Gwr ai enw yn goronoc
a wna dossod yn dywyssoc
  ath gledd rrwng wyth glann
  i ol a welann
ar drychann aurdorchog.

17. *Cyhydedd Naw Ban.* This is a nine-syllable line which is usually arranged into groups of couplets and, as in Meilyr's *Elegy on Gruffudd ap Cynan*, these stanzas run for lengthy sequences without a new rhyme. Here is Einion's example.

Wrthyt greawdyr byt bid vygobeith
Wrthyf byd drugar hywar hyweith
Yth arge neud gwae nyt gwael y gweith
Wrth dynyon gwylon y bo goleith
Wrth hynny Duw vry vrenhin pob ieith
Yth archaf dagnef keinllef kanlleith.

18. *Cyhydedd Hir.* This is a line of nineteen syllables which, for convenience of writing or printing, may be divided into ten and nine, or into sections of five, five, five and four or five, five and nine syllables. The first three sections rhyme together and the fourth carries the main rhyme. Sir John Morris-Jones says that the form was not used alone until the thirteenth century. In the *Black Book of Carmarthen* the first poem ends with a

[1] The Dafydd Nanmor specimens are from his tour de force of an ode to Thomas ap Dafydd ap Thomas.

gwawdodyn byr followed by five couplets of *cyhydedd hir*, and the form also occurs in the *Gododdin*. Here is an example from the work of Dafydd Nanmor.

> Un dwrf pan derrynt
> Ac od gann y gwynt
> A naw erw oyddynt ynn orweiddioc.

19. *Toddaid.* The short *toddaid* of sixteen syllables has already been referred to in the *byr a thoddaid* section. The *toddaid* proper is of nineteen syllables divided into ten and nine, the main rhyme occurring one, two or three syllables before the end of the first line, which in turn rhymes with the middle of the second line. The *toddaid* was generally used with other forms, particularly the nine-syllable couplet and the *cyhydedd hir*. Here is Einion's example.

> Nit digeryd Duw, neut digarat—kyrd
> Neut lliw gwyrd y vyrd o veird yn rat;
> Neut lliaws vrwyn kwyn kanwlat—yghystud
> O'th attall Ruffudd gwaywrud rodyat.

20. *Gwawdodyn.* An old practice of mingling the nine-syllable couplet with the *toddaid* or *cyhydedd hir* was regularised in the fourteenth century into a four-line form known as the *gwawdodyn*. It is unlikely that there is any etymological connection between this term and the name of the tribe which gave the title to the *Gododdin*.[1] Here is Einion's specimen.

> Meddylyeis y dreis o trasyml vryd,
> Medwl medw, gymwyn, anvwyn, ynvyd,
> Medyliaf am Naf, am nawd gyt—esmwyth,
> Nid medwl diffrwyth, mod ymdiffryd.

21. *Gwawdodyn hir.* If more than one couplet preceded the *toddaid* the stanza so formed was known as a long *gwawdodyn*. Einion's example has two couplets before the *toddaid*.

[1] A possible derivation is from *gwawd* meaning poem.

Gwann iawn wyf o glwyf er gloyn vorwyn
Gwae a vaeth hiraeth brif arvaeth wrwyn
Gwyr vyghalonn donn defnyd vyghwyn
Gwnn ar vyrr y tyrr kyn bo terwyn
Am na ddaw y law y lwyn—a bwyllaf
A garaf attaf atteb addwyn.

22. *Hir a thoddaid.* Einion and Dafydd Ddu Athro are both accredited with the invention of this measure which is an extension of the *gwawdodyn.* The *hir a thoddaid* is a stanza of ten-syllable lines followed by a *toddaid.* Here is Einion's example, possibly of his own composition.

Gwynnvyd gwyr y byd oed vod Agharat
Gwennvun yn gyfun ae gwiwuawr garyat
Gwannllun am llud hun hoendwc barablad
Gwynlliw eiry difriw difrisc ymdeithyat
Gwenn dan eur wiwlenn ledyf edrychyat—gwyl
Yw vannwyl yn y hwyl heul gymheryat.

This is one the most frequently employed *awdl* measures today and at the National Eisteddfod a prize is annually offered for a poem (usually on someone's death) in this measure.

23. *Cyrch a chwta.* This stanza, again thought to be an invention of Einion Offeiriad, consists of six seven-syllable lines followed by an *awdl gywydd* couplet. It has never been much used and, as Sir John Morris-Jones says (*Cerdd Dafod*, p. 344) the best specimen is the eighteenth century Goronwy Owen's stanza on the Welsh language.

Neud esgud un a'i dysgo,
Nid cywraint ond a'i caro,
Nid mydrwr ond a'i medro,
Nid cynnil ond a'i cano,
Nid pencerdd ond a'i pyncio,
Nid gwallus ond a gollo
Natur ei iaith, nid da'r wedd;
Nid rhinwedd ond ar honno.

24. *Tawddgyrch cadwynog* differs only slightly from two lines of *rhupunt hir.* The rhyme scheme of the sections, instead of being

b, b, b, a; c, c, c, a, is now b, c, c, a; b, c, c, a. Several modifications and elaborations were introduced into the measure after its invention in the fourteenth century, and here is Dafydd Nanmor's specimen with its tightened *cynghanedd.*

Bogwl kynnenn bugeil kannau
Briwa'r grannau bwrw'r gwyr enwoc
Bar a brynnenn bwrw beiriannau
Bwried rannau brwydr dariannoc.

The reader will have noticed that in the specimens given in sections 22, 23 and 24, each line begins with the same consonant. This device, originally perhaps an aid to memory, is known in Welsh as *cymeriad.*

Another form of *cymeriad* is to repeat the last word of one stanza in the first few words of the next. When such a chain is made complete by the last word of the poem repeating one of the first, the stanza sequence was known as *cyngogion.*

Einion Offeiriad's description of the twenty-four measures concludes with prose triads setting forth the virtues and faults to be observed in poetry and poets. These pieces of traditional teaching, grouped into threes to aid the memory, go beyond technical considerations into morality, as in the triad: *Tri pheth a dyly prydyd eu gochel: llynna, gwragedda a chlerwryaeth.* Three things a poet should avoid, drunkenness, womanizing and wandering minstrelsy.

There are many manuscript copies of Einion Offeiriad's *Grammar* with Dafydd Ddu Athro's editing but the earliest are in the *Red Book of Hergest* and in the *Llanstephan 3 Manuscript.* The early grammars are conveniently assembled in *Gramadegau'r Penceirddiaid* by G. J. Williams and E. T. Jones (Welsh University Press, 1934).

In the above references to Einion I have used the *Llanstephan 3* text, but I have thought it unwise to go back on Sir John Morris-Jones' rearrangement of the order of the measures in his *Cerdd Dafod*, where a much fuller treatment of the whole matter will be found.

Dafydd ap Edmwnd's modification of the twenty-four

measures has already been dealt with, but it may be of interest to append, for what it is worth, Gutyn Owain's conclusion to his version of the rules in the *Llanstephan 28 Manuscript*. "Pump messur kyffredin a vu orau ar odlau a wnaeth Taliessin, y rai a elvid gynt "pump kolofn kerdd Daliesin," nid amgen, toddaid, gwawdodyn byrr, kyhydedd hir, kyhydedd verr, a hupunt byrr; a Rai a'i geilw hwynt "pump kadair kerdd davod." Gwedy hynny y dychymygwyd pedwar mesur eraill, nid amgen, gwawdodyn hir, kyhydedd nawban, byrr a thoddaid, a chlogwrnach, yr hwnn a elwir "dull Kynddelw." Gwedy hynny y dychymygawdd Davydd Ddu Athraw dri messur eraill, nid amgen kyrch a chwta, hir a thoddaid, a thawddygrch kadwynoc. Einion Offeiriad a ddychymygawdd yntau hupynt hir. Davydd ap Edmwnt a ddychymygawdd ddau vessyr yn lle ynglyn o'r hen ganiad ac ynglyn milwr, nid amgen, gorchest beirdd a chadwynvyrr." "Five common measures were the best in the poetry made by Taliesin. They were called of old "the five pillars of Taliesin's song" and they were the *toddaid*, *gwawdodyn byr*, *cyhydedd hir*, *cyhydedd fer* and *rhupunt byr*. Some called these "the five chairs of poetry." After that four other measures were invented, the *gwawdodyn hir*, *cyhydedd nawban*, *byr a thoddaid* and *clogyrnach*, the last being known as Cynddelw's manner. Then Dafydd Ddu Athro invented three more measures, the *cyrch a chwta*, *hir a thoddaid* and *tawddgyrch cadwynog*. Einion Offeiriad invented the *rhupunt hir*. Dafydd ap Edmwnd invented two measures to replace the old style *englyn* and the *englyn milwr*, namely the *gorchest beirdd* and the *cadwynfyr*."

Gutyn Owain's summarization, though interesting as showing how the history of Welsh prosody was regarded towards the middle of the fifteenth century (he wrote in 1455), is not to be taken very seriously, for the *rhupunt hir*, whose invention he gives to Einion, had been used as far back as the *Gododdin*.

Cynghanedd

The word *cynghanedd* means harmony and in poetry it is a means of giving pattern to a line by the echoing of sounds, consonantal and vowel. There are three main divisions of *cynghanedd*:—

Cynghanedd Gytsain, *Cynghanedd Sain* and *Cynghanedd Lusg*.
Cynghanedd Gytsain consists of multiple alliteration.
Cynghanedd Sain has alliteration and rhyme within the line.
Cynghanedd Lusg has internal rhyme only.
Each of these kinds is sub-divided according to the position of the recurring sounds within the line and to the accented or unaccented nature of the syllable at the internal pause and at the end of the line.

Cynghanedd Gytsain

This consists of the repetition of a series of consonants. If the same consonants appear in the same order before the main stress in each half of the line, this is known as *cynghanedd groes*. A straightforward example of this, by Gutyn Owain goes:—

"Troes dilyw tros y dalaith."

There are three permitted ways of arranging the heavy accents in the line and therefore three divisions of *cynghanedd groes*. The line just quoted is an example of *cynghanedd groes gyt-bwys ddiacen*, or unaccented, balanced cross alliteration. It will be observed that the stresses are in exactly the same position in the two halves of the lines, hence *balanced*. Also that each half of the line ends with an unaccented syllable, hence *unaccented*.

Another form of *cynghanedd gytsain* or consonantal harmony, is the *cynghanedd draws*, which differs from *cynghanedd groes* only in that the two sets of consonants are separated by consonants which are not repeated. In the following line from Llywelyn ap Gutyn's comic elegy to Guto'r Glyn the four consonants to be repeated, t, r, s and t, are widely separated.

Tristach yw Cymru trostyn.

This kind of *cynghanedd* too is capable of three kinds of accenting.

The third kind of purely consonantal *cynghanedd* is the *cynghanedd groes o gysswllt*. Here the repetition of the consonants, instead of being neatly balanced in the second half of the line, begins before the main pause in the line.

Serch a rois ar chwaer Esyllt. [Tudur Aled.]

Here the consonants to be repeated are s, r, ch, r, but the repetition begins with the *s* in *rois*, immediately before the pause. Once again there are three possible variations of accent on the syllable at the pause and at the end of the line, both stressed, both unstressed, or one stressed with the other unstressed.

Cynghanedd Sain

In this kind of *cynghanedd* rhyme and alliteration are mingled, for the line is divided into three sections, the first two rhyming with each other, whilst the second and third are linked according to the above rules of consonantal harmony. This time there are four possible arrangements of accent in the second and third sections of the line, both ending in a stressed syllable, or both ending in an unstressed syllable, or the second ending in a stressed syllable with the third unstressed, or the second ending in an unstressed syllable with the third stressed. In the following example from Gutyn Owain the fourth possible arrangement occurs.

Llygaid a ddywaid i ddoeth.

Cynghanedd sain is easier than *cynghanedd gytsain* to attempt in English and was much used by G. M. Hopkins. An example in English would be:—

The road with its load of lads.

Cynghanedd Lusg

A line of *cynghanedd lusg* ends in a word of more than one syllable and the penultimate syllable in that word rhymes with the last syllable in the first half of the line. The following example comes from Goronwy Owen's *Cywydd i Fon*.

Poed it *hedd* pan or*wedd*wyf.

This too is effective enough in English and an example would be:—

A saint in an old painting.

As in *cynghanedd sain* the rhyme may be hidden by a linking with the next word as in Ieuan ap Rhydderch's line:—

Dialwr tre Lywelyn.

The rhyme here is *el*.

The brief summary made above is of the forms of *cynghanedd* established in the fourteenth century and followed ever since. All the examples I have given are from the fourteenth century or later, but rudimentary forms of complex alliteration and internal rhyme are to be found in the oldest Welsh Poetry and Sir John Morris-Jones in *Cerdd Dafod* gives many examples from the Four Ancient Books. A line in the *Stavell Gyndylan* poem in the Llywarch Hen series in the *Red Book of Hergest*, for instance, is an early example of *cynghanedd sain*.

Cynon a Gwiawn a Gwyn

(–on here rhymes with –awn, for *o* and *aw* were frequently interchangeable in Old Welsh).

It was the systematizing of *cynghanedd* and the growing insistence by the master poets on its continuous employment that characterized the end of the fourteenth century and the beginning of the fifteenth.

Rhyme

Rhyme is as old as poetry in Welsh and all three Welsh forms of rhyme are to be found in Aneirin's *Gododdin*.

As in other European languages, rhyme in Welsh consists of a correspondency in the final syllables of two or more words. Such rhyme most often occurs at the end of the line, but internal rhyme has been noted above in the *cynghanedd sain* and *cynghanedd lusg*. Cross-rhyming too has been noted in the *englyn*, *toddaid* and *awdl gywydd* measures, where the syllable at the end of one line rhymes with one in the middle of the next.

In addition to the familiar kind of rhyme there are two kinds of half-rhyme in Welsh. In the first, known as *proest*, the final vowel or consonant only in a word corresponds to that in another. The consonant may be the same and the vowel before it different, the only requirement being that the vowels in half-rhyming syllables shall be of the same kind, for a long vowel may not correspond to a short one. Thus in English *mode* would half-rhyme with *speed* but not with *bid.*

Diphthongs for this purpose are divided into two groups, ae, oe, wy, ei, ai, and aw, ew, iw, ow, yw, uw. Thus *llwyn* half-rhymes with *drain* but not with *dewn.*

Similar vowels at the ends of words are considered to half-rhyme without any correspondency of consonants, thus *lliw–draw*, *tre–tŷ*. Thus in English *toy* would half-rhyme with *way* and *too* with *see.*

Another kind of half-rhyme is where the vowel in the final syllables of two words is the same but the consonants differ. This is sometimes today known in Welsh as *odl wyddelig*, Irish rhyme, though since it occurs in the *Gododdin* it can hardly be of mediæval importation from Ireland. Examples of such half-rhyming from the *Gododdin* are *med–offer*, *esgar–haual*, *enwawc–gwirawt.*

Appendix B

THE SOURCES OF ARTHURIAN LEGEND

★

The spectacular growth of Arthurian romance is to be observed mainly in other languages than Welsh, but Welsh writers and Welsh traditions have played a greater part in this growth than is generally realised, a part which has recently been stressed by Professors Gwyn Jones and Thomas Jones in the introduction to their translation of the *Mabinogion* (Golden Cockerel Press and Everyman Library, 1949). It has been the natural concern of Welsh scholarship to assert the Celtic origins of the complex and enchanting body of story which grew up during the Middle Ages on the continent of Europe, where from the beginning Arthurian legend was known as "the matter of Britain", a term first used in the twelfth century by Jean Bodel in his *Chanson des Saisnes*. That two trends in Arthurian scholarship, pro and anti-Celtic, are still clearly discernible is shown by the most important work on this subject of recent years, Professor J. P. S. Tatlock's *The Legendary History of Britain* (University of California Press, 1950). Professor Tatlock belittles the Celtic element in the work of Geoffrey of Monmouth, Wace and Layamon, as well as the importance of the pre-twelfth century references to Arthur and Myrddin in Welsh poetry. Prof. Thomas Jones, in an important review of this book in *Llên Cymru*, number III, shows that Professor Tatlock has depended on J. Gwenogfryn Evans' altered texts and on the out-of-date translations of Skene. His ignorance of the Welsh language and of the recent findings of Sir Ifor Williams and others therefore invalidates his treatment of Welsh sources and detracts from the usefulness of a book which is otherwise a monument of careful scholarship.

APPENDIX B

Geoffrey of Monmouth claimed to have translated a British book into Latin and said the same of his inclusion of the prophecies of Merlin. These "British books" do not exist today but there is some contemporary evidence of the existence of such books at the time when Geoffrey wrote, and, although he invented a good deal and shamelessly reorganised other material, he could not have been entirely independent of earlier writers. William of Newburgh, a severe critic of Geoffrey, seems to accept that much of the *Historia* is translated from the British (i.e. Welsh) language, for he reproves Geoffrey for adding to the prophecies in translating them into Latin (J. Stevenson, *History of William of Newburgh* (Church Historians of England), London, 1856, volume IV, p. 398).

Geoffrey Gaimar stated that the first book of his metrical *Lestorie des Engles*, written about 1150, was based on a translation ordered by Robert, Earl of Gloucester, and refers as well to another ancient British book kept at Oxford.

> Robert li quens de Gloucestre
> Fist translater icele geste
> Solum les liveres as Waleis,
> K'il aveient, des Bretons reis . . .
> Le bon livere de Oxeford. ll. 6449–6464

Unfortunately, all that remains of Gaimar's *Lestorie* is the second book, based on the Anglo-Saxon Chronicle, the first book, dealing with the Britons and Bretons, having disappeared.

Gerald the Welshman says in his *Expugnatio Hibernica* (Dimock, *Giraldi Cambrensis Opera*, Rolls Series, volume V, pp. 401–2) that when on tour with Archbishop Baldwin he came upon a book of the prophecies of Merlin in a remote part of North Wales. It is difficult to dismiss all these assertions, even if one does not take seriously John of Cornwall's claim to have translated from Welsh in his *Prophecy of Merlin concerning the Seven Kings*, as the bolstering up of political propaganda and early fiction.

Wace used Geoffrey's *Historia* as the main source of his metrical versions of British history, but it must be remembered that he was also familiar with Breton folk tales and legends and that he is the first of all Arthurian writers to mention the Round Table. Layamon, the first Englishman to write about Arthur, writing in English during the first half of the thirteenth century, claimed three books as his authorities and example, those by Bede, Saints Albin and Augustine, and Wace. But Layamon was a village priest in a still very Celtic part of England on the bank of the river Severn, close enough to Wales to have heard of its legends and prophecies, and he refers to these beliefs as though he is familiar with them. Thus he records the passing of the wounded Arthur in the care of fairy girls to the island of Avalon to be made well there by Argante, its queen, and he says that the Britons still expect Arthur to return some day.

Bruttes ileveth yete
that he beon on live
and wunnien in Avalun
mid fairest alre alven
and lokieth evere Bruttes yete
whan Arthur cumen lithe.

Geoffrey of Monmouth says that Arthur is going to be made well of his wounds but does not mention the belief in his return, which is usually taken to be Wace's addition to the story. It is therefore important to have the testimony of Layamon, who knew what the Welsh thought about it, to the belief in Arthur's return.

Merlin and his prophetic utterances came into European literature through Geoffrey's *Historia* and through the *Vita Merlini*, a poem in Latin hexameters written about 1150, possibly by Geoffrey too, but there is ample evidence in Welsh poetry of an old tradition of Merlin's prophecies, and there is a strong probability that Merlin (Myrddin in Welsh) actually lived and wrote at the end of the sixth century. This has been well argued by Miss E. M. Griffiths in section II of her *Early Vaticination in Welsh*.

Earlier testimony to beliefs in Wales about Arthur and to prophecies concerning him is to be found in William of Malmesbury's *De Gesta Regum Anglorum* written between 1125 and 1140.

This critical and truth-loving historian referred to Arthur as the one about whom the Britons raved in empty words but who was worthy to be the subject, not of deceitful tales and dreams, but of true history.

There is no reason therefore to doubt the existence in Wales at the beginning of the twelfth century, and so for centuries before, for such things do not grow up in a day, of wide-spread tales and prophecies linked with the names of Arthur and Merlin, but the meagre remains we have in literature before 1100 yield only puzzling and disappointing fragments of these tales. Gildas, the first British historian, makes no mention of Arthur, although he refers to Mount Badon, traditionally one of Arthur's victories. Many attempts have been made to meet the difficulty created by this omission, the earliest recorded being that of Gerald the Welshman in his *Description of Wales* (Everyman edition, page 191), where he reports the tradition current in Wales that Gildas left out Arthur because the latter had killed Gildas' brother, the prince of Albania, i.e. Scotland. There is no doubt that Gildas was an embittered cleric and since his purpose was to chastise the British leaders from some monastery on the Continent rather than to glorify his country or even to record events, there may be something in the explanation which Gerald gives.

Nennius, writing his *Historia Britonum* about the year 800, gives an account of Arthur's battles, as does also the *Annales Cambriae*, the earliest manuscript of which dates from 955. Convenient translations into English of these passages may be found in the section on Arthurian legend of the *Cambridge Book of Prose and Verse*. The earliest Welsh poetry carries only passing references to Arthur's fame such as a comparison for a warrior's courage in the *Gododdin*, line 1242, and in the elegy on the death of the seventh century Cynddylan (CLlH, p. 52).

Scattered throughout the oldest manuscripts are fragments which constitute evidence of a great body of story developing from about the ninth century onward, a detailed study of which will be found in T. Gwynn Jones' essay on *Celtic Sources of Arthurian Legend* in Aberystwyth Studies, 1924. The *Stanzas of the Graves* in the *Black Book of Carmarthen* contain the famous line on the mystery of Arthur's burial place already quoted in Chapter III, and the grave of Bedivere is recorded.

Bet mab ossvran yg camlan
gvydi llauer kywlavan
Bet bedwir in alld tryvan. [BBC p. xxxii b.]

The grave of Osvran's son is at Camlan
after many battles.
Bedivere's grave is at Allt Tryvan.

Also mentioned are the graves of March and Gwalchmai (Mark and Gawayn).

Again in the *Black Book* there is a poem entitled *Gereint filius Erbin* which gives Arthur as Gereint's leader. In the same manuscript there is a poem which appears to be a dialogue between Arthur and Glewlwyd Gavaelvawr, where Bedivere's prowess is noted but where Cei (Sir Kay) is chiefly glorified.

Oet trum y dial
oet tost y cynial
Pan yuei o wual
yuei urth peduar
yg kad pandelhei
vrth cant idlathei. [BBC p. xlviii b.]

He was heavy in vengeance,
he was terrible in attack;
when he drank from a horn,
he drank as much as four;
when he came to battle,
he killed as many as a hundred.

In the *Book of Taliesin* there is a very strange poem called *Preidieu Annwfyn* which tells of the expeditions of Arthur in his ship Prydwen (Fairface) into the underworld, and which Sir Ifor Williams dates about the year 900. Many journeys are referred to, one of them in search of a cauldron which reminds us of the Irish cauldron of the *Mabinogion*, but not one of the places mentioned in the poem is identifiable. From each of these journeys only seven men returned, a fact which provides a kind of refrain to each section.

These, with the puzzling references in the Triads to three Gueneveres, successively queens to Arthur, are the principal fragments that remain to us of early Arthurian poetry in Welsh.

In prose, however, we have one complete and splendid piece of Arthurian writing, the story of *Culhwch and Olwen*, found in a thirteenth century manuscript but generally accepted as a tenth century redaction of much more ancient material. In this brilliantly composed story, myth, legend and folk tale are on the point of becoming romance and, as Professor Gwyn Jones has indicated,[1] the pattern of future Arthurian romance is established, for the action starts at Arthur's court, from which the young man sets out on his quest of the giant's daughter, there are strange deeds to be achieved heroically and magically, and the giant is to be killed. Wherever the girl walks flowers spring up in her track, and for this she is called Olwen or White Track. A long list is given of the heroes upon whom Culhwch calls for help; there are pages and pages of them and they include Cei, Bedwyr and Gwalchmai, as well as scores of others whose names occur nowhere else. It is in reading such lists that we sense something of our loss in the disappearance of so many tales and story cycles, and form some notion of the repertoire of the Welsh *cyfarwydd* or story-teller.

Amongst the gold-torqued girls whose names Culhwch invokes are Creiddylad, Shakespeare's Cordelia, and the two Iseults. Others less known have names, Tangwen, Teleri, which, as Gwyn Jones aptly remarks, sound like the plucking of the harp.

Arthur's ship Prydwen carries Culhwch and his friends over to Ireland and both *Culhwch and Olwen* and *Preidieu Annwfyn* have cauldrons which are sought over the sea and strange animals of totemic significance. They deal with similar people

[1] Life and Letters, March 1948, and Introduction (with Thomas Jones) to the *Mabinogion*, Everyman edition.

and give the impression of being contemporary, but whereas the tale is well constructed by a master of narrative prose, the poem is as obscure as anything could be.

The author of the twelfth century *Vita Gildae*, perhaps Caradoc of Llancarvan, gives an account of the carrying away of Guenevere by Melwas, but once more the source of this is unknown. So we return to the evidence of the three great Norman-Welshmen of the twelfth century, Geoffrey of Monmouth, Walter Map and Giraldus Cambrensis, and to that of their friends and opponents. It makes little difference here that Geoffrey may have been Breton, as is held by Tatlock and by Koht in his recent *Dawn of Nationalism in Europe*.

We may be permitted to regret the loss of the stories once told by such a person as Bledhericus, *famosus ille fabulator*, whom Giraldus refers to as living a little before his time (*Description of Wales*, page 185), the South Wales story-teller for whom Miss Jessie Weston in her *From Ritual to Romance* made out such a good case as the author of the earliest version of the tale of Perceval and the Quest for the Grail. The stories known by this time as the *Mabinogion* fortunately remain, but they deal chiefly with heroes older than Arthur, with the gods and worthies of pre-Christian Britain. Sir Ifor Williams has shown that we also have verse fragments which once formed the metrical part of story cycles in prose, and the *Stanzas of the Graves* may be a collection of final stanzas recording the burial place of heroes whose deeds have been recounted. The stanza which embodies the mystery of Arthur's resting place may therefore have formed part of an early account of his life and of his strange passing from the world of men.

To the Normans, the Celtic countries contiguous with their western borders, Brittany and Wales, were clearly of great interest and importance, and Arthur had the advantage of being a Celtic, i.e. non-Saxon, hero and so unlikely to arouse rebellious feelings in the subdued Saxons. Thus it was as a result of this Norman interest in this matter of Britain and through the work of Norman-Welshmen and of Englishmen and Normans familiar with Wales and Brittany that this source of story was made known to the rest of the civilised world and available for lovely elaborations in French and German and every other European language. The essentials of Arthurian romance, however, were present in Welsh or in Latin written by Welshmen.

BIBLIOGRAPHY

MANUSCRIPTS

The oldest poetry written down in Welsh is to be found in the ninth century *Juvencus* manuscript, a metrical version of the Gospels in Latin, which is in the Cambridge University Library. For a treatment of these stanzas see BBCS VI and LEWP.

The so-called Four Ancient Books of Wales, first edited by W. F. Skene, Edinburgh, 1868, are the following:—

1. *The Black Book of Carmarthen*. This is a manuscript of the late twelfth century containing much as yet unedited poetry, including the poems associated with Myrddin and the *Stanzas of the Graves*. It is the oldest manuscript wholly in Welsh. A tour de force of printing is its reproduction by J. G. Evans, Pwllheli, 1907.
2. *The Book of Aneirin*. A manuscript of about the year 1250, containing the *Gododdin* and four shorter heroic poems, one of them by Taliesin. Edited by Sir Ifor Williams, 1938.
3. *The Book of Taliesin*. This was probably written at Margam about the year 1275 and contains poems associated with Taliesin and vaticinatory verse which is post-900. Facsimile and text printed by J. G. Evans, 1910.
4. *The Red Book of Hergest*. A manuscript of about the year 1400 which contains a text of the *Mabinogion* and a great deal of poetry, including the Llywarch Hen and Heledd poems. J. G. Evans has printed the following unedited texts:—
   The Mabinogion from the Red Book of Hergest;
   The Poetry in the Red Book of Hergest.
   The Llywarch and Heledd poems have been edited by Sir Ifor Williams, 1935.

Other manuscripts of first importance are:—

The White Book of Rhydderch (MS Peniarth 4), written at Strata Florida about the year 1325 and containing an earlier text of the *Mabinogion* than that of the *Red Book of Hergest*. Recent printings of this *Mabinogion* text have been:—

The White Book Mabinogion, J. G. Evans, Pwllheli, and
Pedeir Keinc y Mabinogi, edited Sir Ifor Williams, 1930.

The Hendregadredd Manuscript. This manuscript of the early fifteenth century, an extremely important collection of twelfth and thirteenth century poetry, was lost until 1910, though most of the poems in it were known in inferior texts. It has been copied and edited by R. Morris-Jones, Sir J. Morris-Jones and T. H. Parry-Williams, 1933.

The Red Book of Talgarth (MS Llanstephan 27) was written about the year 1400 in the same hand as part of the *Red Book of Hergest.* It contains prose and verse, including the *Englynion y Clyweit.*

MS Peniarth 16. Written early in the thirteenth century, this contains triads.

Poetry and other material from these manuscripts, with the exception of the *Hendregadredd* text, was printed in the *Myvyrian Archaiology* (see printed books).

Other manuscripts used in the preparation of this book are the following:—

Gwyneddon 3. This late sixteenth century manuscript contains a good text of some Dafydd ap Gwilym poems and of other poets up to William Midleton. It has been edited by Sir Ifor Williams, 1931.

Mostyn 112. This early seventeenth century manuscript contains a large number of poems of Tomas Prys, perhaps in the author's own hand.

Mostyn 131, a collection of *englynion* in the hand of John Jones, Gelli Lyfdy, written between 1605 and 1618.

Mostyn 158. Elis Gruffydd's sixteenth century chronicle, which has been partly translated into English by M. Bryn Davies, Fuad I University Bulletin, Cairo, 1944 and 1950.

Llanstephan 133 and 134. Both these manuscripts are rich collections of the *cywydd* poets, Dafydd ap Gwilym, Dafydd ap Edmwnd, Dafydd Nanmor, Iolo Goch, Sion Cent and others.

Peniarth 53, a late fifteenth century manuscript edited by Stanton Roberts and H. Lewis, 1927.

Peniarth 76, a manuscript of the second quarter of the sixteenth century, with love poems by Dafydd ap Gwilym and others, edited by Stanton Roberts and W. J. Gruffydd, 1927.

Peniarth 106. This is the only text of the Welsh tragedy of *Troilus and Cressida* (*Troelws a Chressyd*) and was written down by John Jones, Gelli Lyfdy, between 1613 and 1622.

PRINTED WORKS

J. W. H. Atkins: *English Literary Criticism: The Renascence*, Methuen, 1947.

Joseph Bédier: *Les Légendes Epiques*, Champion, Paris, 1926–29.

Sir Idris Bell: *The Development of Welsh Poetry*, OUP, 1936.

Carleton Brown: *Religious Lyrics of the 15th century*, OUP, 1939.

CERNGOCH: *Cerddi Cerngoch*, Lampeter, 1904.
H. M. CHADWICK: *The Heroic Age*, CUP, 1926.
H. M. and N. K. CHADWICK: *The Growth of Literature*, CUP, 1932–1940.
T. M. CHOTZEN: *Recherches sur la Poésie de Dafydd ap Gwilym*, Amsterdam, 1927.
R. G. COLLINGWOOD and J. N. L. MYRES: *Roman Britain and the English Settlement*, OUP, 1936.
W. DINAN: *Monumenta Historica Celtica*, Nutt, 1911. A convenient assembly of references to the Celts in Greek and Latin.
J. GWENOGFRYN EVANS: Facsimiles and Texts of the oldest manuscripts. See Manuscripts.
E. FARAL: *La Légende Arthurienne des Origines à Geoffrey de Monmouth*, Champion, Paris, 1929.
GERALD THE WELSHMAN: *Giraldi Cambrensis Opera*, edited Brewer, Dimock and Freeman, Rolls Series.
The Itinerary and Description of Wales, edited J. Llewelyn Williams, Everyman, 1908.
GILDAS: *De Excidio Brittaniae*, edited Hugh Williams, Cymmrodorion Record Series, 1899.
LADY GREGORY: *Cuchulain of Muirthemne*, Murray, 1919.
E. M. GRIFFITHS: *Early Vaticination in Welsh*, WUP, 1937.
W. J. GRUFFYDD: *Y Flodeugerdd Newydd*, Cardiff, 1909.
Welsh Literature, Encyclopedia Brittannica, 14th edition.
Llenyddiaeth Cymru o 1450 hyd 1600, 1922.
Blodeuglwm o Englynion, Swansea. This has an important introduction on the *englyn* form.
Math vab Mathonwy, WUP, 1928.
Y Flodeugerdd Gymraeg, WUP, 1931.
Rhagarweiniad i Farddoniaeth Cymru cyn Dafydd ap Gwilym, THSC, 1937.
LADY CHARLOTTE GUEST: *The Mabinogion*, Everyman.
L. J. HOPKIN-JAMES and T. C. EVANS: *Hen Gwndidau*, 1910.
KENNETH JACKSON: *Early Welsh Gnomic Poems*, WUP, 1935.
Studies in Early Celtic Nature Poetry, CUP, 1935.
A Celtic Miscellany, Routledge and Kegan Paul, 1951.
A. O. H. JARMAN: *Lailoken and Myrddin*, BBCS IX i.
R. T. JENKINS: *Hanes Cymru yn y Ddeunawfed Ganrif*, WUP, 1928.
D. JERROLD: *Introduction to the History of England*, Collins, 1949.
D. GWENALLT JONES: *Yr Areithiau Pros*, WUP, 1934.
GWYN JONES and THOMAS JONES: *The Mabinogion*, Golden Cockerel, 1948; Everyman, 1949.

BIBLIOGRAPHY

T. GWYNN JONES: *Bardism and Romance*, THSC, 1913-4.
Celtic Sources of Arthurian Legend, Aberystwyth Studies, 1924.
Llên Cymru (4 volumes), Aberystwyth, 1926.
Gwaith Tudur Aled, WUP, 1926.
Y Gelfyddyd Gwta, Aberystwyth, 1929.

W. LEWIS JONES: *King Arthur in History and Legend*, CUP, 1911.

HENRY LEWIS: *Hen Gerddi Crefyddol*, WUP, 1931.
(with others) *Cywyddau Iolo Goch ac Eraill*, WUP, 1937.

SAUNDERS LEWIS: *A School of Welsh Augustans*, Wrexham, 1924.
Braslun o Hanes Llenyddiaeth Gymraeg hyd 1535, WUP, 1932.
Dafydd Nanmor, Llenor, vol. IV.
Tudur Aled, Efrydiau Catholig, vol. I, 1946.

SIR J. E. LLOYD: *History of Wales*, 1911.

J. LLOYD-JONES: *The Court Poets of the Welsh Princes*, Proceedings of the British Academy, vol. XXXIV, 1948. The notes give a valuable list of twelfth and thirteenth century poets and their dates.

SIR THOMAS MALORY: *Morte D'Arthur*, edited by Sir John Rhys, Everyman; and E. Vinaver, OUP, 1948.

WILLIAM MIDLETON: *Bardhoniaeth neu brydydhiaeth*, London, 1593.
Psalmae, London, 1603.

J. C. MORRICE: *Barddoniaeth Wiliam Llyn*, Bangor, 1908.

SIR JOHN MORRIS-JONES: *Cerdd Dafod*, OUP, 1925.

MYRDDIN FARDD: *Cynfeirdd Lleyn*, Pwllheli, 1905.

The Myvyrian Archaiology of Wales: OWEN JONES, EDWARD WILLIAMS and W. OWEN PUGHE; the first attempt to assemble and edit material from the oldest manuscripts; London (3 volumes), 1801-7 and Denbigh (1 volume), 1870.

CARL MULLER: *Fragmenta Historicum Graecorum;* for early references to the Celts by Posidonius and Eusebius.

J. G. O'KEEFFE: *The Adventures of Suibhne Geilt*, Irish Texts Society, XII, 1913.

J. J. PARRY: *Vita Merlini*, Univ. of Illinois Press, 1925.

THOMAS PARRY: *Baledi'r Ddeunawfed Ganrif*, WUP, 1935.
Hanes Llenyddiaeth Gymraeg, WUP, 1944.

T. H. PARRY-WILLIAMS: *Llawysgrif Richard Morris o Gerddi*, WUP, 1931.
Canu Rhydd Cynnar, WUP, 1932.
Hen Benillion, Aberystwyth, 1940.
Welsh Poetic Diction, Proc. Brit. Acad. XXXII, 1946.

T. ROBERTS: *Dafydd ap Edmwnd*, Welsh MSS Soc., Bangor, 1914.
Dafydd Nanmor, WUP, 1923.
(with Sir Ifor Williams) *Dafydd ap Gwilym a'i Gyfoeswyr*. Bangor, 1914.

G. SAMPSON: *Cambridge Book of Prose and Verse; from the Beginnings to the Cycles of Romance*, CUP, 1924.

J. SPEIRS: *The Scots Literary Tradition*, Chatto and Windus, 1940.

J. P. S. TATLOCK: *The Legendary History of Britain*, Univ. of California Press, 1950.

A. W. WADE-EVANS: *Welsh Medieval Law*, OUP, 1909.

J. L. WESTON: *From Ritual to Romance*, CUP, 1920.

SIR WYNN WHELDON: *Cymry Enwog* (short biographies of famous Welshmen), WUP, 1949.

WILLIAM OF NEWBURGH: *History*, edited by J. Stevenson, Church Historians of England, 1856.

G. J. WILLIAMS (with E. J. JONES): *Gramadegau'r Penceirddiaid*, WUP, 1934.

GWYN WILLIAMS: *The Rent that's Due to Love*, translations from Welsh Poetry, Poetry London, 1950.

SIR IFOR WILLIAMS: *Canu Llywarch Hen*, WUP, 1935.
Canu Aneirin, WUP, 1938.
Lectures on Early Welsh Poetry, Dublin, 1944.
The Juvencus Englynion, BBCS, vol. VI.
(with T. ROBERTS) *Dafydd ap Gwilym a'i Gyfoeswyr*, Bangor, 1914.
(with H. LEWIS and T. ROBERTS) *Cywyddau Iolo Goch ac Eraill*, WUP, 1937.
(with J. LL. WILLIAMS) *Gwaith Guto'r Glyn*, WUP, 1939.

W. S. GWYNN WILLIAMS: *Welsh National Music and Dance*, Curwen, 1933.

ADDENDUM: Since this book went to Press the following important work has appeared:—

THOMAS PARRY: *Dafydd ap Gwilym*, WUP, 1952.

THE PRONUNCIATION OF WELSH

Welsh, like Italian but not English or French, is almost a phonetic language, or a language whose spelling gives clear indication of its pronunciation. Generally speaking, one symbol from the alphabet represents one sound only, and any one sound is represented by one symbol only. For instance, if one vowel symbol is used (e.g. o and u in *onn* and *pur*), the vowel sound is pure and single, and cannot be diphthongised as in the English *only* and *pure*. A diphthong is represented by the symbols of its component sounds; thus the Welsh word *taid* and the English *tide* are similarly pronounced.

There are exceptions. The seven vowel letters, a, e, i, o, u, w, y, can all represent short or long sounds, and the difference is indicated by a circumflex accent over the long vowel only when confusion with another word is likely to occur (e.g. *llen* (curtain) and *llên* (literature)). Then there is the troublesome y, whose three sounds will be indicated later.

There is one case of a consonant sound being represented by two different symbols, for the English f sound, as in *fine*, not *of*, is written in Welsh as both ff and ph. The latter symbol is used only when the sound results from the initial mutation of p (e.g. *ei phel* (her ball) from *pel* (ball)).

J, K, Q, V, X and Z do not occur in the modern Welsh alphabet, but the reader of old Welsh will often meet J, K and V used for sounds which are today represented by I, C and U or W.

Ch, Dd, Ff, Ng, Ll, Ph, Rh and Th are letters of the Welsh alphabet. The English sh sound is rendered in Welsh by the letters si, but this is not a letter of the alphabet.

Here is the alphabet with approximate indication of how the sounds should be pronounced. The phonetic symbol is given in brackets after each letter.

A: short (a) as in the Italian *bianco*;
long (a:) as in the English *darn*.

The following diphthongs are formed with a:—ae (a:ε) ai (ai), au (ai) and aw (au). The first does not exist in English, the second is like the ai in *aisle*, the third is similar the fourth is like the ow in *cow*.

B: (b) as in English.

C: (k) as the English k.

Ch: (x) as in the German *sprechen* or Scottish *loch*.

D: (d) as in English.

Dd: (ð) as the th in the English *this*.

E: short (ε) as in the English *pen*;
long (e:) as in the Italian *sera*.
Diphthongs formed with e are:—ei (ai) as in the German *zwei*, eu and ey. The second and the third are indistinguishable from the first in modern Welsh.

F: (v) as in the English v.

Ff: (f) as the English f in *fair*.

G: (g) as the g in the English *gun*.

Ng: (ŋ) as in the English *song*, but in Welsh it can be the first letter in a word, when g has suffered nasal mutation, as in *gardd*, *fy ngardd*.
Ngh is the ng sound followed by a pronounced h.

H: (h) always an aspirate and given more breath than the English h.

I: short (i) as in the English *tin*;
long (i:) as in the English *machine*.

L: (l) as in English.

Ll: (ɬ) is easier to pronounce than is generally thought by those not born to it. It is the unvoiced form of the l sound. To produce it place the tongue in the position for the l sound and then breathe out past the tongue on either or both sides without vibrating the vocal chords. It involves a much greater widening of the mouth than is required in the speaking of English; hence, perhaps, the unwillingness of the English to attempt it.

M: (m) as in English.
Mh occurs at the beginning of a word when p is nasally

mutated (e.g. *pen, fy mhen*). Both m and h are here pronounced.

N: (n) as in English.
Nh occurs at the beginning of a word when t is nasally mutated (e.g. *tad, fy nhad*).
It should be noted that Ng follows G, not N, in the Welsh alphabet.

O: short (ɔ) as in the English *not*;
long (o:) a pure sound as in the Italian *Roma*, not a diphthong as always in English.
Diphthongs formed with o are oe (oɛ), a short o followed by a short e, oi (oi) and ou (oi) as in the English *oil*.

P: (p) as in English, but more explosively uttered.

Ph: as in English.

R: (r) is always rolled and not avoided as in English.

Rh: (rh) requires the pronunciation of both r and h.

S: (s) always as in the English *single*. There is no z sound in Welsh; hence Seion for Zion.
The English sh sound is rendered in Welsh by si. The Welsh word for *shop* (siop) is pronounced exactly as in English.

T: (t) as in English.

Th: (θ) as in the English *think*.

U: (ɨ) This sound lies somewhere between the English ee and the French u, and is variously pronounced in Wales.
The short u (ɨ) is close to the English i, so that *culni* is pronounced rather as *kill-knee* in English.
The long u (ɨ:) is close to the English ee, so that *cul* is pronounced rather like the English *keel*.

W: in Welsh is a consonant and a vowel.
As a consonant it is pronounced as in English.
As a vowel it can be short or long;
short (u) as oo in the English *book*,
long (u:) rather like oo in the English *soon*, but a rounder, purer sound.

Y: represents three vowel sounds, possibly four:—
the short y (ɨ or i). Thus the Welsh *tyn* is very like the English *tin*;
the short y (ə) as in the English *myrtle*;
the long y (ɨ: or i:). Thus the Welsh *dyn* is very like the English *dean*.
This is the one sound in Welsh which must be learnt by experience, for there is no rule to govern its variation.

Those who are familiar with or are prepared to master the international phonetic symbols will find the following book useful:

Welsh Phonetic Reader: S. Jones, University of London Press.

Stress

Welsh is closer to English than to French in being a highly stressed language. (I do not, of course, mean intonation, in which the languages differ vastly.) Stress in Welsh is regular and with very few exceptions occurs on the last syllable but one of the word. A word which occurs in English, Welsh and French may be taken as an example—*personal*, *personol*, *personnel*, respectively. In English the first syllable is stressed, in Welsh the second, in French the third.

Stress is important in *cynghannedd* and unless the reader observes it the rhymes of a *cywydd* cannot be appreciated, for there a stressed syllable always rhymes with an unstressed one.

The Initial Mutations

Reference has been made above to the mutations but an account of them is outside the scope of this book. Anyone who attempts to puzzle out Welsh with the aid of a dictionary only should have a mutation table at his side, for a word which begins with b in its radical, dictionary form may begin with f or m in the form before him. The consonants c, p, t, g, b, d, ll, m, rh, when they are the first letter in a word, may alter in certain situations, under the influence of the sound which immediately precedes them. Here is the table of mutations.

		c	p	t	g	b	d	ll	m	rh
Mutation	soft	g	b	d	—	f	dd	l	f	r
	nasal	ngh	mh	nh	ng	m	n	—	—	—
	aspirate	ch	ph	th	—	—	—	—	—	—

When these mutations occur will be found explained in any Welsh grammar, but the chart may help in the finding of an elusive word in the dictionary. For instance, a word beginning in a text with f may radically begin with either b or m (see soft mutations above), e.g. *braint, y fraint; mam, ei fam.*

Gender

It should be remembered that nouns in Welsh may be masculine or feminine and that their gender may affect the adjectives that qualify them and the pronouns that replace them.

The following Welsh grammars are in English:—

An Elementary Welsh Grammar: Sir J. Morris-Jones, O.U.P. 1922.
Welsh Syntax: Sir J. Morris-Jones, O.U.P. 1931.
The Basis and Essentials of Welsh: Vinay and Thomas, Nelson 1947.

INDEX

INDEX

INDEX